HUMAN FACTORS IN
MANAGEMENT   INFORMATION
SYSTEMS

HUMAN/COMPUTER INTERACTION
A Series of Monographs, Edited Volumes and Texts
SERIES EDITOR
BEN SHNEIDERMAN

Directions in Human/Computer Interaction
Edited by Albert Badre and Ben Shneiderman

Human Factors in Management Information Systems
Edited by Jane Carey

Expert Systems: The User Interface
Edited by James A. Hendler

**Online Communities:
A Case Study of the Office of the Future**
Starr Roxanne Hiltz

Human Factors In Computer Systems
Edited by John Thomas and Michael Schneider

Human Factors and Interactive Computer Systems
Edited by Yannis Vassiliou

Advances in Human/Computer Interaction Vol. 1
Edited by H. Rex Hartson

Advances in Human Computer Interaction Vol.2
Edited by H. Rex Hartson and Deborah Hix

Empirical Studies of Programmers
Edited by Elliot Soloway and Sitharama Iyengar

Empirical Studies of Programmers Vol. 2
Edited by Gary Olson, Elliot Soloway and Sylvia Sheppard

In preparation:

Human-Computer Interface Design Guidelines
C. Marlin Brown

Online Helps: Design and Implementation
Greg Kearsley

Socializing the Human/Computer Environment
Jerry Vaske and Charles Grantham

HUMAN FACTORS IN MANAGEMENT INFORMATION SYSTEMS

edited by

Jane M. Carey

College of Business Administration
Texas A & M University

ABLEX Publishing Corporation
Norwood, New Jersey 07648

Printed in the United States of America.

Library of Congress Cataloging-in-Publication Data

Carey, Jane M.
　　Human factors in management information systems.

　　(Human/computer interaction)
　　1. Management information systems—Human factors. I. Title. II. Series: Human/computer interaction (Norwood, N.J.)
　　T58.6.C365　1988　　　　　　　　658.4'038　　　　　　　　88-1266
　　ISBN 0-89391-448-7

m.R.

Ablex Publishing Corporation
355 Chestnut Street
Norwood, New Jersey 07648

Table of Contents

General Introduction 1

- 1. A Taxonomy for the Study of Human Factors
  in Management Information Systems (MIS) 7
  Jon W. Beard and Tim O. Peterson

SECTION I   THE MACHINE 27

  2. Verification of User Identity via Keyboard Characteristics 29
     John Leggett, Glen Williams, and David Umphress

  3. User Computer Interface (UCI) Guidelines Research
     for Keyboards and Function Keys 43
     Rodger J. Koppa

SECTION II   HUMAN-MACHINE INTERACTION 63

  4. Adaptive General Audience Models: A Research Framework ... 65
     Merle P. Martin

  5. SmartSLIM: A DSS for Controlling Biases
     during Problem Formulation 83
     David B. Paradice and James F. Courtney, Jr.

SECTION III   USER INTERFACE SPECIFICATION TOOLS..........101

  6. Applying Software Engineering Principles
     to the User Application Interface 103
     James A. Sena and L. Murphy Smith

  7. FORMFLEX: A User Interface Tool for Forms Definition and
     Management 117
     Joobin Choobineh

SECTION IV   THE SYSTEM ANALYST....................................135

  8. Cognitive Styles, Project Structure, and Project Attributes:
     Considerations in Project Team Design 137
     Kathy Brittain White

v

SECTION V INFORMATION PRESENTATION 147

9. Factors Affecting Opinion and Knowledge: Responses to
Paper and Online Presentation of Questionnaires 149
Peter R. Newsted

SECTION VI SYSTEM USER DOCUMENTATION 165

10. Theories of Explanation: Expert Systems and Simulation 167
David H. Helman and Jeffrey L. Bennett

SECTION VII END USER INVOLVEMENT 181

11. The Darkside of Office Automation: How People Resist
the Introduction of Office Automation Technology 183
Claudette M. Peterson and Tim O. Peterson

12. Understanding Resistance to System Change:
An Empirical Study...195
Jane M. Carey

13. A Plan for Evaluating Usability of Software Products 207
Eileen F. Kopp and H. JoAnn Timmer

14. End-User Computing: A Research Framework for
Investigating the Training/Learning Process..........................221
Robert P. Bostrom, Lorne Olfman, and Maung K. Sein

SECTION VIII THE END USER...251

15. A Human Information Processing Model of the
Managerial Mind: Some MIS Implications 253
William M. Taggart

Appendix 269
Edward J. Szewczak

Author Index..279

Subject Index..287

For Lenny, Rinny, Erin & Kelly

HUMAN FACTORS IN MANAGEMENT INFORMATION SYSTEMS: Design and Implementation of Successful MIS

Jane M. Carey, editor,
Texas A&M University

Ben Shneiderman, series editor,
University of Maryland

PREFACE

The core of this book revolves around 14 papers presented at the Texas A&M Symposium on Human Factors in Management Information Systems (MIS) on October 8 and 9, 1986 in College Station, TX. Two invited papers by Robert Bostrom of Indiana University and Peter Newsted of the University of Calgary are also included. The book is focused and integrated by a general introduction and eight section headings written by editor Jane M. Carey. The eight sections include

1. The Machine
2. Man–Machine Interaction
3. User–Interface Specification tools
4. The Analyst
5. Information Presentation
6. System-user Documentation
7. End-user/System Involvement
8. The User

This book is intended as a professional reference resource for both deisgners of real-world management information systems (MIS) and academicians who are interested in teaching and researching in the area of MIS. It also has real potential as a textbook for graduate-level students, both as a supplemental reading requirement for graduate-level systems analysis and design courses and MIS courses and as a basic text for a graduate seminar course in human factors. Human factors has been identified as one of eight research areas within the MIS discipline by Mary Culnan (1986). Currently, very few human factors publications focus on human factors within the information system. They tend to isolate man/machine interaction without placing it in an organizational environment. Business professionals and academicians are beginning to understand the importance of human factors as determinants of system success and have few references at their disposal which address this issue. I believe that this book will aid in the understanding of the large view of human factors in a systems context and also provide guidelines and examples to aid in specific domains.

SERIES EDITOR'S PREFACE

The enormous potential benefits of applying human factors techniques to Management Information Systems is attractive to practitioners and researchers. The user interface design techniques that have been successfully applied in many life critical systems (air traffic control, medical systems, etc.) and to personal computer systems are now being refined to suit the demanding needs of MIS. High volume commercial systems such as banking, credit cards, reservations, or order entry can be substantially improved to produce cost savings in training, improved productivity, lower error rates, and increased job satisfaction. Creative environments for decision support, information search, and financial planning models can also be made more attractive through innovative designs.

The opportunity is great, but the progress has been slow until recently. In the past 2-3 years researchers and developers have laid the basis for a broad-based revolution in the design process and the resulting products. Those who wish to eliminate the confusing displays, chaotic menus, incomprehensible instructions, condemning error messages, and bizarre sequences of actions can now take advantage of new software tools, testing methods, design concepts, and emerging standards. There is much work to be done, but the competitive pressure from examples of excellence is already compelling many developers to respond. Those who are joining the "fight for the user" are gathering at conferences, reading the new journals and books, and absorbing the lessons from successful commercial products.

Jane Carey was a pioneer in recognizing this trend and organized a workshop to bring together fellow researchers. The October 1986 meeting generated an enthusiastic atmosphere as the participants shared their experiences and empirical data. Many attendees left with the feeling that the application of human factors to MIS would have a profound effect on future systems.

Dr. Carey worked diligently to have the presentations critiqued and the papers reviewed. She selected the most important papers, encouraged reorganization of some papers, invited new papers on topics that were not sufficiently covered, organized the material in a meaningful sequence, and merged the disparate formats into a uniform and readable style. She and all the contributors deserve credit for creating this landmark book that heralds the marriage of two vital disciplines.

Ben Shneiderman,
University of Maryland,
College Park, MD

General Introduction

USABILITY AS A DETERMINANT OF MANAGEMENT INFORMATION SYSTEM (MIS) SUCCESS

Information is an important resource in an organization. It costs a great deal of time and money to develop systems which provide information to the organization. In order to ensure that an information system (IS) is performing both efficiently and effectively, IS managers must have some measurable criteria on which to base their evaluation. Many researchers have focused their attention on this issue (Alloway & Quillard, 1981; Shneiderman, 1987; Cerullo, 1980) and the following list of criteria is a synthesis of their combined recommendations for determinants of system success:

1. Information accuracy
2. Information timeliness
3. Information relevancy
4. Correct information format
5. Appropriate level of information scope
6. Decision support capability
7. Speed of performance
8. Reduced error rates
9. User satisfaction
10. Ease of learning
11. System responsiveness

12. Enhancement of communication
13. System reliability

Upon close examination of these factors, all of them (with the exception of system reliability) either directly relate to the user or cannot be defined without user input, as in the case of the first five criteria.

From the conceptualization through the implementation and use of an MIS, the user should play a key role. There are various tools and techniques which allow the user to become involved in the development process and aid in the use of the system. Table 1 relates the human factors focus areas to the appropriate stage of system development.

In the early days of systems development, analysts/programmers proceeded through the stages of system development with very little interaction with the user. The primary contact occurred when the system feasibility study was initiated. At certain points during the development of the system, the user would be required to sign off on the system. However, the system would be presented to the user via a narrative document written in very technical terms which often encompassed several hundred pages. The average user would have neither the time nor knowledge to read the technical specification document and would either sign off without understanding the system or would make an attempt to understand the system and bog down the development

Table 1

Relationship between Systems Development Life Cycle (SDLC) Stages
and Human Factors Focus

SDLC STAGES	HUMAN FACTORS FOCUS
Feasibility	*User/analyst interface
	*Composition of development
	Team to include user representative
Requirements analysis	*Data flow diagrams
	*Communication techniques
	*Graphic techniques
System specification	*Prototyping
	*Graphic techniques
	*Fourth-generation languages
Program design & development	*Guidelines for designing the user interface
	*Application generators
	*Prototyping
System test	*User acceptance test
Implementation & production	*Using the man/machine interface
	*Combat of user resistance to change
	*System documentation
	*User training and learning

time severely. Structured and graphic techniques were developed, such as the data flow diagram and structured English, which gave the users a "top down" view of the system which they could understand in order to address this problem.

In general, the trends in software design and system development tools have moved in two directions: (a) towards more user involvement and (b) away from machine orientation toward human orientation. Reasons for the existence of these two trends are:

1. *An increase in the number of novice system users* (Shneiderman, 1982). Due to the invention and inexpensiveness of micro computers, desktop computers have infiltrated the business organization. In the past, access to the computer was limited to those people with a very technical background who understood the computer well but perhaps did not understand the task environment of the systems they were trying to develop. Now attempting to use computers are people who have a good understanding of the task they wish to perform but little or no training or experience with computers;

2. *An increase in office automation.* Such tools as electronic mail, word processing, schedulers, spread sheets, and workstations have been introduced to knowledge workers who have little or no education or training in computer-based skills. In order to enhance rather than degrade office-worker productivity, attention must be paid to the usability of these tools;

3. *Systems that perform more and more complex tasks.* Today's newly developed systems are not attempting merely to perform business transactions and operations which are rather simple and well-structured. They are now performing very complex and poorly-structured tasks, such as forecasting analysis, communications networking, and problem definition. These complex tasks require user input and interaction and, because of this, the user interfaces must be designed in such a manner as to enhance the problem solution or use of the system rather than degrade it;

4. *Newer information systems that have voluntary, rather than required, usage.* If the user is frustrated and alienated by the system, the user will not use the system when it is not required. Decision support systems, expert systems, and communications systems are often voluntary systems. Other means of accomplishing the task exist. The user may elect to bypass the computer-based system to accomplish the task rather than undergo the frustration of dealing with a system which is difficult to learn and use;

5. *Newer systems that are critical to the support of the organization* (Shneiderman, 1982). Life-support systems in hospitals, air-traffic-control systems, on-line reservation systems, Point of Sale (POS)

terminals, and so forth must be reliable and easy to use if the organization cannot survive without them.

Toward a Taxonomy for HUMAN FACTORS in MIS

The first chapter in this book presents a taxonomy for human factors in MIS. It is around this taxonomy that the book is organized, based upon a representation of the interaction between the computer (actual hardware) system , the analyst, and the user. It was developed by Jon W. Beard and Tim O. Peterson under the direction of Jane M. Carey. It is an attempt to synthesize and categorize the diverse and disjointed research efforts in the area of human factors in MIS. Figure 1 illustrates the taxonomy. At the far left is a computer terminal which signifies the machine itself and the ergonomic issues related to human factors. In the foreground of the diagram is a human symbol which signifies the user characteristics which impinge on human-machine interaction. These user characteristics include user attitude, user cognitive style, user personality and experience, and so forth (Zmud, 1979). At the right of the diagram is another representation of a human being which signifies the systems analyst and his or her involvement in system development and implementation. In between the computer symbol and the human symbols are five circles which represent five distinct areas of research in human factors in MIS.

1. Human-machine Interaction
2. User Interface Specification Tools
3. Information Presentation
4. System User Documentation
5. End User/System Involvement

These five circles represent specific research areas in human factors in MIS and form the framework of this book. A brief introduction to each section has been included for further explanation and to integrate the particular articles which have been assigned to each section.

Computer-based management information systems have been in existence only for approximately 30 years. There is little agreement on definitions and theory in MIS. To impose another diverse discipline, such as human factors, upon MIS can lead to confusion and lack of clarity. This book has two main goals. One is to provide the reader with specific tools and guidelines which allow the incorporation of human factors engineering into system development, design, and use. The other is to provide a taxonomy for the study of human factors in MIS. This taxonomy provides a framework for research as well as under-

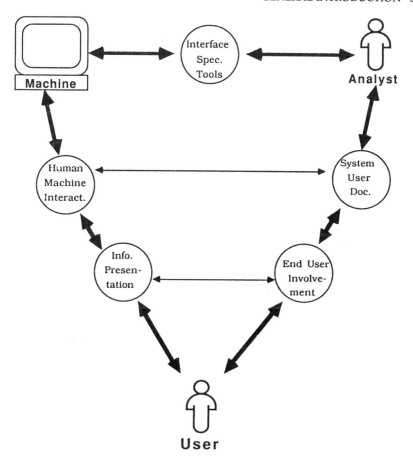

Figure 1. Taxonomy for Human Factors In MIS

standing. The nature of management information systems and human system interaction is changing all the time. This taxonomy is flexible enough to withstand changes and dynamic enough to allow insertions and deletions as required by new directions in human factors design and research findings.

REFERENCES

Alloway, R.M., & J.A. Quillard (1981, September). Top priorities for the information systems function. Unpublished Manuscript, Center for Information Systems Research-Massachusetts Institute of Technology.

Cerullo, M.J. (1980). Information success factors. *Journal of Systems Management. 31*, 6–13.

Culnan, M.J. (1986). The intellectual development of MIS, 1972–1982: a co-citation analysis. *Management Science*, 32, 156–172.

Shneiderman, B. (1982). The future of interactive systems and the emergence of direct manipulation' In Y. Vassiliou, (Ed.) *Human factors and interactive computer systems*. Norwood, NJ: Ablex.

Shneiderman, B. (1987). *Designing the User Interface*. Reading, MA: Addison Wesley.

Zmud, R.W. (1979). Individual differences and MIS success: a review of the empirical literature. *Management Science*, 25, 966–979.

CHAPTER 1

A Taxonomy for the Study of Human Factors in Management Information Systems (MIS)

Jon W. Beard
and
Tim O. Peterson
Texas A&M University

Human factors in Management Information Systems (MIS) is a relatively new, but growing, field of research. One reason for the interest in this topic seems to be the "...intellectual recognition of the fact that all systems are man-machine systems and that if the human part of the system is not performing effectively then it is unlikely that the technical part of the system will be efficient either" (Mumford, 1971, p. 918). Although the field of research is growing and many new topics are being explored, it is important to stop momentarily to examine where the field is and where it seems to be headed. This snapshot will provide the reader with a Gestalt view of the human factors field. This manuscript reviews the historical roots of human factors, synthesizes the many diverse definitions into one working definition, and develops a taxonomy of human factors.

AN OPENING THOUGHT

No longer the exclusive tool of specialists, computers have become both commonplace and indispensible. Yet they remain harder to use than they should be. It should be no more necessary to read a 300-page book of instructions before using a computer than before driving an unfamiliar automobile. But much more research in both cognitive and computer science will be required to learn how to build computers that are that easy to use. That is why our industry is paying increasing attention to the field of applied psychology called human factors, or ergonomics. Equally neglected has been human factors at the level of systems design. We know that system architecture has significant and widespread

7

implications for user friendliness, but we know next to nothing about how to make fundamental architectural decisions differently, in the interest of human factors. (Shackel, 1985).

INTRODUCTION

Computer-based information management is a relatively new technology which is seeing increasing use by individuals and organizations to meet information needs. However, this new technology is often difficult to understand and sometimes even more difficult to use and, in many cases, the blame can be laid on design of the human-machine interface. Because of these design problems, much of the potential in this new technology lies dormant and will remain untapped until the technology is adapted to the information systems' end-users. The scientific study of this relationship between humans and their work environment is called human factors or ergonomics (Chapanis, 1965; Murrell, 1965).

Culnan (1986), in her article on the intellectual development of MIS, identifies eight central themes at the core of the MIS discipline. One of those major themes is human factors. Shneiderman (1982) has identified three basic factors responsible for the growing awareness and concern over the relationship between human factors and computer-based information systems. First, the computer-user populace is rapidly expanding to include both novice users and noncomputer-trained individuals. Second, more organizations are becoming increasingly dependent on computer-based information systems. Despite this, Shneiderman argues, studies indicate that performance by users is poor, even among expert users. Third, because of the complexity of information needs and the availability of faster processing in more life-critical situations, systems such as medical intensive care, nuclear reactors, air traffic control, fire and police dispatch, manned spaceflight, and military command and control are incorporating computers. Finally, it is now possible for the computer to enhance human intellect through programmer/artist workstations with decision support systems (DSS), expert systems, and through retrieval and simulation. The importance of the human-machine interface in these situations cannot be overemphasized. As Shneiderman (1987) states, "Human engineering, which was seen as the paint put on the end of a project, is now understood to be the steel frame on which the structure is built" (p. v).

For these reasons it is important to develop a framework around which human factors in computer-based information systems can be studied. This paper begins with a brief historical overview of the field of human factors. Next, a working definition of human factors in MIS is provided. Finally, a taxonomy for the study of human factors and MIS is developed.

HISTORICAL PERSPECTIVE OF HUMAN FACTORS
(Preinformation Systems)

Human factors as a separate field of study has a relatively short history dating back only to the turn of the century. In 1898, empirical studies were made by Frederick W. Taylor to discover the best design of shovels and the optimum weight per shovelful. The main interest of the study was in work rates and worker motivation. Frank B. Gilbreth's study of brick layers in 1911 set a pattern for work improvement when he invented a scaffold that could be easily raised or lowered so that the bricklayer could work at the most convenient levels at all times. Gilbreth believed that work methods provide the basis for differences in skill and effectiveness at various stages of training (Huchingson, 1981, p.10). These two studies were the pioneering efforts in the branch of industrial engineering now known as time-and-motion study.

Until World War II, the primary focus of time-and-motion engineering was on the human as a worker or a source of power. At this same time, machines began to appear that made demands upon operators' sensory, perceptual, judgmental, and decision-making abilities instead of upon their muscular power (Chapanis, 1965). "The formalized interest in human factors stemmed from technological advances in the development of elaborate military, space, and electronic systems" (Huchingson, 1981, p.9). For example, relationships such as radar operation and information overload, optical distortion and windscreen design of high-speed aircraft, and sudden decompression and operator performance in pressurized aircraft were being studied. The questions about design and use could not be answered by common sense or by the principles of motion economy found in time-and-motion theories. "Equipment seemed to be so complex that it exceeded the capabilities of men to operate it" (Huchingson 1981, p. 10). The new experts in the field were behavioral scientists psychologists, physiologists, anthropologists, and physicians instead of engineers, "because the primary load that modern machines place on their human operators is a mental load" (Chapanis, 1965, p. 11). A special branch of psychology, engineering psychology, developed around this important research area. The research conducted on workers and their work environment led to the field called human factors.

HISTORICAL PERSPECTIVE OF HUMAN FACTORS
(Postinformation Systems)

Computerized information systems began to appear in the same postwar period that interest in human factors was growing and the first two decades of the data-processing era saw attention given to effective human-machine relationships focused in broad sweeping areas such as the development of human-oriented langauges to replace machine langauge and interactive terminal input to replace the "unfriendly" batch systems. Screen dialog and psychological issues were not addressed for quite some time. The primary concern was on the efficient use of the central processing unit and storage media. Little effort was made to develop easy-to-use, or "user friendly," systems. This was to be expected, because the majority of the users were computer proficient. Also, the use of computers was quite rare and expensive and, therefore, access was effectively limited. The interface between the human and computer-based information system was often the computer operator's console which used machine-dependent languages. According to Martin (1973), the systems were "designed from the inside, out"(p. 3). In other words, the user had to adapt to the particular style that the programmer or machine designer chose to use, rather than having the system adapted to the user's preferred style of interaction.

The year 1969 was a landmark for human factors research. *Ergonomics* published a special issue of papers to be presented at the International Symposium on Man-Machine Systems. *IEEE Transactions on Man-Machine Systems* reprinted the articles. This reprint gave the human factors literature a much wider circulation. In the same year, the *International Journal of Man-Machine Studies* began publication of a quarterly journal devoted to human factors research (Gaines 1985, p. 3). A few books essential to the growth of human factors also began to appear. Sachman's *Man-Computer Problem Solving* (1970) and Weinberg's *Psychology of Computer Programming* (1971) "did much to stimulate interest in the possible applications of human factors principles in computer science" (Gaines 1985, p. 4). Weinberg writes in his book, "at the moment programming   sophisticated as it may be from an engineering or mathematical point of view   is so crude psychologically that even the tiniest insights should help immeasurably" (p. ii). In another influential book, James Martin (1973) states that "it is essential to take into account the shortcomings of both human and computer. Man is limited in what he can achieve at the terminal, and accomplishments will vary very widely between different persons"(p. 3). In addition, "conferences on almost any computing topic felt it timely to have a section on the human factors associated with it" (Gaines 1985, p. 4).

More recently, Ben Shneiderman has written *Software Psychology: Human Factors in Computer and Information Systems* (1980). This book brought together many of the research techniques used in testing the human factors of systems and discussed some of the problems which can be encountered in designing, developing, and testing good systems that are oriented to the human user.

Shneiderman has also written *Designing the User Interface: Strategies for Effective Human-Computer Interaction* (1987) which explains and develops these ideas, techniques, and technologies even further. This rapidly growing literature base and awareness of human factors, coupled with the dramatic growth in computer use due to the reduction in computing costs and increase in processing availability, have triggered a rapidly increasing number of human factors studies and articles.

With the growing use of MIS within business and industry, it has become quite clear that it is necessary to study the physical and cognitive aspects of human-computer interaction in order to improve productivity. This increased awareness of human needs has led to studies and improved technologies for using more fully the potential of both humans and computers.

HUMAN FACTORS: A DEFINITION

It is important to develop mental anchors so that researchers have a shared understanding of the topic under study. Hussain and Hussain (1984) in their textbook, *Information Resource Management*, define human factors as "the physiological, psychological, and training factors to be considered in the design of hardware and software, and the development of procedures to ensure that humans can interface with machines efficiently and effectively" (p. 625).

Still another definition can be found in the introduction to Woodson's *Human Factors Design Handbook* (1981). Here the definition of human factors is

> "...the practice of designing products so that the user can perform required use, operation, service, and supportive tasks with a minimum of stress and a maximum of efficiency. To accomplish this, the designer must understand and acknowledge the needs, characteristics, capabilities, and limitations of the intended user and design from the human out, making the design fit the user instead of forcing the user to fit the design." (p. vii)

The more traditional definition of human factors has been "the scientific study of the relationship between humans and their work environment" (Murrell, 1965; Chapanis, 1965). In a somewhat less traditional manner, Thomas (1982) defines human factors as "using what we know about the way people really are to design systems and tools that help make people more productive and happier". His point is that the study of human factors is more than just the scientific study of the human-machine interaction; it is also the use of this knowledge in the design and development of MIS that is important. In addition, this definition makes it clear that the study of human factors must be the study of people and computers as they really are, not as we think they should be or want them to be. Finally, this definition recognizes the importance of both increased performance and improved quality of work life.

Ergonomics is defined as "the science of human engineering which combines the study of human body mechanics and physical limitations with industrial psychology" (Hussain & Hussain, 1984, p. 624). Although ergonomics is a commonly used term and is sometimes used synonymously with human factors, we wish to make a clear distinction between the two. Some of the human factors citations mentioned here attempt to be all inclusive. However, we see two distinct streams of research. These two categories are the physical aspects of human-computer interaction (ergonomics) and the cognitive aspects of the interaction (human factors). Ergonomics deals with topics such as work station and furniture design, lighting, noise, keyboard height and arrangement. There is already a substantial body of literature in this important area. (See Huchingson, 1982 ; Osbourne & Gruenberg, 1984; Woodman, 1984 for good presentations of this information.) The cognitive attributes or human factors concentrate on the actual conscious (and subconscious) mental activities that occur during the use of the computer. Although the terms human factors and ergonomics are sometimes used interchangeably, the distinction between them seems to be based on the physical versus cognitive dimension of the human-computer relationship. Obviously, complete understanding of both the physical and cognitive attributes of human-computer interaction does not yet exist. For our purposes, however, we wish to emphasize the cognitive dimension rather than the physical dimension.

From the array of definitions above, it is easy to see that human factors has been defined in almost as many ways as the number of people who have written about it. We feel it is time to break with this tradition. In an effort to do just that, we have attempted to integrate these different and yet similar definitions. With this in mind, we propose that:

> Human factors is the scientific study of the interaction between people, machines, and their work environment. The knowledge gained from this

study is used to create systems and work environments which help to make people more productive and more satisfied with their work life.

A number of different taxonomies exist which break human factors into separate categories of research. The AFIPS Taxonomy Committee has developed the Taxonomy of Computer Science and Engineering. In this taxonomy, human factors engineering (ergonomics) is defined as "the art and science of building powerful but easy to use graphical man-machine dialogs" (Part 7.9.6.5, p. 331). The subcategories are the workstation organization "how user friendly the physical terminal is," the operator interface "how easy to use, forgiving, reliable, powerful, responsive, etc., the application package is," and the programmer interface "how easy to use, reliable, powerful, well-documented, etc. the hardware and support software are." *Ergonomics Abstracts* has it's own classification scheme consisting of 11 major categories. These categories are human characteristics, performance related factors, information presentation and communication, display and control design, workplace and equipment design, environment, system characteristics, work design and organization, health and safety, social and economic impact of the system, and method and techniques. As can be seen below, there is some overlap between this taxonomy and the taxonomy we propose for human factors in MIS but the *Ergonomics Abstracts* classification scheme is much broader than ours and includes topics basically outside the realm of human factors research in MIS.

Like many other fields, especially those as young and diverse as human factors, it is often difficult to determine the research streams which are currently being examined, as well as the most significant references on these topics. What is needed is a human factors taxonomy that would help researchers and students of human factors to form a schema of the research streams within the field. In the final section of this paper, such a taxonomy is developed.

TAXONOMY

In an attempt to define more clearly the major research themes on human factors, we have divided the literature into five categories. This typology is an attempt to group the related research into more clearly defined units for ease of use and reference. It should be understood, however, that overlapping among categories still exists. The categories are:

- Human-Machine Interaction
- Interface Specification Tools
- Information Presentation

- System-User Documentation
- End-User Involvement

Each of these will be briefly explained and discussed below.

Table 1 provides a matrix of the major works and the five categories which make up the taxonomy. This table identifies the significant works in each category and the overlap between the categories and the manuscripts. *Human-Machine Interaction* refers to the different ways in which the user and the computer communicate. These communication modes include the use of keyboards and monitors, speech input and output (Hahn, 1982; Bierman, 1985), vision (eye-tracking) (Bolt, 1984), touch screens, light pens, the use of a mouse, and a digitizing tablet. This interface is facilitated through the use of specially designed natural command languages (Bierman, 1985; Black, 1981; Hahn, 1982), menus, icons, and graphics (Hahn, 1982). Direct manipulation (Shneiderman, 1987), where the objects and actions of interest are visible; actions are rapid, reversible, and incremental; and where complex command language sequences have been replaced with direct manipulation of the object of interest, best represents the apparent direction of development in this area. Although the actual physical design and arrangement of these items are closely related to, and may overlap, the category of Human-Machine Interaction, its primary focus is on the efficiency and effectiveness of the different tools and techniques which facilitate human-computer interaction. The significant works in this category are Weinberg (1971), Martin (1973), and Shneiderman (1980, 1987).

Although there are many works which define and discuss aspects of the human-machine interface in more detail than either Weinberg or Martin, these two were the first to define this broad research area and much subsequent research in human factors developed from their seminal frameworks and suggestions. Shneiderman (1980, 1987) synthesized and clarified much of the work prior to 1980 and his work also helped to focus contemporary research.

Interface Specification Tools are more formal techniques for detailed design of the point of interaction between people and computers. Some of these techniques consist of the use of flowcharts, system diagrams, data-flow diagrams, Warnier-Orr techniques, Nassi-Shneiderman techniques, and ultimately system shells and prototyping. All of these have been used with varying degrees of success to define and explain the details of the interface but there still does not seem to be a good and widely accepted technique for clearlypecifying the details of the human-computer interface. These specifications should describe the system: what it does, how it does it, who it does it with. As stated in the opening thought, the system architecture has significant and widespread impli-

TABLE 1

A Taxonomy to Manuscript Matrix

Of Human Factors Research in MIS

Author(s) Publication Year	Man-Machine Interaction	Interface Specification Tools	Information Presentation	System User Documentation	End User Involvement
Alty & Ritchie, 1985		*			
Andriole, 1983	*		*	*	
Barber, 1981	*				*
Barber, 1982	*				*
Barber & Hewitt, 1981	*				*
Bass, 1985	*	*			*
Bateman, 1983	*				
Beynon, 1985		*			
Biermann et al., 1985	*				
Black, 1981	*	*	*		*
Blaser & Zoeppritz, 1983	*				
Bolt, 1984	*		*		
Brod, 1984	*				
Brown, 1984	*		*	*	
Card et al., 1983			*		
Carroll & Carrithers, 1984	*				
Clowes, 1985		*			
Cockton, 1985		*			
Curtis, 1981	*	*	*		
Dehning et al, 1980	*	*	*		
Dix & Runciman, 1985		*			
Erhlich & Saloway, 1984		*	*		
Fountain & Norman, 1985		*			
Fowler et al., 1985	*		*		
Glen, 1985			*		
Good et al., 1983	*	*			*
Goos & Hartmanis, 1981	*				

TABLE 1

A Taxonomy to Manuscript Matrix
Of Human Factors Research in MIS

Author(s) Publication Year	Man-Machine Interaction	Interface Specification Tools	Information Presentation	System User Documentation	End User Involvement
Green et al., 1983	*	*	*		
Grued, 1980	*		*		
Hahn, 1982	*				
Hammond & Barnard, 1984		*	*		
Harrison & Thimbleby, 1985		*			
Heppe et al., 1985	*				
Herot, 1982	*				
Hill, 1983	*	*			
Hlltz & Turoff, 1985	*		*		
Houghton, 1984	*			*	
Hulme, 1984			*		
Jacob, 1984		*			
Johnson & Cook, 1985	*	*	*	*	
Kasschau et al, 1982	*	*	*	*	*
Kidd, 1984			*		
Malone, 1984	*	*	*	*	
Martin, 1973	*	*	*	*	*
Mills, 1985				*	
Monk, 1984	*	*	*		
Morland, 1983	*	*	*		
Naffah, 1982	*	*	*	*	
Norman, 1984	*	*	*		
Osborne, 1985			*		
Otte, 1982	*	*	*	*	
Reid, 1984	*				
Reisner, 1984		*			

TABLE 1

A Taxonomy to Manuscript Matrix
Of Human Factors Research in MIS

Author(s) Publication Year	Man-Machine Interaction	Interface Specification Tools	Information Presentation	System User Documentation	End User Involvement
Reisner, 1984		*			
Reitman-Olson/ Bruenenfelder, 1982	*	*	*	*	
Roberts, 1985			*		
Salvendy, 1984	*	*	*	*	
Savage & Habinek, 1984	*	*		*	
Schneider, 1982	*	*		*	
Sheppard et al, 1984		*	*	*	
Shneiderman, 1980	*	*	*	*	*
Shneiderman, 1982	*	*		*	
Shneiderman, 1983	*		*	*	
Shneiderman, 1986	*	*	*	*	*
Sime & Coombs, 1983	*			*	
Smith, 1985				*	
Sutcliffe, 1985		*			
Thimbleby, 1984	*				
Thomas, 1982	*			*	
Thomas & Schneider, 1984		*			
Turner et al, 1982	*				
Vassiliou, 1982	*		*	*	
Vassiliou & Jarke, 1982	*	*			
Weinberg, 1971	*		*		
Wilson, 1985	*				

cations for user interfacing but we know next to nothing about how to make fundamental architectural decisions in this light (Shackel, 1985). The works of Fountain and Norman (1985), Card, Moran, and Newell (1983), and Reisner (1981, 1984) do seem to show promise. But because there is, at present, no good interface design tool available, it is often difficult to design the interface and get feedback from the future system users. Some of the key works in this area are Black (1981), Fountain and Norman (1985), Jacob (1984), and Schneider (1982).

Information Presentation is how the data is portrayed to the system user. The form of this presentation could be graphic, numeric, alphanumeric, tabular, text (hard copy), audible, tactile, or some other form. "With the early computers, a manager would often have dumped on his desk an indigestible printout   sometimes several hundred pages long. Now the manager is more likely to request information when he needs it, and receive data about a single item or situation..." (Martin, 1973, p. 6). This category also includes the use of artificial intelligence (AI) or expert systems to tailor information presentations to an individual's cognitive style. Ehrlich and Saloway (1984) and Shneiderman (1983) have provided foundation works on this topic.

System-User Documentation discusses the needs and techniques of producing documentation in a form and style suitable for the everyday users of the system whether expert or novice. Documentation is very important in explaining and teaching the user how to accomplish desired tasks. Documentation includes operation manuals, system messages, and both on-line and manual help facilities. Some key works in this area are Brockman (1986), Brown (1984), and Houghton (1984).

End-User Involvement is the last category. It is an often overlooked aspect in developing easy-to-use systems which consists of the methods used to get users directly involved in the design, development, testing, implementation, and maintenance of the system. At least part of the design problem seems to be that the analyst/designer is working from his or her own perceptions of the computer and of the user's needs. Although not completely without merit, this process often includes unrealistic expectations of user knowledge and an often mistaken idea of user desires and requirements. Additional study of this problem is needed. Seminal work in this category was done by Good et al. (1984).

DISCUSSION

As Figure 1 shows, the five categories we have defined form a network of relationships among the computer, the user, and the analyst/ programmer/ developer. Each category represents a major link in the human factors research literature. Some factors directly affect the relationship between the computer, the user, and the analyst while other factors indirectly influence the specified relationships. Specifically, the analyst and the computer are linked by the category we have called Interface Specification Tools. These tools describe the point of interaction between the analyst and the computer. The analyst and the user interact through the two categories of System User Documentation and User Involvement. Finally, the link between computer and user, which is the focus of increasing concern with human factors, is characterized by the categories of Human-Machine Interaction and Information Presentation.

The three participants in this relationship the computer, the analyst, and the user form an intriguing and complex relationship. The analyst

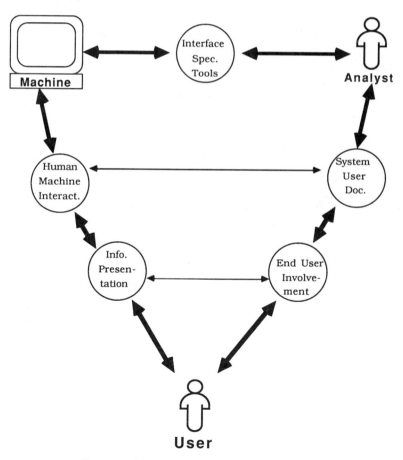

Figure 1. Taxonomy for Human Factors in MIS

views the computer from an expert's point of view and an often technical perspective. The user views the computer as a potentially useful tool but from a more general orientation. These two views are quite different and are often incompatible and in conflict. This type of relationship has been explained by Newcomb (1953, 1961) as the co-orientation model. According to his model, if an object (the computer) is important to us, we expect others to whom we are attracted or with whom we interact to also like the object and view it from our perspective. A "strain toward symmetry," an attempt to reach a common understanding or viewpoint, can develop from the discrepancies between the two possibly different orientations. The resolution of these different perspectives is possible only when the analyst begins to understand the needs, requirements, and desires of the user in order to properly design and produce the system. Users must also aid in this resolution by understanding the limitations of the computer systems they desire as well as by developing a thorough and specific understanding of their own needs. Thomas (1982), in his definition of human factors, alludes to these often divergent views. In order to be successful in improving human-computer interaction, it is becoming more evident that we as designers and analysts need to view the relationship as it really is, not as we think it should be or as we want it to be.

The five categories we have defined have some overlap and are interrelated. However, two relationships are particularly strong. *Human-Machine Interaction* and *System User Documentation* are very closely related. The documentation provides detailed information to the user on how to use the tools provided to successfully interact with the computer. *Information Presentation* and *End-User Involvement* are also very closely tied together. For example, through user involvement with the analyst, the system can be designed so that information is presented in a useful and appropriate way.

Table 1 should help the reader visualize the amount of research in each category. In addition, it shows the overlap of research between categories. Here, the categorization for each article is indicated with an asterisk under its category or categories. Some of the pieces even span our whole human factors taxonomy. From this table, a pattern seems to be evident. Some categories contain a large number of references, indicating a well-developed topic. Other categories have very few references, indicating an emerging topic.

In conclusion, it seems that research in human factors of MIS is moving within a network of categories which relate the computer, analyst, and user. Other areas of human factors research are related in varying degrees. Some of these areas, or others not yet identified, may evolve and grow into this network of relationships. With further research and understanding of each category, someday we may be able to develop computer systems which are not only user-friendly, but also make the users more productive and satisfied in their work environment.

A CLOSING THOUGHT

If the point of contact between the product and the people becomes a point of friction, then the industrial designer has failed. If, on the other hand, people are made safer, more comfortable, more eager to purchase, more efficient or just plain happier the designer has succeeded (Dreyfus, 1955).

ACKNOWLEDGEMENT

The authors appreciate the helpful comments made by Claudette Peterson on drafts of this paper and the assistance of Caryl Beard in its preparation.

REFERENCES

Alty, J.L., & Ritchie, R.A. (1985). A path algebra support facility for interactive dialogue designers. In P. Johnson & S. Cook (Eds.), *People and computers: designing the interface* (pp. 128–137). New York: Cambridge University Press.

Andriole, S.J. (1983). *Interactive computer based systems: design and development*. Princeton, NJ: Petrocelli Books.

Barber, G.R. (1981). Embedding knowledge in a workstation. In N. Naffah (Ed.), *Office information systems* (pp. 341–354). New York: North-Holland.

Barber, G.R. (1982). User interfaces for problem solving support. In Y. Vassiliou (Ed.), *Human factors and interactive computer systems* (pp. 191–206). Norwood, NJ: Ablex.

Barber, G.R. & Hewitt, C. (1981). Foundations for office semantics. In N. Naffah (Ed.), *Office information systems* (pp. 363–382). New York: North-Holland.

Bass, L.J. (1985). A generalized user interface for applications programs (II). *Communications of the ACM, 28,* 617–627.

Bateman, R.F. (1983). A translator to encourage user modifiable man-machine dialogue. In M.E. Sime & M.J. Coombs (Eds.), *Designing for human-computer communication* (pp. 157–172). New York: Academic Press.

Benbasat, I., Dexter, A.S., & Masulis, P.S. (1981). An experimental study of the human/computer interface. *Communications of the ACM, 24,* 752–761.

Beynon, M. (1985). Definitive notations for interaction. In P. Johnson & S. Cook (Eds.), *People and computers: designing the interface* (pp. 23–34). New York: Cambridge University Press.

Biermann, A.W., Rodman, R.D., Rubin, D.C., & Heidlage, J.F. (1985). Natural Language with discrete speech as mode for communication. *Communications of the ACM, 28,*

628–636.

Black, J.B. (1981). An invited article: facilitating human-computer communication. *Applied Psycholinguistics, 2*, 149–177.

Blaser, A., & Zoeppritz, M. (Eds.) (1983) *Enduser systems and their human factors.* New York: Springer-Verlag.

Bolt, R.A. (1984). *The human interface: where people and computers meet.* Belmont, CA: Lifetime Learning Publications, Wadsworth.

Brod, C. (1984). *Technostress: the human cost of the computer revolution.* Reading, MA: Addison-Wesley.

Brown, P.J. (1984). Error messages: the neglected area of the man/machine interface. *Communications of the ACM, 26*, 246–249.

Card, S.K., Moran, T.P., & Newell, A. (1983). *The psychology of human-computer interaction.* Hillsdale, NJ: Lawrence Erlbaum.

Carroll, J.M., & Carrithers, C. (1984). Training wheels in a user interface. *Communications of the ACM, 27*, 800–806.

Chapanis, A. (1965). *Man-machine engineering.* Belmont, CA: Wadsworth.

Clowes, I., & Hopkins, C. (1985). User modelling techniques for interactive systems. In P. Johnson & S. Cook (Eds.), *People and computers: designing the interface,* (pp. 35–45). New York: Cambridge University Press.

Cockton, G. (1985). Three transition network dialogue management systems. In P. Johnson & S. Cook (Eds.), *People and computers: designing the interface,* (pp. 138–147). New York: Cambridge University Press.

Culnan, M.J. (1986). The intellectual development of MIS, 1972-1982: a co-citation analysis. *Management Science, 32*, 156–172.

Curtis, B. (Ed.). (1981). *Tutorial: human factors in software development.* Stratford, CT: IEEE Computer Society Press.

Dehning, W., Essig, H., & Maass, S. (1981). *The adaptation of virtual man-computer interfaces to user requirements in dialogs.* New York: Springer-Verlag.

Dix, A.J., & Runciman, C. (1985). Abstract models of interactive systems. In P. Johnson & S. Cook (Eds.), *People and computers: designing the interface,* (pp.13–22). New York: Cambridge University Press.

Dreyfus, H. (1955). *Designing for people.* New York: Simon and Schuster.

Ehrlich, K., & Saloway, E. (1984). An empirical investigation of the tacit plan knowledge in programming. In J.C. Thomas & M.L. Schneider (Eds.), *Human factors in computer systems* (pp. 113–133). Norwood, NJ: Ablex.

Fountain, A.J.,& Norman, M.A. (1985). Modeling user behavior with formal grammar. In P. Johnson & S. Cook (Eds.), *People and computers: designing the interface* (pp. 3–12). New York: Cambridge University Press.

Fowler, .J.H., Macaulay, L.A., & Fowler, J.F. (1985). The relationship between cognitive style and dialogue style: an explorative study. In P. Johnson & S. Cook (Eds.), *People and computers: designing the interface* (pp. 186–198). New York: Cambridge University Press.

Gaines, B.R. (1985). From ergonomics to the fifth generation: 30 Years of human-computer interaction studies. In B. Shackel (Ed.), *Human-computer interaction-INTERACT 84* (pp. 3–7). New York: Elsevier.

Galitz, W.O. (1985). *Handbook of screen format design.* Wellesley, MA: QED Information Sciences.

Glen, J.A. (1985). Mathematical students and computers: an interface for experimentation. In P. Johnson & S. Cook (Eds.), *People and computers: designing the interface* (pp. 282–289). New York: Cambridge University Press.

Good, M.D., Whiteside, J.A., Wixon, D.R., & Jones, S.J. (1984). Building a user-derived interface. *Communications of the ACM, 27*, 1032–1043.

Goos, G., & Hartmanis, J. (Eds.), (1981). *Directions in human factors for interactive systems.* New York: Springer-Verlag.

Green, T.R.G., Payne, S.J., & van der Veer, G.C. (Eds.), (1983). *The psychology of computer use.* New York: Academic.

Grued, R.A. (1980). Towards better interactive systems: methodology and problems in human-computer interaction. In T. Sata and E. Warman (Eds.), *Man-machine communication in CAD/CAM* (pp. 89–93). New York: North-Holland.

Hahn, W.V. (1982). The contribution of artificial intelligence to the human factors of application software. In A. Blaser & M. Zoeppritz (Eds.), *Enduser systems and their human factors* (pp. 128–138). New York: Springer-Verlag.

Hammond, N., & Barnard, P. (1984). Dialogue design: characteristics of user knowledge. In A. Monk (Ed.), *Fundamentals of human-computer interaction* (pp. 127–164). New York: Academic.

Harrison, M., & Thimbleby, H.W. (1985). Formalising guidelines for the design of interactive systems. In P. Johnson & S. Cook (Eds.), *People and computers: designing the interface* (pp. 161–171). New York: Cambridge University Press.

Heppe, D.L., Edmondson, W.H., & Spence, R. (1985). Helping both the novice and advanced user in menu-driven information retrieval systems. In P. Johnson & S. Cook (Eds.), *People and computers: designing the interface* (pp. 92–101). New York: Cambridge University Press.

Herot, C.F. (1982). Graphical user interfaces. In Y. Vassiliou (Ed.), *Human factors and interactive computer systems.* Norwood, NJ: Ablex.

Hill, I.D. (1983). Natural language versus computer language. In M.E. Sime & J. Coombs (Eds.), *Designing for human-computer communication* (pp. 55–72). New York: Academic.

Hiltz, S.R., & Turoff, M. (1985). Structuring computer-mediated communication systems to avoid information overload. *Communications of the ACM, 28,* 680–689.

Houghton, R.C., Jr. (1984). Online help systems: a conspectus. *Communications of the ACM, 27,* 126–133.

Huchingson, R.D. (1981). *New horizons for human factors in design.* New York: McGraw-Hill.

Hulme, C. (1984). Reading: extracting information from printed and electronically presented text. In A. Monk (Ed.), *Fundamentals of human-computer interaction* (pp. 35–47). New York: Academic.

Hussain, D., Hussain, K.M. (1984). *Information resource management.* Homewood, IL: Irwin.

Jacob, R.J.K. (1984). Using formal specifications in the design of a human-computer interface. *Communications of the ACM, 26,* 259–264.

Johnson, P., & Cook, S. (Eds.), (1985). *People and computers: Designing the interface.* New York: Cambridge University Press.

Kasschau, R.A., Lachman, R., & Laughery, K.R. (Eds.), (1982). *Information technology and psychology: prospects for the future.* New York: Praeger.

Kidd, A. (1984). Human factors problems in the design and use of expert systems. In A. Monk (Ed.), *Fundamentals of human-computer interaction* (pp. 237–247). New York: Academic.

Malone, T.W. (1984). Heuristics for designing enjoyable user interfaces: lessons from computer games. In J.C. Thomas & M.L. Schneider (Eds.), *Human factors in computer systems* (pp. 1–12). Norwood, NJ: Ablex.

Martin, J. (1973). *Design of man-computer dialogues.* Englewood Cliffs, NJ:Prentice-Hall.

Monk, A. (Ed.), (1984). *Fundamentals of human-computer interaction.* New York: Academic.

Morland, D.V. (1983). Human factors guidelines for terminal interface design. *Communications of the ACM, 26,* 484–494.

Mumford, E. (1971). A comprehensive method for handling the human problems of computer Interaction. *In Information Processing 71* (pp. 918–923). New York: North-Holland.

Naffah, N. (Ed.), (1982). *Office information systems*. New York: North-Holland.

Newcomb, T.M. (1953). An approach to the study of communicative acts, *Psychology Review, 60,* 393–404.

Newcomb, T.M. (1961). *The acquaintance process*. New York: Holt, Rinehart & Winston.

Norman, D.A. (1985). Design rules based on analyses of human error. *Communications of the ACM, 26,* 254–258.

Osborne, D.J. (1985). *Computers at work: A behavioral approach*. New York: John Wiley.

Otte, F.H. (1982). Consistent user interfaces. In Y. Vassiliou (Ed.), *Human factors and interactive computer systems* (pp. 261–276). Norwood, NJ: Ablex.

Reid, P. (1984). Work station design, activities and display techniques. In A. Monk (Ed.), *Fundamentals of human-computer interaction* (pp. 107–121). New York: Academic.

Reisner, P. (1982). Formal grammar and human factors design of an interactive graphic system. *IEEE Transactions on Software Engineering, 7,* 229–240.

Reisner, P. (1984). Analytic tools for human factors of software. In A. Blaser & M. Zoeppritz (Eds.), *Enduser systems and their human factors,* (pp. 94–121). New York: Springer-Verlag.

Reisner, P. (1984). Formal grammar as a tool for analyzing ease of use: some fundamental concepts. In J.C. Thomas & M.L. Schneider (Eds.), *Human factors in computer systems* (pp. 53–78). Norwood, NJ: Ablex.

Reitman-Olson, W.B.W., II, & Bruenenfelder, T.M. (1982). A general user interface for creating and displaying tree-structures, hierarchies, decision trees, and nested menus. In Y. Vassiliou (Ed.), *Human factors and interactive computer systems* (pp. 223–241). Norwood, NJ: Ablex.

Roberts, P.S. (1985). Intelligent computer-based training. In P. Johnson & S. Cook (Eds.), *People and computers: designing the interface* (pp. 264–272). New York: Cambridge University Press.

Sachman, H. (1970). *Man-computer problem solving*. Princeton, N.J.: Auerbach.

Salvendy, G. (Ed.), (1984). *Human-computer interaction advances in human factors/ ergonomics*. New York: Elsevier.

Savage, R.E., & Habinek, J.K. (1984). A multilevel menu-driven user interface: design and evaluation through simulation. In J.C. Thomas & M.L. Schneider (Eds.), *Human factors in computer systems* (pp. 165–186). Norwood, NJ: Ablex.

Schneider, M.L. (1982). Ergonomic considerations in the design of command languages. In Y. Vassiliou (Ed.), *Human factors and interactive computer systems* (pp. 141–162). Norwood, NJ: Ablex.

Shackel, B. (1985). Designing for people in the age of information. In B. Shackel (Ed.), *Human-computer interaction-INTERACT'84* (pp. 9–18). New York: Elsevier.

Sheppard, S.B., Bailey, J.W., & Bailey, E.K. (1984). An empirical evaluation of software documentation formats. In J.C. Thomas & M.L. Schneider (Eds.), *Human factors in computer systems* (pp. 135–164). Norwood, NJ: Ablex.

Shneiderman, B. (1980). *Software psychology: human factors in computer and information systems*. Cambridge, MA: Winthrop.

Shneiderman, B. (1982). The future of interactive systems and the emergence of direct manipulation. In Y. Vassiliou (Ed.), *Human factors and interactive computer systems* (pp. 1–28). Norwood, NJ: Ablex.

Shneiderman, B. (1983). Human factors of interactive software. In A. Blaser & M. Zoeppritz (Eds.), *Enduser systems and their human factors* (pp. 9–29). New York: Springer-Verlag.

Shneiderman, B. (1987). *Designing the user interface: strategies for effective human-computer interaction*. Cambridge, MA: Winthrop.

Sime, M.E., & Coombs, M.J. (Eds.), (1983). *Designing for human-computer communication*. New York: Academic.

Smith, J.J. (1985). SUSI   A smart user-system interface. In P. Johnson & S. Cook (Eds.), *People and computers: designing the interface* (pp. 211–220). New York: Cambridge University Press.

Sutcliffe, A.G. (1985). Use of conceptual maps as human-computer interfaces. In P. Johnson & S. Cook (Eds.), *People and computers: designing the interface* (pp. 117–127). New York: Cambridge University Press.

Thimbleby, H. (1984). User interface design: generative user engineering principles. In A. Monk (Ed.), *Fundamentals of human-computer interaction* (pp. 165–179). New York: Academic.

Taxonomy of Computer Science and Engineering (1980). Arlington, VA: AFIPS Press.

Thomas, J.C. (1982). Organizing for human factors. In Y. Vassiliou (Ed.), *Human factors and interactive computer systems* (pp. 29–46). Norwood, NJ: Ablex.

Thomas, J.C., & Schneider, M.L. (Eds.). (1984). *Human factors in computer systems.* Norwood, NJ: Ablex.

Turner, J.A., Jarke, M., Stohr, E.A., Vassiliou, Y., & White, N. (1982). Human factors and interactive computer systems. In Y. Vassiliou (Ed.), *Human factors and interactive computer systems* (pp. 163–190). Norwood, NJ: Ablex.

Vassiliou, Y. (Ed.). (1982). *Human factors and interactive computer systems.* Norwood, NJ: Ablex.

Vassiliou, Y., & Jarke, M. (1982). Query languages   a taxonomy. In Y. Vassiliou (Ed.), *Human factors and interactive computer systems* (pp. 47–81). Norwood, NJ: Ablex.

Weinberg, G.M. (1971). *The psychology of computer programming.* New York: Van Nostrand Reinhold.

Wickens, C.D. (1984). *Engineering psychology and human performance.* Columbus, OH: Charles E. Merrill.

Wilson, M.D., Barnard, P.J., & MacLean, A. (1985). Analysing the learning of command sequences in a menu system. In P. Johnson & S. Cook (Eds.), *People and computers: designing the interface* (pp. 63–75). New York: Cambridge University Press.

Woodson, W.E. (1981). *Human factors design handbook: information and guidelines for the design of systems, facilities, equipment, and products for human use.* New York: McGraw-Hill.

SECTION I

The Machine

This section focuses on the characteristics of the actual hardware that relate to human use of the computer system. It is represented by the machine in the taxonomy diagram (see Figure 1 of the General Introduction). The study of how the physical design of a machine fits the people using it is called *ergonomics*. Such issues as the tilt of a terminal screen, keyboard layout, use of color, height and position of the keyboard, and so forth are ergonomic issues. The overall goal in ergonomics is to enhance the performance of the system by improving the fit between man and machine. A machine which is difficult to use physically can very easily detract from, rather than enhance, system performance.

The physical body of a human being has certain characteristics which cannot be altered. Finger dexterity, muscle endurance, and visual processing are a few such characteristics. When the design of a machine does not take these given characteristics into consideration, the result can lead to degradation rather than improvement of performance.

An example of poor ergonomic fit between man and machine is the typewriter keyboard. The original keyboard was designed in a particular manner to keep the keys from sticking. The object was to separate the frequently used keys as far from each other as possible. That meant that the fingers had to travel farthest to reach those keys and consequently slowed down the typing process. The Dvorak-type keyboard has been designed to minimize the amount of finger travel by placing the frequently used keys in the center of the keyboard. Very few organizations have adopted this keyboard, however, and most of us are still struggling with the original layout on both typewriter and the computer keyboards.

If ergonomics is primarily concerned with the physical side of man/machine interaction, what is the relationship between human factors and ergonomics? The answer to this question differs from discipline to discipline. The traditional human factors engineer will tell you that they are one in the same. The human factors engineer is concerned with many machines other than the computer and in many cases the relationship between the human and the other machines is that of operator rather than user. In other words, the task environment is often that of physical work rather than mental work. For the most part, human factors engineers are concerned, foremost, with the performance of the system; secondarily, they realize that goodness of fit between the man and the machine impacts system performance.

Professionals in other disciplines, such as organizational behavior, psychology, and MIS, often separate the physical use of and interaction with the machine from the psychological interactions. Such aspects as ease of use, enhancement of learning, recall aid, task enhancement, information presentation, and so forth are termed human factors. The ergonomics issues are kept separate from the psychological issues. This orientation often stresses individual satisfaction with the system as the primary goal.

There is a great deal of overlap between the two areas and it is sometimes difficult to separate the physical from the psychological. The total human being is both physical and psychological in composition and the two components cannot be isolated from each other.

The two papers in this volume which focus on ergonomics (represented by the machine in Figure 1) are "UCI Guidelines Research for Keyboards and Function Keys" by Rodger Koppa of the Texas Transportation Institute, Texas A&M University, and "Verification of User Identity via Keyboard Characteristics" by John Leggett, Glen Williams, and David Umphress, from the Computer Science Department, also at Texas A&M University. Both papers center on the physical aspects of computer and user, and they both describe empirical studies which support their findings.

CHAPTER 2

Verification of User Identity via Keyboard Characteristics

John Leggett
Glen Williams
and
David Umphress
Texas A&M University

The implementation of safeguards for computer security is based on the ability to verify accurately the identity of authorized computer system users. The most common form of identity verification in use today is the password. The password has many poor traits as an access control mechanism, however. To overcome the many disadvantages of simple password protection, we are proposing the use of the physiological characteristics of keyboard input as a method for verifying user identity.

After an overview of the problem and summary of previous research, a pilot study is described which was conducted to determine the possibility of using keystroke characteristics as a means of identity verification. Due to the promising results of the pilot study, the last section of the paper describes proposed future experimentation.

INTRODUCTION

Overview of Problem and Proposed Solution

Control of access to computer systems and networks is becoming increasingly important as computers are entrusted with more sensitive applications and more valuable information. In recent years, much emphasis has been placed on increasing the accessibility to computers in order to accommodate the user and to enhance user-computer interaction. This increased accessibility has posed new threats to system security and has emphasized the need for more adequate safeguards against unauthorized access and misuse of computer resources. Central

29

to the implementation of safeguards for computer security is the ability to verify accurately the identity of authorized computer system users (Brand & Makey 1985; Cole, 1978; National Bureau of Standards, 1977; Warfel, 1984).

A survey by Wood (1977) shows that the password is the overwhelming choice as a personal identifier. Passwords are inexpensive and easy to implement. However, passwords suffer from the disadvantage of being open to compromise without knowledge of their disclosure. Warfel (1984) points out that a stolen password is frequently used many times before anyone realizes it has been compromised. Also, the degree of security provided by the password is largely dependent upon the possible number of combinations from which it is chosen (Brand & Makey, 1985; National Bureau of Standards, 1977). Most passwords are limited in length to eight or less characters and most are chosen to be familiar words, both of which reduce the allowable combinations and increase the likelihood that the password will be compromised by observation or determined guesswork. Once compromised, the computer system has no way of telling an imposter from an authorized user, because the password is assumed to be secret.

Another disadvantage of the password is that it is a Static Identity Verifier. Normally, the user is asked for the password at log-in time and the system assumes that the user is the same person until log-off time. It is quite common, though, for a user to be away from the keyboard during a session. An imposter would then be able to key information through the user's keyboard without detection.

To overcome the many disadvantages of simple password protection, we are proposing the use of the physiological characteristics of keyboard input as a method for verifying user identity. In this way, the password can be replaced with a passphrase and knowledge of the passphrase will not in itself compromise security. This method will allow a higher level of security through a simple extension to the common use of passwords. Likewise, continued surveillance of the keystrokes would allow a Dynamic Identity Verifier. An imposter would have a much more difficult time trying to breach security by keying information at a logged-in keyboard, because the imposter's keyboard profile would not match the user's keyboard profile. Through the use of both of these techniques, a much higher level of security would be available at minimum cost and minimum user inconvenience.

PREVIOUS RESEARCH

Background

Cole (1978) proposes six areas of information protection: identification, local access control, remote access control, information flow control, threat monitoring, and protection assurance. He maintains these areas are hierarchical in nature; the security of one area is contingent on the strength of the previous area. Thus, according to Cole (1978), identification of the user is the primary issue that must be addressed in the protection of information. The security system must (a) determine who is requesting access to resources (b) verify the requester's identity. Cost, accuracy, and robustness play important roles in the selection of an identifier. In general, the identification process may be categorized as being based on knowledge (e.g., passwords), artifacts (e.g., keys), or personal characteristics (e.g., fingerprints) (National Bureau of Standards, 1978). The form of identification selected is determined by operational requirements.

Of the three categories of identifiers, personal characteristics give the greatest promise of identity monitoring (Cotton & Meissner, 1975; Forsen, Nelson, & Staron, 1977; National Bureau of Standards, 1978). Woodard (1979) points out that the strength of identifiers based on personal characteristics is two-fold. First, with proper selection, the identifier is unique to the individual. Second, identifiers are not easily transferred from one individual to another. Research is thus focused on determining those personal characteristics that are unique, easily measurable, and relatively stable over time.

Automated identification using characteristics based on physiological or morphological attributes was initially investigated by forensic medicine specialists. In the mid-1960s, the Federal Bureau of Investigation, together with the National Bureau of Standards conducted studies on automated fingerprint recognition (Wegstein, 1970) and voice recognition (Doddington, 1975). The emphasis of this work was on law enforcement and consequently of interest mostly to criminologists. In the early 1970s, however, personal characteristics were introduced as identity verification mechanisms for secure entry to controlled areas (Rennick & Vitols, 1975). User acceptability and convenience sparked the use of hand geometries and signatures in the recognition process. After extensive work on access control for physical resources, Cotton and Meissner (1975) suggested that logical resources, such as information, could be reliably protected by the use of personal characteristics. Although they advocated integrating recognition devices directly into computer terminals, the level of technology at that time made this prohibitive. However, the interest in security and user identification prompted the National Bureau of Standards to develop a set of guidelines describing the use and effectiveness of personal identifiers (National Bureau of Standards, 1977). It was at this time that Meissner (1976) proposed a set of evaluation criteria for identifiers. His work also included a formal scenario for the use of identifiers: train the recognition device, accept samples, compare samples to reference patterns, assess differences, and accept or reject the sample. Because personal characteristics identification moved from forensics to access control, research has been channeled primarily into the areas of fingerprint, voiceprint, hand geometry, and signature recognition.

PSYCHOLOGY OF KEYSTROKING

As early as the turn of the century, psychology experiments demonstrated that the mechanics of human actions are predictable in the performance of repetitive, routine tasks. In 1895, observations of telegraph operators showed that each operator had a distinctive pattern of keying messages over telegraph lines (Bryan & Harter, 1899). Further, operators often recognized who was transmitting information simply by listening to the characteristic pattern of dots and dashes.

Just as the telegraph key served as a common input medium in days past, the keyboard is the most common computer input device today. Keying patterns are rich in qualities unique to individuals. Shaffer (1970, 1973) suggests that typing is a motor programmed skill; keystroke movements are organized in advance of their actual execution. Thomas and Jones (1970) postulated that part of the brain was being used as a short-term buffer. The typist looks at text, loads a certain amount of text into the buffer, then outputs the text onto the keys of the keyboard. Shaffer (1976, 1982) proposes that the rhythm with which the buffer is emptied is determined by an "executive pacer." Gentner's (1983) research goes a step further to show that although the typing process exhibits an overall rhythm, individual keystroke times are affected by hand position, finger length, and learning habits. This argument is strengthened by computer simulation of the typing process (Rumelhart & Norman, 1982). Cooper (1983) demonstrates that limitations on the buffer size cause typists to group text into discrete, predictable units. Card, Moran, & Newell (1980) take advantage of this "cognitive partitioning" to model user-computer interaction during a session at an interactive terminal. The keystroke-level model is designed to evaluate the cognitive processes required in the operation of text editors.

IDENTIFICATION BASED ON KEYSTROKES

The use of keystroke characteristics for identification was suggested by (Spillane, 1975). His approach was oriented toward access control for physical facilities. He proposed to associate a unique phrase with each individual and to use phrase content, time between keystrokes, and force of each keystroke as identifying attributes. However, such a system was never designed (Spillane, personal communication with D. Humphress, 1984). In 1977, the Air Force conducted a study to evaluate those personal characteristics that offered the highest potential for access control (Forsen et al., 1977). Typing style was one of the 30 attributes examined. Experiments in this area consisted of having each participant type his or her name and the name of all other participants. Although the project showed that access control via typing style received a great degree of user acceptability, names proved to be too short for positive personal identification. In 1980, the Rand Corporation produced some preliminary results on authentication by keystroke timing under a National Science Foundation grant (Gaines, Lisowski, & Shapiro, 1980). Even though their experiment was "based upon a small and imperfect sample of data" Shapiro concluded: "This is an important area of research, positive results are expected in future related research, and preliminary analysis strongly suggests the existence of typing 'signatures.' " However, further experimentation was not conducted (Shapiro, personal communication with D. Umphress, 1984). Finally, Barton and Barton (1984) suggest the use of keyboard characteristics in the determination of passwords, although they do not propose any recognition scheme.

SUMMARY

It is clear that a need exists for better access control to computer systems. Previous research indicates that keyboard characteristics may have the discriminating power necessary for identity verification. The next section of this paper will describe a pilot study which was conducted to determine the feasibility of using keystroke characteristics as a means of identity verification. For a complete discussion of this experiment, please see the paper by Umphress and Williams (1985). Due to the success of the pilot study, the last section of this paper will describe proposed future experimentation.

DESCRIPTION OF PILOT STUDY

Introduction

The pilot study consisted of the design, implementation, and evaluation of an experiment in identity verification based on keystroke digraph latency times. A digraph is defined as two adjacent letters; for example, the word fish consists of the three digraphs: fi, is, sh. A digraph latency time is the time elapsed between the keypresses for the letters of the digraph.

The psychological models of Card et al. (1980), Shaffer (1978, 1982), Gentner (1983), and Cooper (1983) provided the common base for determining which keystrokes characterize an individual's keying patterns. The keystroke-level model was used initially to decide that the only keystrokes within words would be evaluated; that is, no mental preparation time (Tm) was included, only the time to press the keys. The works of Gentner and Shaffer indicated that digraph latencies within words might give the ability to discriminate required for distinguishing among keyboard profiles. Finally, Cooper's work indicated that pause points in keystroking occur between words as well as within words that are longer than six to eight characters.

The general experimental procedure consisted of having the participants generate a keyboard reference profile followed, at a later date, by a keyboard test profile. All test profiles were compared to all reference profiles and a value of low, medium, or high was assigned, indicating the level of confidence that the same individual typed both the reference and test profiles.

THE EXPERIMENT

The generation of the reference and test profiles consisted of accepting keystrokes and storing them with a time stamp. Time was divided into intervals of .01s. The keystrokes were then filtered as follows:

1. The typed text was compared to the original text and any word containing an error was discarded. This was done to remove any possibility of mental preparation times due to the recognition of an error.

2. Intraword digraph times were then generated for the first six characters of each word.

3. Finally, latencies over .75 in duration were discarded. A latency this large indicates unfamiliarity with the keyboard or some sort of mental preparation time and is not suitable for inclusion in a particular digraph's statistics.

Two keystroke characteristic measures were generated from the filtered key-stroke data. The first measure was the overall mean and standard deviation of the filtered keystrokes. The second measure was the mean digraph time of each digraph in the filtered keystrokes.

Two measures were used to compare test profiles to reference profiles. For the first measure, test-profile digraph latency times were compared with reference-profile digraph latency means. If the test digraph latency time was within 0.5 sd (using the reference profile standard deviation) of the reference digraph latency mean, then this digraph latency was counted as valid. The ratio of valid digraph latencies to total digraph latencies was then computed. The test profile passed the "digraph test" if the ratio was greater than 0.6. The values of 0.5 and 0.6 used above were empirically determined.

The second measure consisted of comparing the test-profile mean to the reference-profile mean using the standard two-tailed T-test for a population mean assuming a normal distribution. The null hypothesis was that the mean test-profile latency is equal to the mean reference-profile latency. An alpha level of 0.05 was used to determine whether the test profile passed the "overall test".

The combined results of the tests were used to indicate the degree of confidence that the same person keyed both test and reference profiles. A high confidence was assessed if both tests passed, a medium confidence was assessed if only one test passed, and a low confidence was assessed if neither test passed.

EXPERIMENTAL RESULTS AND EVALUATION

Seventeen programmers, ranging in keyboard proficiency from touch-typists to those with few formal typing skills, participated in the experiment. The participants were asked to submit two typing samples. The first sample consisted of approximately 1,400 characters and served as a reference profile. The second sample, of approximately 300 characters, was used as the test profile. Comparison of all test profiles to all reference profiles showed that, in most instances, a high confidence was assigned in cases where the same individual typed both the test profile and reference profile. This is shown in Figure 1 on the main diagonal. A few medium confidences were assessed when the test profile and reference profile typist were not the same, but in general a low confidence was assigned in this case.

Two measures are commonly computed when evaluating security mechanisms: false alarm rate (FAR) and imposter pass rate (IPR). The FAR indicates the degree to which the methodology fails to recognize authorized individuals. A FAR of 2% would indicate that, on the average, authorized individuals would be rejected in 2 out of 100 attempts. The FAR for this experiment was calculated as the ratio of low and medium confidence scores on the diagonal to the total number of

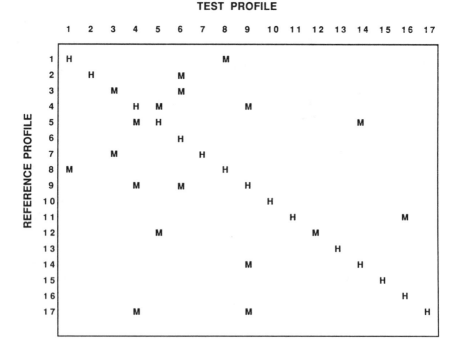

Figure 1. Comparison of test reference profiles H = high confidence, M = medium confidence, blank = low confidence (Umphress and Williams 1985)

scores on the diagonal; this gives a FAR of approximately 12% (2:17). The IPR indicates the degree to which the methodology fails to reject imposters. An IPR of 3% would indicate that, on the average, imposters would be accepted in 3 out of 100 attempts. The IPR for this experiment was calculated as the ratio of medium and high confidence scores outside the diagonal to the total number of scores outside the diagonal; this gives an IPR of approximately 6% (16:272). Obviously one would like the FAR and IPR to be 0, but, for initial experimentation these rates were encouraging. It should also be noted that there was no high confidences assigned off the diagonal and no low confidences assigned on the diagonal.

Other measures considered for evaluation are cost, time, and user convenience. The cost is dependent on the implementation. For this experiment the extra cost was nil since the microcomputer had a programmable clock and the capability for isolating each keystroke. Most microcomputers have these same facilities. The time to compute the various measures is minimal and could be done in real-time quite easily. Finally, the biggest benefit is user convenience; the user can be accomplishing a useful task while identity is being verified.

PROPOSED FUTURE EXPERIMENTATION

Introduction

We propose to identify those characteristics which make up the keyboard profile and to use the profiles to enhance the access control mechanism. In particular, to enhance the static use of passwords, we are proposing the use of a passphrase in conjunction with the user's keyboard profile as a Static Identity Verifier. The computer system can then check that the correct secret passphrase was input and also verify user identity based on the profile. An imposter, having stolen the passphrase, is still unable to breach the security mechanism. A simple log file will indicate that an imposter is attempting to use the passphrase.

A similar scheme is proposed for Dynamic Identity Verification. The user's keyboard characteristics will be monitored during the entire logged-in time. These characteristics will be matched against the user's keyboard profile and a confidence level assigned indicating the probability that the current keystroker is the owner of the current profile. This will allow a continual verification of the identity of a user. An imposter would not be able to successfully use a logged-in keyboard during the absence of a user.

List of Objectives

The specific objective are as follows:

1. We will evaluate keyboard actions to determine those characteristics which will give the necessary discriminating power for identity verification. Typical keyboard actions would include the digraph latency times of: left hand only (e.g., *ce*), right hand only (e.g., *li*), left-right and right-left transitions (e.g, *fo*, *ma*), and medials (e.g, *en*, *ly*). Gaines et al. (1980) have suggested that the latency times of the five digraphs (*in, io, no, on,* and *ul*) are sufficient to distinguish righthanded touch typists from one another in a reliable way. We will certainly try to determine the smallest set of actions possible, thereby validating or invalidating the RAND findings. Other keyboard actions might include error rates, capital letter digraphs, and particular trigraphs and tetragraphs. The evaluation of keyboard actions will consist of a large amount of keyboard data capturing from many individuals. Satisfying this objective will give the basic data (now unavailable) necessary for successful completion of the following objectives.

2. We will develop two scoring algorithms based on the keyboard

actions identified in objective one. The first scoring algorithm will be used to verify statically the identity of a user at initial log-in time. The second scoring algorithm will be used to verify dynamically verify the identity of a user throughout the total logged-in time. The output of the algorithms will indicate the probability that the keystroker is the claimed authorized user. Satisfying this objective will give the methodology necessary to use keystroke characteristics as an identity verifier.

3. We will conduct controlled experiments to determine the FAR and IPR of the methodologies determined in objective 2. Satisfying this objective will give an indication of the degree of success of the methodologies identified in objective 2.

4. In addition to the FAR and IPR of objective 3, we will evaluate the methodologies determined in objective two and the use of keystroke characteristics for identity verification in general by considering the following factors:

    a. Resistance to deceit

    b. Susceptibility to circumvention

    c. Convenience to user

    d. Time to make accept/reject decision

    e. Processing requirements

    f. Interfacing requirements

    g. Cost of use, protection, distribution, and logistical support

Experimental Procedure

For Objectives 1 and 2 (evaluating keyboard actions and developing scoring algorithms) we will employ an iterative procedure consisting of

1. enrolling several users by generating reference profiles based on keyboard characteristics;
2. having the same users generate test profiles based on the same keyboard characteristics;
3. computing correlations among all users;
4. evaluating the discriminating power of these keyboard characteristics; and
5. adjusting the keyboard characteristics for the next iteration.

Software has been written which will collect the raw data by capturing each keystroke along with a time stamp. Several filtering programs have also been written and several more filters will be required. By using the same data and applying a different filter, we may shorten the iterative procedure above by removing the user from the loop. This iterative procedure will continue until we have identified those keyboard characteristics which give the most discriminating power across a broad range of keyboard samples. Accomplishment of Objective 3 will require the execution of two distinct experiments. The first experiment will use Scoring Algorithm 1 to attempt to statically verify the identity of a user at log-in time. The procedure for Experiment 1 will be as follows:

1. Approximately 50 authorized users will be enrolled by producing reference profiles based on typing a passphrase of at least 60 characters and at most 75 characters. A typical passphrase might consist of: first name, last name, password, and phrase; for example, "john leggett curlyjoe once upon a midnight dreary while I pondered" (66). The passphrase will be typed approximately five times for enrollment.
2. The passphrases for all authorized users will be collected, published, and distributed to each experimental participant.
3. Each authorized user will be instructed to:
4. log-in as himself 10 times;
5. log-in as an imposter of all the authorized users one time;
6. log-in as an imposter of a particular other authorized user 10 times.
7. After each accept or reject decision, the system will ask the user if it made the right decision and record the responses.
8. The FAR and IPR will be generated by the system automatically.

The second experiment will use Scoring Algorithm 2 to attempt to verify dynamically the identity of a user throughout a longer typing sample. The procedure for Experiment 2 will be as follows:

1. Approximately 50 authorized users will be enrolled by producing reference profiles based on typing a passage of approximately 1000 words.
2. Each authorized user will be instructed to:
3. identify himself and type the passage; and
4. identify as an imposter of a particular other authorized user and type the passage.
5. After each accept or reject decision, the system will ask the user if it made the right decision and record the responses.
6. The FAR and IPR will be generated by the system automatically.

It is anticipated that the methodology for Experiment 2 will accept or reject the user as soon as possible. In these cases, the number of characters typed up to the decision point will be recorded. This count will give an indication of the number of characters necessary for verifying identity or verifying lack of identity. As much as possible, the basic data from all experiments will be captured in order to provide other researchers a base of keystroke data.

The accomplishment of Objective 4 (evaluation on multiple criteria) will be a subjective assessment after having had the experience of executing the experiments. Discussion will follow the guidelines established by the National Bureau of Standards (1977).

Proposals for the accomplishment of the above study are currently being reviewed by the appropriate funding agencies.

SUMMARY

The immediate benefit of a successful methodology for using keystroke characteristics as an identity verifier would be a much higher level of security with very little investment in time or materials and very little inconvenience to the user. Any organization which is responsible for the safekeeping and secrecy of personal information (e.g., banks, police, government) would benefit from the methodology. If the techniques discovered are highly successful, the results could make a major impact on system security in a broad range of applications.

REFERENCES

Barton, B., & Barton, M. (1984). User-friendly password methods for computer-mediated information systems. *Computers and Security, 3*, 186–195.

Brand, S.D., & Makey, J.D. (1985). *Department of Defense password management guideline.* Fort George G. Mead, MD: DOD Computer Security Center.

Bryan, W.L., & Harter, N. (1899). Studies in the telegraphic language. *Psychological Review, 6*, 345–375.

Card, S.K., Moran, T.P., & Newell, A. (1980). The keystroke-level model for user performance time with interactive systems. *Communications of the ACM, 23*, 396–410.

Cole, D. (1978, January). Design alternatives for computer network security. (*National Bureau of Standards Special Publication No. 500–21, 1.* Washington, D.C.: U.S. Government Printing Office.

Cooper, E. (1093). *Cognitive aspects of skilled typewriting.* New York: Springer-Verlag.

Cotton, I.W., & Meissner, P. (1975). Approaches to controlling personal access to computer terminals. *Computer Networks Symposium,* (pp. 32–38). New York: IEEE.

Doddington, G.R. (1975). Speaker identification for entry control. *Proceedings of Wescon.* Western Electric Show and Convention, El Segundo, CA.

Forsen, G., Nelson, M., & Staron, R. (1977). Personal attributes authentication techniques. Rome, NY: Rome Air Development Center (RADC). (*Tech. Rep. No. TR-77-1033*).

Gaines, R.S., Lisowski, W., Press, S.J., & Shapiro, N. (1980). Authentication by keystroke timing: some preliminary results. (*Rand Report No. R-2526-NSF*). Santa Monica, CA: Rand Corporation.

Gentner, D.R. (1983). Keystroke timing in transcription typing. In W.E. Cooper (Ed.), *Cognitive aspects of skilled typewriting* (pp. 95–120), New York: Springer-Verlag.

Meissner, P. (1976). Evaluation of techniques for verifying personal Identity. *Proceedings of the 15th Annual Technical ACM-NBS Symposium* (p. 119–127). New York: ACM.

National Bureau of Standards. (1977). Evaluation of techniques for automated personal identification. *FIPS Publication No. 48.* Washington, D.C.: U.S. Government Printing Office.

National Bureau of Standards. (1978, June). Considerations in the selection of security measures for automatic data processing systems. (*NBS Special Publication 500-23*). Washington, D.C.: U.S. Government Printing Office.

Rennick, R.J., & Vitols, V.A. (1975). MUFTI- A multifunction identification system. *Proceedings of Wescon.* Western Electric Show and Convention, El Segundo, CA.

Rumelhart, D., & Norman, D.A. (1982). Simulating a skilled typist: A study of skilled cognitive motor performance. *Cognitive Science, 6,* 1–36.

Shaffer, L.J. (1970). The basis of transcription skill. *Journal of Experimental Psychology, 84,* 424–440.

Shaffer, L.H. (1973). Latency mechanisms in transcription. In S. Kornblum (Ed.), *Attention and performance, 4,* (pp. 435–446). New York: Academic.

Shaffer, L.H. (1976). Intention and performance. *Psychological Review, 83,* 375–393.

Shaffer, L.H. (1978). Timing in the motor programming of typing. *Quarterly Journal of Experimental Psychology, 30,* 333–345.

Shaffer, L.H. (1982). Rhythm and timing in skill. *Psychological Review, 89,* 109–122.

Spillane, R.J. (1975). Keyboard apparatus for personal identification. *IBM Technical Disclosure Bulletin, 17,* 3346.

Thomas, E.A.C., & Jones, R.G.A. (1970). A model for subjective grouping in typewriting. *Quarterly Journal of Experimental Psychology, 22,* 254–367.

Umphress, D. & Williams, G. (1985). Identity verification through keyboard characteristics. *International Journal of Man-Machine Studies, 23,* 263–273.

Warfel, G.H. (1984). Identification technology. *Auerbach data security management,* (pp. 1–11). Pennsauken, NJ: Auerbach Publishing.

Wegstein, J. (1970). Automated fingerprint identification. (*National Bureau of Standards Technical Note 538*). Washington, D.C. U.S. Government Printing Office.

Wood, H. (1977). The use of passwords for controlled access to computer resources. (*National Bureau of Standards Special Publication 500-9*). Washington, D.C.: U.S. Government Printing Office.

Woodard, J.P., & Maier, J.J. (1979). Automatic entry control for military applications. *1979 Carnahan Conference on Crime Countermeasures,* (pp. 65–76). Lexington: University of Kentucky.

CHAPTER 3

User Computer Interface (UCI) Guidelines Research For Keyboards and Function Keys

Rodger J. Koppa
Texas A&M University

This paper presents the results of several experiments conducted upon many different keyboards at the Texas Transportation Institute since 1983. The thrust of these experiments has been to collect data to support the standardization of keyboards for military use. The results of the experiments are reported and a consensus computer keyboard is presented.

INTRODUCTION

Since 1983 the Texas Transportation Institute (TTI) has been engaged in a program of survey and research into issues of layout, function key designation, physical characteristics of keys, innovative types of keyboard input devices, and even some development guidelines for quick reference guides for the use of software programs. Sponsorship of this program has come from the U.S. Army's Human Engineering Laboratory (HEL), headquartered at Aberdeen Proving Grounds, Maryland. The underlying theme of what otherwise may seem to be a very mixed bag of work is standards for keyboard-type data-entry devices for a very special class of users—military recruits under combat conditions for whom no assumptions can be made concerning previous experience, training, level of education, or motivatio--other than perhaps panic.

To date, only a few guides have been available to assist designers of military command and control systems in specification of keyboard interfaces, particularly at the tactical level: notably, the long-obsolete MIL-STD-1280, a few hints in MIL-STD-1472 (lately expanded to an

43

entire section), and more recently, a chapter in DOD-HDBK-761 on full keyboard layouts. Industry, in the meantime, has come up with a variety of different keyboard layouts which differ in function-key nomenclature, locations, cursor-key approach, and even some fundamental issues such as numeric arrangement of keypads, the perennial "telephone" versus "calculator" controversy. The arrangement of small keyboards (or keypads as they are usually called) is even more chaotic, even though such keypads are finding their way into many industries and such special-purpose equipment as the user interface. Most design guides are eloquently silent concerning 3x3, 3x4, or 4x4 keypads. A well-equipped forward command post may have three or four keyboards, as many keypads, plus communication devices, all built by different manufacturers, varying from slightly to radically different keyboards.

The emphasis in this program of research has been on that class of devices for which the greatest need seemed to exist for developing a basis for standards for the military—the small keyboard or keypad. Some studies are planned in the future that concentrate on the full keyboard, and one survey and one empirical study of the full keyboard have been done since TTI began this program.

4 x 4 KEYPAD LITERATURE SURVEY

This very limited survey was completed in 1983 for the HEL. Two basic kinds of keypads were researched: those which support single-input-at-a-time entry and those which support multiple-press entry or "chord" keypads. At the time of this literature search, the fundamental question of bottom-up (calculator) versus top-down (telephone) layouts (Figure 1) had not been researched for almost a generation and a new user population, much more used to touch-tone (R) phones and pocket calculators, warranted consideration. The suspicion was and is strong, however, that consistency of layout and function designation is much more important than the layout per se.

Alphabetic entry with a restricted keypad, if it is to be unambiguous (as telephone alphabetic entry is not), requires some strategies involving sequential or simultaneous key encoding. Various strategies such as shift keys, matrix denotation, combinations of multiple shift keys, and use of keys under a chord scheme that involved pressing keys in spatial patterns that were symbolic or at least mnemonic were found in the literature.

Research on function keys, such as "ENTER", "+", and "2nd", revealed no firm industry guidelines yet something of a consensus of

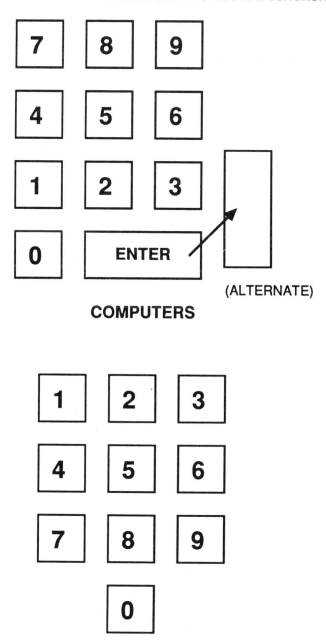

Figure 1. Telephone vs. caculator keypads

location for these keys emerged from a survey of a number of commercially available keypad devices. They tend to be located in a C-shape encircling the numeric/alphabetic keys, with ENTER (or its analogous function) at the lower righthand corner of the pad (Figure 2). Some of these consensus configurations for different sizes of small keypads are sketched here (Figure 3).

The literature appeared to favor labels over templates for any kind of keyboard, even though many software programs now feature a screen presentation of function-key redesignation (such as the Wordstar processor with which this presentation is being composed!).

Chord or multiple simultaneous entry keyboards have been of interest for many years. They have, of course, been in use for centuries in musical instruments and, since 1920 or so, with special purpose machines such as the Stenotype machine. The chief disadvantages of chord keypads are the long training times generally needed and the high error rates found, even with trained operators. Nevertheless, a well-(human) engineered chord keypad held some promise for use as a UCI for certain military applications.

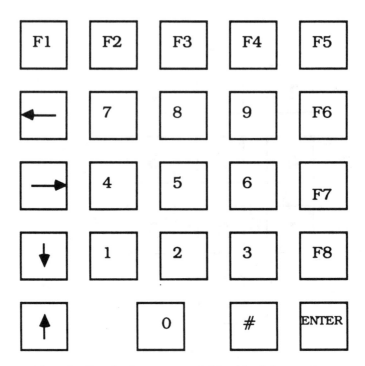

Figure 2. Function keys suuround right side of character keys

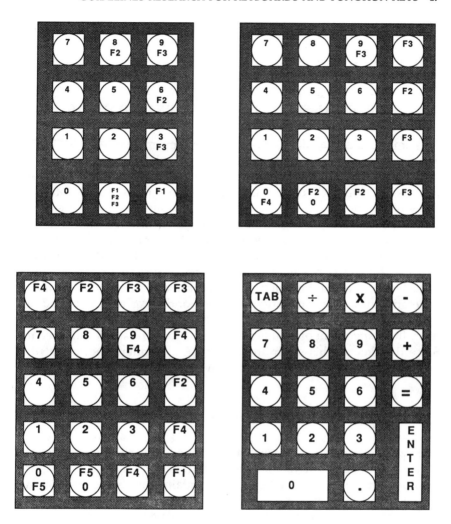

Figure 3.   Industry concensus keypads of various martix size

A CONSENSUS KEYBOARD

Although a recommended full keyboard appears in DOD-HDBK-761, it struck some of us at A&M as being somewhat at variance with industry practice as the "PC Generation" came of age. Several researchers accordingly embarked upon a survey of all the leading microcomputers available in the local area and mapped their keyboard layouts onto a wall-sized template blown up from the one that appears in MIL-STD-

1280. This keyboard, as close as one can get to a "consensus," is shown in Figure 4 side-by-side with the 761 layout. Many similarities exist, but there are some differences.

EMPIRICAL STUDY 1: KEYPAD ARRANGEMENTS

This small study was designed to answer the simple question, "Which arrangement is best for numeric entry, calculator or telephone?" A population of research participants reasonably representative of military recruits, 105 high-school vocational education seniors, busily entered a series of random seven-digit number sets. The numbers were presented from an audio tape, with a suitably motivating message that exhorted participants to be accurate because their "life might depend it!" No corrections were allowed. Entry speed and errors formed the dependent variables for this one-way analysis of variance design.

Results supported the null hypothesis of no difference; the upcoming generation has some familiarity with both kinds of arrangement and can operate either one reasonably well (Figure 5). But, obviously, consistency in arrangement of a numeric keypad should be strictly adhered to. Since the time of this study the Army HEL, I understand, adopted a recommendation of the "telephone" layout for all numeric keypads.

INITIAL STUDY OF ALPHABETIC ENTRY STRATEGY

The same research participants also entered four-character nonsense syllables using one of two strategies with this keypad (Figure 6). Either the operator designates the key which contains the character which he or she intends to input, and then (using the bottom row of keys) which of the three is meant (Strategy A) or (Strategy B), just the opposite, which of three possibilities is intended, and then the key on which the character in question is found. To no one's overwhelming surprise, Strategy A won hands down, especially with regard to errors (Figure 7). This study was felt to be just the opening salvo in a series of encoding strategy studies.

FOLLOW-ON STUDY OF ENCODING STRATEGIES

Taking its cue from the previous study, a follow-on project has recently been completed which looks at three additional methods of encoding

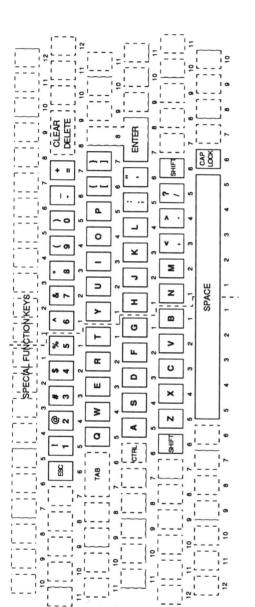

THE TEXAS TRANSPORTATION INSTITUTE CONSENSUS COMPUTER KEYBOARD

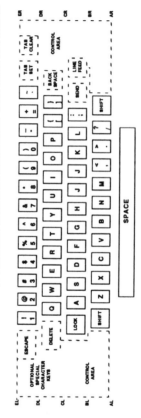

MIL-HDBK-761 SUGGESTED COMPUTER KEYBOARD

Figure 4.   A comparison of the TTI consensus keyboard with MIL-HDBK-761 keyboard

49

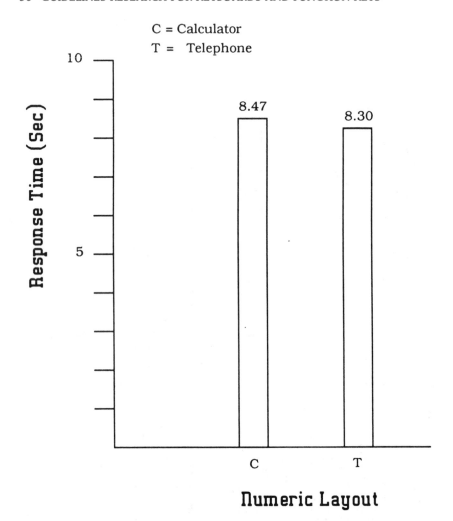

Figure 5. Mean entry times for telephone and calculator layout keypads

the same (worst-case) nonsense syllables and runs a baseline using Strategy A above (Figure 8).

- *Three-Press.* A given character may take one, two, or three key presses, depending on whether it is left, center, or right.
- *Two-press.* Same as above, but only two letters per key.
- *Shift-key.* Same layout as two-press, but the second character is denoted by pressing a shift or "second" key, as is commonly used today on calculators and similar keypad entry or control devices.

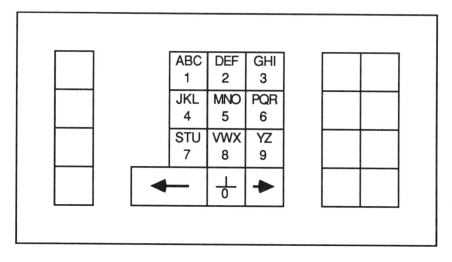

Figure 6.   Experimental keypad for alphanumeric entry

The results of this study are shown in Figure 9. To at least some of the researchers' surprise, the two-press keypad turned out to be fastest and scored lower on errors as well. The Strategy A and shift-key approach tied for the red ribbon, with the three-press a very distant third.

EFFECT OF KEY DISPLACEMENT ON TYPING PERFORMANCE

In combat situations, the fewer moving parts a device has, the less likely it is to jam, stick, freeze, bend, or become contaminated. Nowhere is this more true than with keyboard entry devices. Keyboards regularly become inoperative in office environments, because of coffee spills, cigarette ash, food, and rough handling. The office is a white chamber compared to a battlefield. Membrane-type keyboards or, at any rate, keyboards that have no obvious moving parts, are thus very attractive to military information system designers, if some of the inherent disadvantages of these devices can be overcome. But the first question is, "Just how much difference can be expected with keyboards which have no kinesthetic, or auditory, feedback, as compared to conventional keyboards?" To get a feel for how performance might change with amount of key displacement, an intermediate-travel condition was included in the study as well as no displacement and full displacement. In order to make a no displacement keyboard which was otherwise identical to the (Apple II +) conventional keyboard, a membrane input

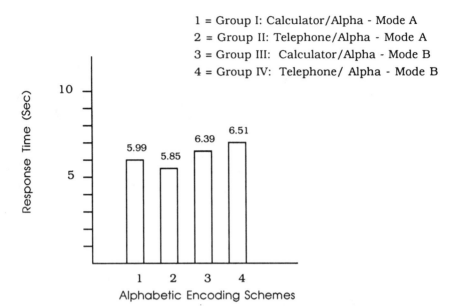

1 = Group I: Calculator/Alpha - Mode A
2 = Group II: Telephone/Alpha - Mode A
3 = Group III: Calculator/Alpha - Mode B
4 = Group IV: Telephone/ Alpha - Mode B

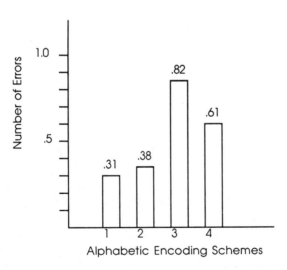

Figure 7. Entry time and errors with the use of alphabetic entry schemes

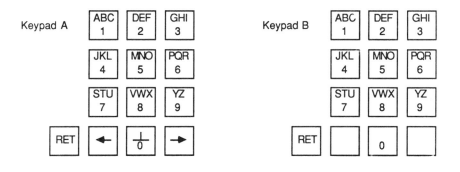

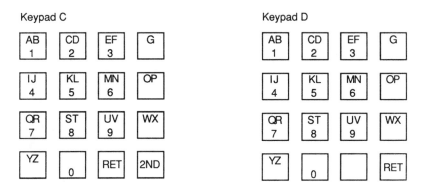

Figure 8. Alternative keypads for encoding strategy study

(sketchpad) device was overlaid by an acetate sheet on which was cemented Apple keys with center inserts to make the input to the membrane and hence to the computer.

Research participants, who were stratified according to typing skill, input lists of 10-digit random numbers and lists of 3-character nonsense syllables. The results of this study indicate that numeric entry speeds were not affected by differences in displacement. Alphabet character input, however, was slowest when no displacement was provided and intermediate when full displacement was provided. Accuracy was also affected by displacement, with those having no-displacement keyboards doing the worst (Figure 10). "Worst" is a highly relative term, however,

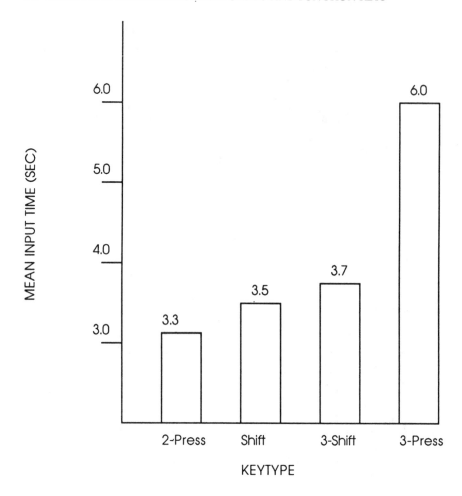

Figure 9. Mean encoding time for four-letter group

because performance differences were really minor and acceptable for the no displacement condition. Highly skilled typists were the least affected by displacement and adapted to any of the three displacement modes. As far as preference is concerned, research participants preferred the medium-displacement keyboard and disliked the no-displacement version.

Future research into the use of no-moving-part keyboards will focus on issues such as substitute feedback for the lost kinesthetic component—clicks or sounds of some kind or perhaps a "clicker deformation of a substrate that has no operational significance". Also, stair-step as well as other "land- scaping" configurations for the keyboard will be studied to help develop design criteria for no-displacement keyboards for military use.

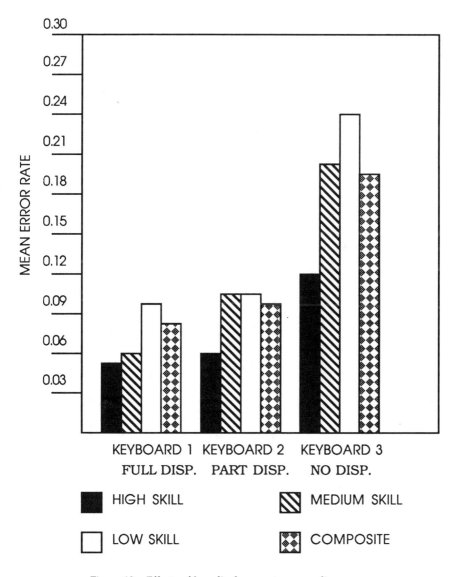

Figure 10. Effects of key displacement on encoding errors

AN EXPERIMENTAL STUDY OF A 5-KEY
HANDPRINT CHORD KEYBOARD

The final study I would like to describe from our HEL research program was of the utility of a 5-key "handprint" chord keyboard with integral display (Figure 11).

This device—the Microwriter, made in the United Kingdom—is cur-

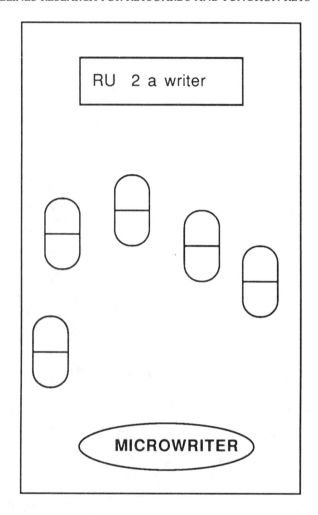

Figure 11. "Handprint" five-finger chord keypad (microwriter)

rently available. In this project, research participants who had no previous computer experience were trained to input textual material and random numbers/nonsense syllables using this handprint keyboard or the Strategy A 4x4 keypad described earlier, the one in which the operator designates a key on which a wanted character occurs and then indicates with three special designator keys at the bottom of the array which character is meant (Figure 12). Participants were trained for 5 days in 30-min sessions, one per day. Those who used the handprint keyboard were assigned to one of two strategies for learning: the use of mnemonic information (Figure 13) or a simple diagram of the pattern of finger and thumb presses required for any given character (Figure 14). Performance at the end of 5 days as measured by speed and errors in input of numbers and characters was still on the increase with both keypads.

The Microwriter has great appeal for operators who have the use of only one of their hands, either because of disability or because the other hand is doing something like flying a helicopter. It is easy to imagine variants of this concept for use with the feet by such persons as bilateral upper amputees. TTI found that the Microwriter had 10 times the error rate of the 4x4 for the more challenging encoding of letters, as compared to double the error rate for the encoding of numbers (Figure 15). But speed differences were minimal, and some leveling off of performance increases was evident at the 5th day of training. The mnemonic system

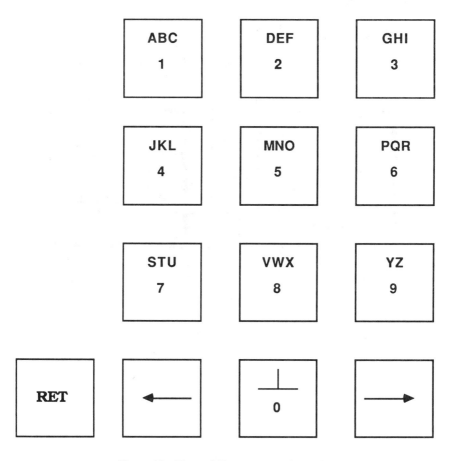

Figure 12.   Three-shift comparison keypad

Figure 13. Mnemonic aid for learning microwriter keystrokes

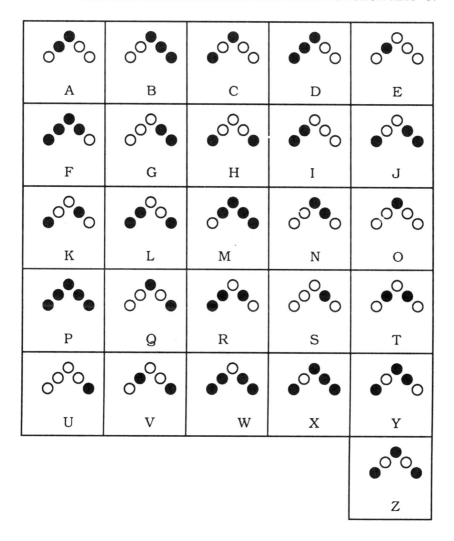

Figure 14.   Encoding scheme for micro writer keystrokes (no mnemonics)

did not seem to help in learning the Microwriter. Rate-of-information transfer varied between 48 and 56 characters per min, roughly 10 words a min—a far cry from performances achievable by even novice typists on a standard keyboard! It can be concluded that the Microwriter can be a somewhat practicable substitute for a more conventional partial keyboard in specialized situations, but that it is still a partial keyboard and cannot in all likelihood compete with the performance attainable with a full keyboard. Where this kind of keyboard is used, the software is going

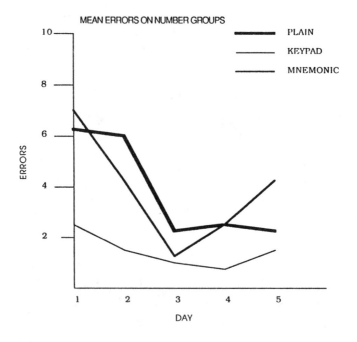

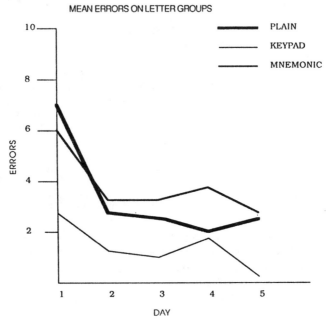

Figure 15.   Performance on chord keypad vs. 3-shift keypad

to have to incorporate a lot of redundancy to cope with the high error rate. With long experience, it may well be that the error rate will approach or match that obtainable with other methods of encoding information with a partial keyboard.

FUTURE PLANS

Strategies for Providing Input Feedback

There continue to be many advantages to the use of flat or "membrane" keyboards and keypads, particularly if they can be materialized on the display screen itself and effectively used. As the TTI research has shown, a significant disadvantage to the use of such input devices is the performance decrement seemingly produced by lack of "feel." What is the best approach for providing this lost feel? Through auditory cues, raised overlaps that snap, or other means not now considered?

Guidelines for the Production of Quick Reference Guides

Previous research not here reported concentrated on guidelines for the writing of quick reference guides (QRG) for use as job aids for data entry. These guidelines will be further refined and extended to a number of different user-computer interaction situations. The products of this work will include (a) basic principles (b) a methodology for developing documentation and (c) resources that have some empirical basis to them, as compared to general how-to texts on technical writing. This project is designed to complement work being performed under HEL sponsorship by Dr. Thomas Duffy and his associates at Carnegie-Mellon University but the scope will be limited to cards, screen menus, and similar job aids.

Function Allocation on Full Keyboards

This study will be a continuation of work presently in progress, but with emphasis on the full keyboard. Fixed and assignable functions will be studied, with emphasis upon placement. Verification of nomenclature and of abbreviations for functions that were established in the current study will be made.

Displaced Template Strategies for Keypads

During the current project, a preliminary investigation of displaced templates or layout diagrams that are screen presented is in progress. Such a strategy, correctly done, can give maximum, multilayer flexibility to an otherwise featureless keyset. Size, type of feedback to indicate input, and mode designation are the dominant research themes in this projected study.

ULTIMATE GOAL

After a number of other TTI HEL issues, as well as data from other programs, are addressed, the ultimate goal will be the complete reissue of MIL-STD- 1280, "Military Standard Keyboard Arrangements," and a new chapter on Input/Control in MIL-STD-1472C, "Human Engineering Design Criteria for Military Systems, Equipment, and Facilities." These revamped standards will serve as Department of Defense guidelines for military hardware and software designers well into the 1990's.

REFERENCES

Huchingson, R.D., Lampen, L.J., & Koppa, R.J. (1985, May). *Keyboard design and operation: A literature review, 1,* (final report). College Station, TX: Texas Transportation Institute.

Koppa, R.J. (1985, June). *A study of data entry keyboards: the 4 x 4 keypad* (Tech Research No. 4–85), Aberdeen Proving Ground, MD: U.S. Army Human Engineering Laboratory.

Lampen, L.J. (1985). The effect of key displacement on typing performance. Unpublished master's thesis, Department of Industrial Engineering, Texas A&M University, College Station.

MIL-STD-1280. (1969). Military standard keyboard arrangements (latest revision).

MIL-STD-1472C. (1983). Human engineering design criteria for military systems, equipment, and facilities (latest revision).

Palko, K.D. (1986). Development of human factors guidelines for computer software quick reference guides. Unpublished master's thesis, department of Industrial Engineering, Texas A&M University, College Station, TX.

Stealey, S.L. (1985). A comparative study of 4 x 4 keypad arrangements and alpha entry modes. Unpublished master's thesis, department of Industrial Engineering, Texas A&M University, College Station, TX.

Wolstein, A.S. (1986). An experimental study of a six-key handprint chord keyboard. Unpublished master's thesis, Department of Industrial Engineering, Texas A&M University, College Station, TX.

SECTION II

Human-Machine Interaction

An interface is the point of contact between two entities. The interface between human and computer may take on various characteristics. These characteristics include media, dialogue, and manipulation techniques. The trend in interface design has been to move from machine-oriented input/output media, such as punch cards in a batch environment, to user-oriented input/output media, such as visual display terminals and voice synthesis in an interactive environment.

Dialogue design options include menus, forms, system command-languages, and natural language command-languages. Quite a large body of research exists in the area of dialogue design (see Chapter 1). In general, it appears that menu driven systems are best suited for novice users because of ease of use and learning. Form filling is appropriate for routine data entry. System command-languages are the most demanding but also the most flexible interfaces and should be reserved for expert users only, not novice users because of the heavy memory load required to utilize them. Natural languages which contain a few user-oriented, but flexible, commands are appropriate for nonroutine data inquiry systems such as query languages for data bases.

The manipulation techniques available to users include keystrokes, function keys, touch screens, the mouse, and digitizing tablets. The most frequently used technique is the keystroke. The use of direct manipulation techniques such as the mouse and digitizing tablet has increased as graphic packages have increased in sophistication and popularity.

Regardless of the choice of media, dialogue, or manipulation technique, the key issue is the adherence of these options to effective design guidelines suggested by researchers (see Chapter 1 for citations).

The area of human-machine interaction has been the most thoroughly researched of the five areas of human factors delineated by the taxonomy which provides the framework for this book (see Chapter 1). Of course, more research is needed, particularly as new techniques are introduced which impact human-machine interaction. It does seem that there is direction, purpose, and a growing cumulative tradition surrounding research in this area that is uncharacteristic of much of MIS human factors research.

The two selections which focus on human-machine interaction in this section are "Adaptive General Audience Models: A Research Framework" by Merle P. Martin of the California State University at Long Beach, Department of MIS and "SmartSLIM: A DSS for Controlling Biases during Problem Formulation" by David B. Paradice and James F. Courtney, Jr., both of Texas A&M University, Department of Business Analysis and Research.

The Martin paper focuses on the design of the user interface to meet the need of both novice and expert users and gradations in between. He presents a model which supplies the "general" user or audience with an interface which dynamically adapts to the needs of the user rather than a static interface which requires adaptation on the part of the user.

The Paradice-Courtney paper presents an interface which is the point of contact between the user and a decision support system. The primary purpose of this interface is to control biases during problem definition. It is a "smart" interface and draws upon the principles of artificial intelligence research for its base.

CHAPTER 4

Adaptive General Audience Models: A Research Framework

Merle P. Martin
California State University, Long Beach

General audience models are defined as interactive applications designed for users of a broad range of expertise (i.e., novice through experienced). Adaptive general audience models first select appropriate processing paths based upon specific user characteristics, then alter these paths as the characteristics of the user change over time. This paper describes the structure of adaptive general audience models, proposes a framework for comprehensive research of such models, and discusses some issues germane to that research.

INTRODUCTION

It is common in the communications and arts disciplines to define authorship, creation, or design in terms of reaching toward a particular audience. In this context, the designer either reaches toward an audience limited to specific interests (e.g., classical music) or to a more general audience (e.g., Christmas music). Often, the designer reaches toward a broad range of audience interest but designs his or her work to mean different things to different people.

The term "audience-directed model" refers to the situation where a programmer, either consciously or unconsciously, directs his or her program to a user audience of a specific range of computer expertise. When the direction is limited to a narrow range of such expertise (e.g., novice), then the resulting product is defined as a limited audience model. When the direction is toward the broadest range of audience computer expertise, the resulting product is defined as a general audience model. There is some evidence in the literature for support of general audience models (Nesdore, 1983; Selander, 1981). While there are few published accounts of the actual implementation of such models, Tektronix's interactive graphics model (Monzeico, 1982) and Micro Pro's Wordstar (Micro Pro, 1983) are examples of commercial models accommodating users at varying levels of expertise.

Adaptive general audience models first select appropriate processing paths to match specific user characteristics, then alter these paths as the characteristics change over time. The structure of an adaptive general audience model is shown in Figure 1.

The structure proceeds in the following sequence:

1. There is a perceived need for the use of models that both address a broad range of user computer expertise and adapt to the user as his or her model needs change.

2. A triggering question(s) is posed to the user. This question seeks to differentiate between different levels of some user characteristic, such as computer knowledge, application area knowledge, or specific model experience.

3. The triggering question differentiates between different classes of users, such as novices, intermediate, casual or experienced (Carey, 1982; Cuff, 1980). Each category of user is directed to an appropriate model-processing path.

4. Alternate processing paths are differentiated by their relative use of programmed coaching techniques, such as automatic help functions, warnings, highlighting, and default values (Maguire, 1982).

5. The intermediate, or casual, user begins with the processing path possessing a considerable amount of coaching overhead. At some point in time when it is determined that this user has sufficiently "warmed up," the level of coaching is gradually decreased.

6. After some period of time, enough coaching overhead is eliminated to bring the intermediate user onto the experienced processing path.

7. The novice user is initially assigned to the processing path with considerable coaching overhead. After a specific learning period, the level of coaching is gradually reduced and the novice begins movement toward the experienced (minimum coaching) processing path.

8. The gradual reduction of coaching overhead culminates in the novice user being brought onto the experienced track.

9. Users can conceivably find themselves in a processing path too difficult for effective performance, given current user characteristics. An escape mechanism allows these users to reenter the model at a point with more coaching overhead.

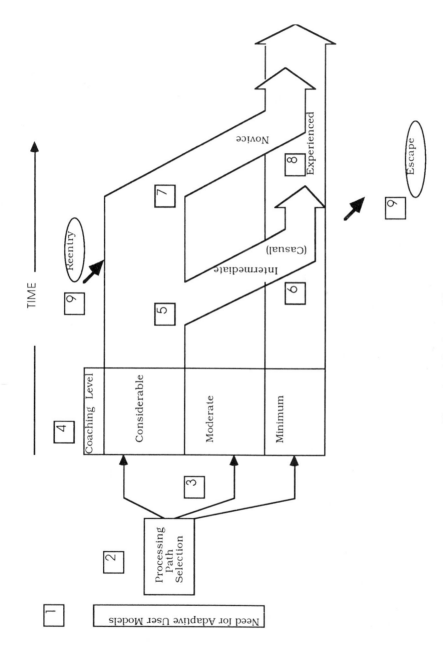

Figure 1. Adaptive model structure

Research Framework

Research in the Management Information System (MIS) field has proven to be of an expeditious and haphazard nature (Courtney, DeSanctis, & Kasper, 1983). What is needed is more programmatic research, where the path towards knowledge is systematic and comprehensive (McGrath, 1964). The structure shown in Figure 1 provides a checklist for programmatic research in adaptive general audience models. The research framework suggested includes:

1. Is there a demonstrated need for adaptive general audience models?
2. What triggering mechanisms are best used to select alternate user processing paths?
3. What types of alternate user processing paths should be included in an adaptive general audience model?
4. What is the appropriate coaching level (human factors mix) for each user processing path?
5. What is the proper adaptive path for casual users? (5 and 6 on Figure 1).
6. What is the appropriate adaptive path for novice users? (7 and 8 in Figure 1).
7. What escape mechanisms are best used for "lost" model users? (9 in Figure 1).

The above research questions are tactical in nature. There are several issues that are more strategic in that they are applicable to how we do research. These strategic issues can best be structured using McGrath's (1964) classification of data-collection methods to include (a) field studies, (b) experimental simulation, (c) laboratory experimentation, and (d) computer simulation. The discussion that follows briefly addresses issues germane to the tactical, then strategic, elements of this research framework.

Tactical Research Issues

1. Need for research.

A general audience model is more costly to develop than are limited audience models. This is because development of the general audience model requires that alternate user paths must first be decided upon, when programmed. Making the general audience model adaptive increases the amount of programming code and, thus, the development time required. Although it has been shown that general audience models perform better than limited audience models under certain conditions (Martin & Fuerst, 1986b), such demonstrated superiority may not be sufficient to justify the need for adaptive general audience models.

It has been suggested that inexperienced model users learn so fast that the expense of developing alternate user paths is not justified (Branscomb & Thomas, 1984). This position must be questioned in two respects. First, there is some evidence that the relative level of human factors coaching included in a model may have something to do with user learning rates (Martin & Fuerst,, 1986a). These findings suggest that if novice users are not provided with a model environment specifically directed to novices, these users may have a difficult time learning the model (Figure 2).

Second, the time it takes a novice user to lose his or her novice status may not be as important as the relative number of persons that are in a learning, or training, status at any one point in time. Figure 3 contains the results of a queuing model with experienced user turnover used as system arrival rates, and novice training times as system service rates. Note that, except for the combination of minimal turnover and rapid training rates, the percentage of time in which at least one novice is in training is significant (Martin & Fuerst, 1986a).

In any case, it is clear that more comprehensive research on the needs for adaptive general audience models is required. Two directions for such research are (a) learning patterns for novice and other types of users and (b) user employment patterns in industry, specifically those patterns determining the expected number of users in training (novices) at any point in time. Approaching this subject from these different directions could lead to an electric assessment of the need for general

Subject/Model Combination		Daily Costs ($000)		Percent Change
		1st 5 Days	Last 15 Days	
Novice Subjects	Using Novice-Directed Model	5.7	5.1	-10.5
	Using Experienced-Directed Model	5.4	5.7	+5.6
Experienced Subject Using Experienced Model		5.2	5.2	0

Figure 2. Changes in subject performance on juror simulation model (Martin and Fuerst 1986a)

Annual	Length of Novice Training (weeks) - (S)					
Turnover Rate * (A)	1	2	3	4	5	6
.05	.019	.038	.058	.077	.096	.115
.10	.038	.074	.109	.143	.175	.207
.15	.056	.109	.206	.206	.251	.293
.20	.074	.143	.251	.265	.319	.370
.25	.092	.175	.293	.319	.382	.438
.30	.109	.206	.370	.370	.438	.500
.35	.126	.236	.332	.416	.490	.554
.40	.143	.265	.370	.460	.537	.603
.45	.159	.293	.405	.500	.579	.646
.50	.175	.319	.438	.537	.618	.685

* Based on 20 total data entry personnel

Figure 3. Probability of having at least one novice in training (queuing model)

audience models and, more specifically, adaptive general audience models.

2. Triggering mechanism.

Some means must be established for determining which of many alternate processing paths is best suited for the user. The simplest procedure is to ask the user one or more questions pertaining to his or her expertise, then to select a processing path based upon the user's response. There is some evidence, however, that novice users tend to overestimate their level of computer knowledge (Martin, 1986). Thus, for the characteristic of computer knowledge at least, there is some question as to the efficacy of allowing users to determine the processing path.

Another approach is to base automatic selection of a processing path upon some computer-captured characteristic, such as number of times the individual has used the model, error rates, or user response time to system requests. It is difficult enough to program such mechanisms but the truly complex aspect of this approach is to determine at what levels of performance to differentiate between classes of users.

Experimentation must be conducted to determine which of these types of triggering mechanisms (and, within each type, which specific method) does a better job of leading the model user to the most appropriate processing path.

3. Alternative user processing paths.

Users have been classified into a myriad of types. Some authors have defined the differences between novice and experienced users (Carey, 1982; Klensin, 1982; Stewart, 1980). Other authors have discussed the causal and the naive user (Branscomb & Thomas, 1984; Kennedy, 1975; Thimbleby, 1980). The terms *competent* and *expert* also appear (Chapin, 1983). The characteristics underlying such classification have also been varied. Gilford (1982) described users in terms of computer experience. Chapin (1983) discussed the same users in terms of computer knowledge and frequency of contact with the specific model. Laxas and Olson (1978) include the importance of applications knowledge in differentiating between users.

It is clear that some consolidating research must be done to define model users in a more precise fashion. As a start, terms such as computer knowledge and computer experience must be correlated with each other to determine whether or not they are independent, rather than cohabitating, states. Next, the relative importance of computer, model, and applications knowledge/experience must be established. This should allow us to establish a common, measurable continuum of user skills.

Finally, some sort of multivariate analysis (i.e., cluster analysis) must be performed so that we can discretely describe progressions along the continuum from the naive to the expert user. Only through such efforts toward consistent definition of user classes can replicable research be conducted on alternate user processing paths.

4. Coaching level.

Maguire (1982) presented a framework of four human factors principles affecting man-machine dialogue. This included (a) the nature of the message, (b) the extent of an automatic user "help" function, (c) response time for both "echoing" of user inputs and execution of user requests, and (d) the complexity of the processing path the user must traverse. Other authors have discussed the use of default values (Wasserman, 1978), screen discontinuation (Simpson, 1982), help functions (Selander, 1981), and menu depth and breadth (Snowberry, Parkingson, & Sisson, 1983; Tullis, 1982). Few of these techniques have been statistically demonstrated by themselves to have an impact upon model users (Willeges & Willeges, 1984).

This author (1984) suggested the human factors/user computer knowledge structure shown in Figure 4. In addition, models programmed according to this structure were found to differentiate significantly between novice and experienced users (Martin & Fuerst, 1986b). However, no research has yet been published regarding the relative impact of different types of coaching (human factors) techniques (see Figure 4). For example, does the use of highlighting increase user performance more than the use of automatic help functions? More research has to be done on effective coaching techniques, the relative impact of such techniques, and the means by which these techniques can be translated into programming code.

5. Casual user.

Carey (1982) defined the casual user as one who is an experienced user of a computer model but who has infrequent contact with that model. This type of user has become rusty and needs a refresher period before he or she can assume experienced user status. The causal user would seem to be more a phenomenon of management information systems than of transaction processing systems, because transaction processing system usage is a more integral part of user roles at that level.

An adaptive general audience model would attempt first to direct the causal user to the model with a considerable amount of human factors coaching. Then, after a sufficient warm up period, the adaptive mechanism would decrease this level of coaching over some period of time until the causal user was using the processing path with the minimum level of coaching.

Three research questions surface here. First, what constitutes the category of casual user? Cuff's (1980) definitions must be expanded to include enough measurable criteria to allow a model's adaptive mechanism to service properly this type of user. Second, how long should the casual users' warmup period be? Casual user learning patterns must be studied to answer this question. Finally, how quickly (and by what means) should the casual user be plummeted from the processing path with considerable coaching overhead to the path with a minimum level of coaching overhead? One scenario for an experiment here would be the effect of alternate transition paths of instant, rapid, gradual, and no transition at all, on casual user performance.

HUMAN FACTOR	HUMAN SUBFACTOR	USER COMPUTER KNOWLEDGE	
		NOVICE	EXPERIENCED
Nature of Message	1. Tone	Explanatory and Polite	Short and to the Point
	2. Use of Humor	Careful	None
	3. Bypasses	None	Allow
	4. Warnings	Many	Rarely
	5. Screen Format	Menu	Inquiry
	6. Input Verification	Always	Rarely
	7. High-lighting	Some (Judiciously)	Little
	8. Defaults	With Explanation	Without Explanation
	9. Screen Discontinuation	Prompt and Keyed Response	Keyed Response Without Prompt
Help Function	1. Procedures	Full, Unsolicited	Upon Request
	2. Values		
Response Time	1. Mean	Minimize within Variance	Minimize
	2. Variance	Minimize	Minimize within Mean
Path Process	1. Menu Structure	Depth	Breadth
	2. Overall Screen Density	Minimize	Maximize

Figure 4. Human factors (coaching mix)

6. Novice users.

The same types of questions surface here as for casual users. What are the identifiable characteristics of the novice user? When has the novice user garnered requisite skills to no longer be a novice? What lengths and types of training differentiate the novice from the experienced user? The level of coaching may well have some influence on whether or not the novice learns (Martin & Fuerst, 1986a). In an experiment using a juror processing simulation model, it was shown that novices' performance improved over time when using a model directed to novices, but did not significantly improve when using a model directed to experienced users. (See Figure 2). In addition, this study showed that, after a short learning period (5 simulated juror processing days), novice user performance on novice models was as good as experienced user performance on a model directed to experienced users.

As with the casual user, experiments should be conducted on learning rates of novice users so that adaptive general audience models can be programmed to detect when, and at what rate, the novice processing path should be altered. Of course, a more precise definition of novice users will be necessary before such experimentation can effectively be conducted on a more than limited basis.

7. Escape mechanisms.

At least one study has shown that novices may tend to overestimate their relative level of computer knowledge (Martin, 1986). If the initial triggering mechanism discussed above is dependent upon the user's accurate assessment of his or her own computer knowledge, then it is likely that the wrong user processing path will be selected. It must be stressed that the study cited dealt only with computer knowledge rather than skill surrogates such as applications or specific model knowledge or experience.

However, the results of this study seem sufficient to suggest that the use of model path escape mechanisms may improve performance for users trapped in an incorrectly selected path. It would be interesting to add to experiments assessing alternate user paths an additional treatment which includes an escape path. Similarly, it might prove beneficial to test different types of escape mechanisms under laboratory conditions. The control group for such an experiment would be, of course, a model with no escape mechanism.

Strategic Research Issues

McGrath (1964) describes the four classes of research settings as field studies, experimental simulations, laboratory experiments, and computer simulations. Field studies include all types of investigations which use data from real organizations. Case-study observations and questionnaire or interview surveys are the most common types of field studies. The field study has the advantage of operational realism, as compared with laboratory experiments and computer simulation. However, field studies exhibit less precision, less control, and less freedom to manipulate variables of primary concern. Thus, field studies are less susceptible to findings of statistical significance.

Experimental simulations are models of an organization under quasi-laboratory conditions. These simulations involve interaction of human beings, much as in management games or in prototype development. Such simulations represent a compromise between setting realism and research precision and control.

Laboratory experiments reject the reality of the organization setting. Instead, a few critical values are lifted from the real world and isolated to determine their interaction. Often the object is not to determine what typically can happen but, instead what can be made to happen at variable extremes (Mook, 1983). The sacrifice in reality is compensated for by the achievement of precision, control, and freedom of manipulation. Laboratory experiments are always accompanied by some statements of statistical significance.

Computer simulations, sometimes referred to as mathematical models, are distinguished from experimental simulation by the fact that computer simulations are closed there is no human intervention. All variables of interest are built into the formulation of the model itself. Computer simulations present the greatest departure from organizational reality. They also represent the data collection methodology with the greatest research control. The computer simulation, once constructed, is free from all effects of confounding variables.

Implicit in the comparison of these four research alternatives are Cooke and Campbell's (1976) definitions of internal and external validity. Internal validity has to do with the question of whether or not experimental results or nonresults are the result of spurious variables. Internal validity is associated with the degree of experimental control. External validity deals with whether or not study results generalize to other persons, settings, and time.

Although not discussed in Cooke and Campbell's treatise, internal and external validity are inversely interrelated. Much as with Type I and Type II errors in hypothesis testing, as one is increased the other must decrease. Mook (1983) suggests, as an example, that internal validity be optimized and, within that optimization, that external validity be maximized. The key point is that a researcher cannot optimize both internal and external validity at the same time.

Figure 5 is adapted from McGrath (1964). It is modified to include the effects of the different types of research settings on internal and external validity. Note that, in a complete programmatic research framework, the four types of data collection methodologies are used in consort with one another. Also note that the research path progresses from limited internal and maximum external validity to maximum and minimum external validity, then back down the scale.

A Total Research Framework

A total research framework can be constructed by combining the tactical structure of Figure 1 with the strategic framework of Figure 5. The resultingtructure is shown in Figure 6.

The cell asterisks represent the proposed types of research settings by adaptive model category that should be emphasized in the next several years. This proposed research framework is based upon examination of current literature on this topic.

The suggested framework is briefly described as follows:

Need for adaptive models.

Industrial firms must be surveyed (field study) to determine the distributions of (a) user turnover rates and (b) model training times. Estimation of these parameters, in addition to typical training methodologies (e.g., how many novices a supervisor can train at one time), will allow development of models that simulate typical Transaction Processing Systems (TPS) and MIS training environments;

Triggering mechanisms.

Experimental simulations should be conducted more specifically to determine the accuracy by which novice and experienced users judge their status. Do novice users tend to overestimate their capabilities? Do experienced users trust their experience? Laboratory experiment should be conducted to determine which type of triggering does a better job of leading model users to the most appropriate processing paths. Here the treatments of user versus computer selection can be tested against blocking factors comprising different types of computer models;

Alternate user paths.

We must gather data from the field pertinent to the ingredients comprising user expertise, the relative strength of each of these ingredients, and the milestones along the expertise continuum whereby we can mark the progression from one type of user to another (e.g., novice to intermediate). Such gathered data would seem particularly amenable to statistical analysis by multivariate methods such as multiple regression, discriminant analysis, and cluster analysis;

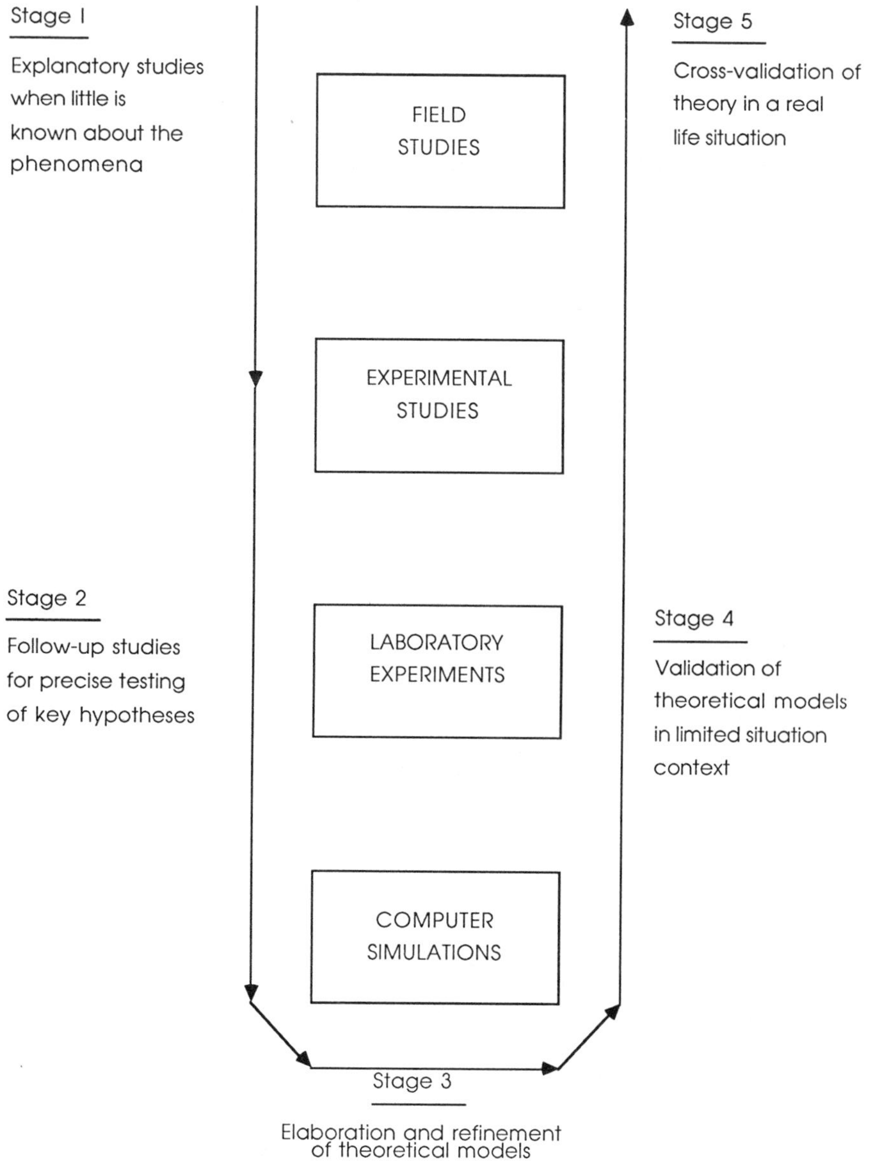

Stage 1

Explanatory studies
when little is
known about the
phenomena

Stage 5

Cross-validation of
theory in a real
life situation

FIELD
STUDIES

EXPERIMENTAL
STUDIES

Stage 2

Follow-up studies
for precise testing
of key hypotheses

LABORATORY
EXPERIMENTS

Stage 4

Validation of
theoretical models
in limited situation
context

COMPUTER
SIMULATIONS

Stage 3

Elaboration and refinement
of theoretical models

Figure 5. Research (adapted from McGrath (1964))

Coaching (human factors) levels.

We must amass evidence as to whether or not, or to what degree, the various human factor principles suggested by Maguire and others improve user performance. In addition, various combinations (or packages) of these techniques must be tested as to their applicability to differing levels of user, novice through experienced. Both interactive (experimental simulations) and more controlled experiments seem most germane to this task;

Casual user paths.

How soon and with what speed does a rusty user become experienced again? This question can be answered by field observation (e.g., user questionnaires), experimental simulation (e.g., one-way glass observation of different model users), or laboratory experiments tracing user characteristics over terms (Martin & Fuerst, 1986a);

Novice user paths.

The same types of analysis can be done for the seasoning of novice users as for the refamiliarization of casual users;

Escape mechanisms.

Both experimental simulations with subject interaction and laboratory experiments can be conducted to test different types of escape mechanisms and, indeed, whether any type of escape mechanism is a significant feature for computer models in general and adaptive models in particular.

For each cell of the ensuing research matrix shown in Figure 6, one must then develop a study specific dimension which includes at least the following checklist items adopted from Cooke and Campbell (1976):

1. Internal validity (controlling spurious events)
   a. random assignment of subjects
   b. insulation between treatment groups c. experiment discipline (preventing disturbances)
   d. duration of the experiment
2. Statistical conclusion validity (power of statistical tests)
   a. research hypotheses (e.g., one-tail)
   b. most powerful test (e.g., one-tail rather than two-tail)
   c. sample (cell) size
   d. handling multiple comparisons
3. Construct validity (proper measurement)

Tactical Stages of Research on Adaptive General Audience Models	McGrath Data Collection Method			
	Field Study	Experimental Simulation	Laboratory Experiment	Computer Simulation
1. Need	*			*
2. Triggering Mechanisms		*	*	
3. Alternate User Paths	*			
4. Coaching (Human Factors) Levels		*	*	
5. Adaptive Casual User Paths	*	*	*	
6. Adaptive Novice User Paths	*	*	*	
7. Escape Mechanisms		*	*	

Figure 6.   Total research framework

    a. measurement instruments
    b. measurement reliability
    c. surrogate variables
    d. missing data and outliers
4. External validity (generalizing results)
    a. subject selection (e.g., use of volunteers)
    b. research setting (how close to reality)
    c. future research path

All of this then comprises a structured and total research framework for investigation of adaptive general audience models.

CONCLUSION

In order to assess effectively the impact of human factors on management information systems, we need a systematic and comprehensive approach that will lead to more programmatic research. This paper has presented one such approach as it relates to the specific research topic of adaptive general audience models. However, it seems clear that this framework is also suitable to other research topics as well.

Progress towards knowledge in a burgeoning field is often slow, painful, and meagerly rewarding. Yet, that structured path must be taken if true knowledge is to be assured. Both the application of human factors in MIS in general, and the use of adaptive models in particular, are new research pursuits. They require a structured framework such as that discussed in this paper, if we are to assess effectively their worth, their costs, and their applicabilities.

REFERENCES

Branscomb, L., & Thomas, J. (1984). Ease of use: A system design challenge. *IBM Systems Journal, 23* (3), 224–235.

Carey, T. (1982). User differences in interface design. *Computer, 15,* 14–20.

Chapin, R. (1983). Human factors in application programming. *Infosystems, 30,* 102–104.

Cooke, T. & Campbell, D. (1976). The design and conduct of quasi-experimental and true experiments in field settings. In M.Dunnette (Ed.), *The handbook of industrial and organizational psychology,* Chicago, IL: Rand McNally.

Courtney, J., DeSanctis, G., & Kasper, G. (1983). Continuity in MIS/DSS laboratory research: The case for a common gaming simulation. *Decision Sciences, 14,* 419–439.

Cuff, R. (1980). On casual users. *International Journal of Man-Machine Studies, 12,* 163–187.

Foley, J., Wallace, V., & Chaw, P. (1981). The human factors of graphics interaction: Tasks and techniques. (*Report No. GWU-II ST-81-3*), Washington, DC: George Washington University.

Gilford, D. (1982). Warming up to computers. *Proceedings on the Conference on Human*

Factors in Computer Systems.

Kennedy, T. (1975). Some behavioral factors affecting the training of naive users of an interactive computer system. *International Journal of Man-Machine Studies, 7,* 817–834.

Klensin, J. (1982). Short-term friendly and long-term hostile? *SIGSOC Bulletin Proceedings: Part II Human Interaction and the User Interface, 13.*

Laxas, K., & Olson, G. (1978). Human information processing in navigational display. *Journal of Applied Psychology, 63,* 734–740.

Maguire, M. (1982). An evaluation of published recommendations of the design of man-computer dialogues. *International Journal of Man-Machine Studies, 16,* 237–262.

Martin, M. (1984). Designing decision support systems for a broad range of user experience, unpublished doctoral dissertation, Texas A & M University, College Station, TX.

Martin, M. (1986). Triggering adaptive audience directed models, *Proceedings of the Southeast Section of the American Institute of Decision Sciences.*

Martin, M., & Fuerst, W. (1986a). Novice user training: A study of different model orientations, Manuscript submitted for publication.

Martin, M., & Fuerst, W. (1986b). Using computer knowledge in the design of interactive system, Manuscript submitted for publication.

McGrath, J. (1964). Toward a 'theory' of method for research in organizations, In W.W. Cooper, H.L. Leavitt, & M.W. Shelly (Eds.), *New Perspectives in Organizational Research,* New York: Wiley.

MicroPro. (1983). *Word Star reference manual,* San Rafael, CA: Micro Pro International.

Mook, D. (1983). In defense of external invalidity, *American Psychologist, 38,* 379–387.

Monzeico, H. (1982). A human/computer interface to accommodate user learning stages, *Communications of the ACM, 25,* 100–104.

Nesdore, P. (1983). Friendly to all or none, *Computerworld, 17,* 54.

Ramsey, H., & Atwood, M. (1979). Human factors in computer systems: A review of the literature, *(Tech. Report No. SAI-79-111-DEN),* Englewood, CO: Science Applications.

Selander, S. (1981). Several approaches for improving user cordiality in the design of on-Line systems for novice users, *Proceedings of the Eighteenth Annual Computer Personnel Research Conference.*

Simpson, H. (1982). A human-factors style guide for program design, *BYTE, 7,* 108–132.

Snowberry, K., Parkingson, & Sisson, N. (1983). Computer display menus, *Ergonomics, 26,* 699–712.

Stewart, T. (1980). Communications with dialogue, *Ergonomics, 23,* 909–920.

Thimbleby, H. (1980). Dialogue determination, *International Journal of Man-Machine Studies, 13,* 295–304.

Tullis, T. (1980). The formatting of alphanumeric displays: A review and analysis, *Human Factors, 25,* 657–682.

Wasserman, D. (1978). The design of idiot-proof interactive systems, *Proceedings of the conference on American Federation of Information Processing Societies.*

Willeges, B., & Willeges, R. (1984). Dialogue design considerations for interactive computer systems, *Human Factors Review.*

CHAPTER 5

SmartSLIM: A DSS for Controlling Biases during Problem Formulation

David B. Paradice
and
James F. Courtney, Jr.
Texas A&M University

Decision-making activities frequently begin with the recognition of a problem situation. Furthermore, decisions are usually a function of the decision maker's perceived structure, or formulation of the current problem. Although human information processors frequently exhibit many types of bias during problem formulation, DSS research aimed at supporting accurate problem formulation processes has been minimal. This paper describes research to develop a DSS which specifically supports unbiased problem formulation.

INTRODUCTION

Decision support systems (DSS) have evolved as tools that attempt to support decision-making processes in problem contexts characterized by novelty and large search spaces. Additionally, there may be no algorithmic approach to the solution. Problems with these characteristics are said to be ill-structured. Examples of ill-structured problems include developing strategies to increase sales volume or decrease costs, not only in a strategic sense, but also by understanding and manipulating the relationships of the resources which come under control of the middle manager.

Although much research has been done in the DSS area, very little of it has been directed at supporting the process of formulating the proper structure of the problem at hand. The process of managerial problem formulation is characterized by hypothesizing relationships in domains of variables in which the relationships are uncertain, temporal, and dynamic.

DSS seek to support decision makers by obviating problems which result from the biases and limitations of human cognitive processes. Biases can lead to incorrect solutions or, worse, incorrect formulation of the problem. Solving the wrong problem is known as committing an "error of the third kind" (Raiffa, 1968).

Statistics is a science of information (Hora, 1985). As such, it provides a number of theoretical tools which should support the decision-making process. Intuitively, the use of statistical methods should increase decision-making effectiveness. The inclusion of such capabilities in a DSS is certainly not a novel idea (see, e.g., Bonczek, Holsapple, & Whinston, 1981, Sprague & Carlson, 1982, Wang & Courtney, 1982). However, little prior research has focused specifically on the use of such methods to support the problem formulation stage of managerial decision making.

Similarly, recent developments in the area of artificial intelligence have demonstrated techniques that may be usefully employed to support problem formulation. This paper discusses research which examines a methodology for incorporating techniques from several disciplines into a DSS to support unbiased managerial problem formulation. A prototype system (SmartSLIM) based on this methodology is described. The ability of SmartSLIM to address 27 types of bias described by Sage (1981) is discussed.

SIMON'S INTELLIGENCE-DESIGN-CHOICE MODEL

Problem formulation is defined here as the process of determining (a) the domain of variables in which the problem exists and (b) the relationships of the variables in that domain to each other and to the problem at hand. Problem formulation occurs during the intelligence stage of Simon's (1960) intelligence-design-choice model of decision making.

During the intelligence stage, the decision maker scans the environment for situations requiring decisions. These situations typically take the form of problems which must be resolved or opportunities which may be exploited. Problems have been defined as deviations from expected results (Pounds, 1969). Opportunities are situations in which the decision maker perceives that conditions exist where it is possible to increase wealth (Ahituv & Neumann, 1982).

Each of these definitions alludes to knowledge of the variables of the problem domain and relationships among them. An "expected result" clearly indicates that some source of information has been the focus of attention, and that the source is capable of assuming a range of quantities. In the second definition, the variable is "wealth," and the decision maker perceives that conditions exist in which other aspects (variables) of the "problem" domain may be manipulated which will result in increasing the value of the variable "wealth."

PRIOR RESEARCH IN PROBLEM FORMULATION

Mintzberg, Raisinghani, & Theoret (1976) note that little is known about the problem formulation phase of the decision-making process, although much of the prior research in the area would appear to indicate that most humans are not particularly adept at it. Problem formulation has been found to be biased by many variables, including:

1. the initial formulation of the problem (Duncker, 1945);
2. which critical stimulus affects the problem solver first (Johnson, 1946, Judson & Cofer, 1956);
3. the system that undertakes the process of formulating the problem (Ackoff, 1979, Reitman, 1964);
4. the perceived deviation from expectations (Pounds, 1969);
5. the environment of the problem space (Newell & Simon 1972);
6. the ability to decompose complex, unfamiliar situations into simpler, more familiar situations (Newell & Simon, 1972, Reitman, 1964);
7. the creativity (Taylor, 1975); and
8. the experience (Rowe, 1977) of the person formulating the problem.

Mintzberg et al. (1976) refer to "problem diagnosis" as "probably the single most important routine, since it determines in large part, however implicitly, the subsequent course of action" (p. 274). Mitroff, Emshoff, & Kilmann (1979) state that in typical organizational environments, problem forming and defining are as important, if not more so, than problem solving.

However, due to cognitive limitations, problem formulation strategies employed by humans are not failsafe, nor, in many cases, even rational. For example, the results of a study by Pruitt (1961) indicated that the amount of information required before changing a decision exceeded a rational strategy based on the expected value of all possible strategies. Research by Tversky and Kahneman (1974, 1981) demonstrated that individuals tend to use heuristics and biases that violate Bayesian normative principles.

Sage (1981) lists 27 biases which may affect the decision-making process (Figure 1). Many of these biases could be collectively labeled "biases due to inability to interpret results of statistical analyses." In many cases, the biases occur in the earliest stages of formulating the analysis (i.e., problem). The Gambler's Fallacy (number 12 in Sage's list) is an incorrect formulation of the situation at hand.

PRIOR RESEARCH IN MODEL BUILDING

In order to compensate for their cognitive limitations and biases, decision makers have turned increasingly to the use of models. Research by Kasper (1983) and others (for a review, see Libby, 1983) has demonstrated that model development and use significantly improve the decision-making process.

More recently, research has addressed the importance of formulating the correct problem (Volkema, 1983). Pracht (1984), for example, has researched the use of graphical structural modeling tools to support the problem formulation process. Loy (1986) extended Pracht's work to the group decision-making environment. McLean and Shepherd (1976) note that ". . . the derivation of model structure is analogous to the framing of hypotheses and . . . these models should be scientifically tested" (p. 41).

Tversky and Kahneman (1974) have concluded, however, that people fail to infer from lifelong experience ". . . such fundamental statistical rules as regression toward the mean or the effect of sample size sampling variability" (p. 1130). Lacking tools that specifically address interpretation of statistical methods, the subjects in prior experiments may have been solving the wrong problem.

SMARTSLIM: A DSS FOR CONTROLLING BIASES

The business management laboratory/systems laboratory for information Management (BML/SLIM) software system provides an excellent environment for investigating the viability of developing an expert system for managerial problem formulation. BML (Jensen & Cherrington, 1977) is a computer simulation of a variety of decision-making functions of the management of a manufacturing firm. Decisions to be made include setting product price levels, production levels, number of sales representatives, advertising expenses, and raw materi-

Biases Associated with Judgment and Choice

1. Adjusting and anchoring from a particular piece of data.
2. Using easily available data only.
3. Being influenced by the number of occurrences of an event.
4. Estimating conservatively.
5. Being influenced by the way information is presented.
6. Being influenced by the data presented first.
7. Desiring self-fulfilling prophecies.
8. Being influenced by the ease of recall of a piece of information.
9. Attributing higher validity to data which confirms expectations.
10. Confusing strong opinion with fact.
11. Attributing past error with "chance events".
12. Assuming the the unexpected occurrence of a "run" of some events enhances the probability of occurrence of an event that has not occurred. (The Gambler's Fallacy)
13. Utilizing a decision rule due to its familiarity.
14. Remembering events which are irrelevant.
15. Feeling control over events.
16. Believing two independent events covary.
17. Ignoring quality of evidence (as with small sample size).
18. Being influenced by the order in which information is received.
19. Being unable to evaluate the impacts of choices not selected or hypotheses not tested.
20. Being influenced by the amount of data.
21. Being influenced by data redundance.
22. Being influenced by the number of stimuli based on prior experience.
23. Ignoring the "regression toward the mean" effect.
24. Giving too much weight to results from small samples.
25. Seeking only information with confirms one's views.
26. Accepting spurious events as commonplace.
27. Choosing an alternative which is desired to be associated with a given event.

Figure 1. Biases associated with judgement and choice (source: Sage, 1981, pp. 647-648)

als purchased. BML may simulate a firm marketing one or two products in one or two market areas, with up to eight firms competing in any one industry.

As subjects compete in the simulation, BML generates a database of historical information for each firm. The SLIM software originally provided a basic capability to access this database (Courtney & Jensen, 1979). SLIM has evolved into a decision support system which now incorporates advanced statistical analysis and modeling capabilities. Participants in a BML simulation use the SLIM software to create models that analyze the data in the database. Subjects have immediate access to data for their firm, but only delayed access to data for other firms. Additionally, SLIM adds a random error component to data for other firms to simulate the uncertainty inherent in such data.

The latest version of the SLIM system, SmartSLIM, focuses on supporting the problem formulation processes of managers. In particular, SmartSLIM attempts to address the biases listed by Sage (1981) that emanate from improper interpretation of statistical results.

Space limitations preclude a detailed discussion of design aspects of the SmartSLIM system (see Paradice & Courtney, 1986; and Paradice, 1986). A brief description of the process of "training" the SmartSLIM system will be given next. Then, a sample scenario is given, demonstrating system usage. Finally, the ability of the system to address Sage's list of biases is examined.

KNOWLEDGE ACQUISITION

SmartSLIM employs causal modeling techniques as a method of acquiring knowledge about a business problem-domain. Causal modeling is a statistical method particularly attractive as a decision-making aid in a business problem context, because causal relationships are frequently sought in problems in the business domain (Blanning, 1984).

One form of causal modeling draws on the method of path analysis to examine relationships among variables (Asher, 1983). The goal of path analysis is to provide plausible explanations of observed correlations by constructing cause-and-effect models of relations among variables. Although an observed correlation can never be used as proof of a causal relationship, very convincing arguments for causality can be constructed from (a) statistical inference, (b) postulated relationships developed from knowledge of the subject matter, and (c) common sense.

Figure 2 shows the conceptual model of the SmartSLIM system. In repeated sessions with SmartSLIM, users hypothesize and test relationships between items in BML's simulated organizational database. The

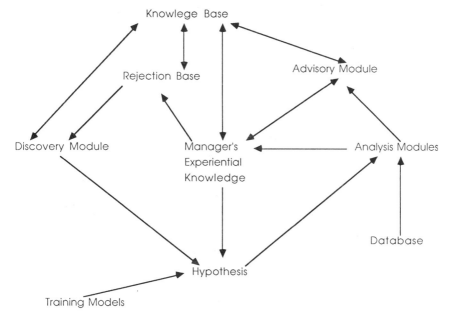

Figure 2.   Conceptual model of the SmartSLIM system

database is cross-sectional in nature, containing data on over 30 firms in a single period in time. Hypotheses are tested using the CAUSE command, which constructs linear (step-wise) regression models (see Figure 3).

The results of the regression are presented to the user, at which time the user may either accept or reject these results. Upon acceptance, the system asks the user for further information regarding the nature of the relationship between the variables in the regression model. For example, the system seeks to determine if any time lag between the variables is involved, whether one variable acts as a constraint on the other, whether the relationship is causal or better described as correlational, definitional, or compositional, and the extent of agreement the user has with the statistical results.

This knowledge acquisition process is repeated for each independent variable that is retained in the model. Note in Figure 3 that the variable quality control (QC) was not retained in the model constructed by SmartSLIM. Although it is certainly reasonable to hypothesize that the level of quality-control expenditures impacts sales volume, SmartSLIM (objectively) indicates that this variable does not contribute to the overall best multivariate model of sales volume in the current problem domain. Hence, SmartSLIM may mitigate a potential user bias by indicating that

> CAUSE SV(F1-*),PRICE(F1-*),ADV(F1-*),BO(F1-*),QC(F1-*):

QC WAS NOT RETAINED IN THE BEST MODEL.
THE VARIABLES RETAINED IN THE MODEL ACCOUNT FOR 73.5%
OF THE VARIATION IN SV.

A ONE UNIT INCREASE IN PRICE RESULTS IN A -8763.3 DECREASE IN
SV. A MORE EXTREME COEFFICIENT FOR PRICE WOULD BE
OBTAINED ONLY 3.58 TIMES IN 100,000,000.

SHOULD THIS RELATIONSHIP BE STORED FOR FUTURE REFERENCE? Y

ON A SCALE OF 1 TO 10 WHERE 10 INDICATES STRONG AGREEMENT,

HOW DO YOU AGREE WITH THIS? 8

HOW MANY QUARTERS PASS BEFORE PRICE AFFECTS SV? 0

IS SV LIMITED BY THE SIZE OF PRICE? N

DOES A MINIMUM LEVEL OF PRICE GUARANTEE SOME MINIMUM
LEVEL OF SV? N

IS THIS RELATIONSHIP DEPENDENT ON OTHER CONDITIONS? N
ENTER A DESCRIPTION OF THIS RELATIONSHIP:
INCREASES IN PRICE RESULT IN DECREASES IN SALES VOLUME.

Figure 3.   An excerpt from the dialogue examining the hypothesis that price,
advertising, back orders, and quality control impact (causes sales volume

quality control should not command too much attention in attempts to
change sales volume.

The information gained during knowledge acquisition is stored in a
knowledge base and used to construct models dynamically in later
sessions. SmartSLIM draws upon a "tool kit" of structural modeling,
path analysis, and linear statistical techniques to synthesize the knowledge in the knowledge base. The system will construct the best model it
can, using these techniques, and can act in an advisory role. The
following scenario gives a brief indication of the operation of the system.

A SAMPLE SCENARIO

Assume that the knowledge acquisition phase described above took
place in an organization and was conducted by various middle-

management personnel. The system has synthesized and integrated this knowledge into a knowledge base containing relationships of variables in the organizational environment. A description of how this knowledge may be used to facilitate unbiased understanding of the business environment can now be made.

Typically, in the use of computer-based systems, management personnel tend to validate a system by checking that certain obviously correct outputs are generated. For example, sample cases with known results may be input to a simulation package to verify that the package produces the correct result. In the case of an intelligent system, the system would be required to demonstrate knowledge of certain fundamental relationships. SmartSLIM uses a statistical technique known as path analysis to infer relationships. Path analysis is performed by invoking the PATH command. For example, the user might check the relationship between price and sales volume, as shown in Figure 4. SmartSLIM has indicated that price and sales volume are believed to be negatively correlated. Other fundamental relationships could be expected to be validated similarly.

Convinced that the system has some basic knowledge of the business

---

> PATH PRICE, SV:
WOULD YOU LIKE EXPLANATIONS (Y/N)ℕ

PRICE -> SV
CONTRIBUTION: -0.62844
NOTE: THIS DIRECT PATH CONTRIBUTION IS NOT INCLUDED IN THE TOTAL

TOTAL CONTRIBUTION OF INDIRECT PATHS IS 0.00000
THE CORRELATION BETWEEN PRICE AND SV IS
-0.44682
NO INDIRECT PATHS.
THE DIRECT PATH EXISTS IN THE KNOWLEDGE BASE
(AGREEMENT = 8).

Figure 4. Stored knowledge of the relationship between price and sales volume

domain, the user would then instruct the system to construct more complex models. The user may desire to determine what the system knows regarding the relationship between cost of goods sold and price (Figure 5).

Although SmartSLIM was not given direct knowledge of the relationship of cost of goods sold to price, it has constructed a relationship through the indirect paths between these two variables. Not only has the system been able to construct a relationship, it also has given an indication of the direction of the relationship by analyzing the signs of the sequences between the variables. Interestingly, in this case the system has determined that the direction of the relationship is opposite to the direction indicated by the correlation, an indication that either the knowledge base needs more training in this area or that the intervening variables in the problem domain have greater influence in the relationship. Note also that on a scale of 1 to 10, SmartSLIM assigns only a value of 3 to its confidence in this relationship.

```
> PATH COGS, PRICE:
WOULD YOU LIKE EXPLANATIONS (Y/N)?  N


COGS -> RMO -> RMI -> PVFS -> PRICE
CONTRIBUTION:  -0.26881


COGS -> RMO -> RMI -> FGUC  -> PRICE
CONTRIBUTION:  0.02573


COGS -> RMO -> RMI -> PVFS -> FGI -> PRICE
CONTRIBUTION:  0.06827


THE TOTAL CONTRIBUTION OF INDIRECT PATHS IS -0.174799
THE CORRELATION BETWEEN COGS AND PRICE IS -0.45539
E - I ANGLE = 26.56505  DEGREES.
ON A SCALE OF 1 TO 10 WHERE 10 IS STRONG BELIEF,
THE SYSTEM ASSIGNS A VALUE OF 3 TO THE OVERALL
CONCLUSION THAT INCREASES IN COGS INCREASES PRICE.
```

Figure 5. Constructed knowledge of the relationship between cost of goods sold and price

Finally, the user may wish to have SmartSLIM construct a model incorporating all of the system knowledge regarding sales volume. This process is shown in Figure 6 using the MODEL command. In this case, the user indicates an interest in increasing sales volume by specifying the optional INCREASE keyword.

Here, the system has once again gone to the knowledge base and dynamically constructed a model. First, variables that are related to sales volume in a noncausal manner are reported. Then any variable known to influence sales volume directly has been included in a model. Again, a stepwise regression approach is taken to estimate the coefficients in the model, giving the user a current (as of the most recent database update) estimation of the relationships involved. Then, any polynomial relationships are constructed and presented. SmartSLIM scans the entire knowledge base when it constructs models. In doing so, the system can draw on knowledge acquired during training sessions with different users. Consequently, entirely new models may be constructed combining knowledge acquired from many users. This approach may overcome the biases inherent in constructing models based solely on knowledge acquired from a single user.

Because the user specified the INCREASE keyword, SmartSLIM has generated a list of potential variables that could be manipulated in order to achieve the goal of increasing sales volume. This list includes advertising expense, price, raw material inventory, and back orders.

The user indicates that more information about the relationship between sales volume and price is desired (Figure 6). The system responds with detailed information about this relationship which is drawn from the knowledge base. This information leads the user to examine ways of achieving a new goal: how to decrease price. This investigation is initiated by requesting more information about price. The system now responds that variables that can be manipulated to achieve this goal include sales commission, advertising ex- pense, and quality control.

In this case, SmartSLIM has assumed an advisory role, assisting the user in learning about relationships in the business domain that are under user control. This type of active participation on the part of the system may be one of its greatest assets in controlling user bias.

SAGE'S LIST OF BIASES

An original goal of the system was to provide tools that support decision-making processes in a routine business problem environment in such a way that common human biases are mitigated. Sage's (1981)

```
> MODEL INCREASE SV:

THE FOLLOWING IS KNOWN ABOUT SV:

SV IS CORRELATED WITH RMI.

SV IS CORRELATED WITH PVFS.

SV IS DEFINED BY SALE.


THE FOLLOWING MODEL HAS BEEN CONSTRUCTED:
CAU SV(F1-*), ADV(F1-*), PRICE(F1-*), SREP(F1-*),

        BO(F1-*),QC(F1-*):

EXTIMATES FOR THE MODEL ARE:
0.6824 AVD -0.8145 PRICE -0.3702 BO
BO HAS A LAGGED EFFECT NOT WELL MODELED HERE.
SREP WAS EXCLUDED FROM THE MODEL.
QC WAS EXCLUDED FROM THE MODEL.
THIS MODEL EXPLAINS 82.5881% OF THE VARIATION IN SV.


SV HAS THE FOLLOWING POLYNOMIAL RELATIONSHIP WITH ADV:
SV = 0.1822 E06 + 0.90580 E05 ADV -0.55090 E05 ADV ^

IN ORDER TO INCREASE SV
INCREASE ADV
DECREASE PRICE
INCREASE RMI
DECREASE BO

TYPE "MORE " FOR MORE MODELING INFORMATION,

TYPE "END" TO EXIT THE MODEL COMMAND,

OR TYPE ONE OF THE VARIABLE NAMES JUST LISTED

FOR MORE INFORMATION ABOUT THAT RELATIONSHIP:  PRICE

A ONE UNIT CHANGE IN PRICE PRODUCES A -0.638 DECREASE

IN SV.   AGREEMENT LEVEL FOR THIS RELATIONSHIP IS 8.


TYPE "MORE " FOR MORE MODELING INFORMATION,

TYPE "END" TO EXIT THE MODEL COMMAND,

OR TYPE ONE OF THE VARIABLE NAMES JUST LISTED

FOR MORE INFORMATION ABOUT THAT RELATIONSHIP:  MORE

IN ORDER TO DECREASE PRICE
DECREASE COM
DECREASE ADV
DECREASE QC

TYPE "MORE " FOR MORE MODELING INFORMATION,

TYPE "END" TO EXIT THE MODEL COMMAND,

OR TYPE ONE OF THE VARIABLE NAMES JUST LISTED

FOR MORE INFORMATION ABOUT THAT RELATIONSHIP:  END
```

Figure 6.   Modeling and advisory action of the system regarding goal of increasing sales volume

list of biases will be used as a checklist against which the system components may be evaluated.

Adjusting and anchoring from a particular piece of data.

When confronted with large amounts of information, a decision maker may choose a particular piece of information as an initial starting point, or anchor, and then adjust that value improperly in order to incorporate the rest of the information. SmartSLIM controls for this bias by testing empirically the extent to which specific relationships between data items are supported. Furthermore, the system treats all relationships equally when synthesizing the knowledge in the knowledge base.

Using easily available data only.

Decision makers tend to use only easily available data. Because SmartSLIM accesses data automatically from the organization's database, all data is equally accessible. One may argue that only data that resides in the database is easily accessed, hence this bias is not addressed. It is assumed that data items that are important to the organization and not in the database can be added.

Being easily influenced by the number of occurrences of an event.

The likelihood of occurrence of two events is often compared by contrasting the number of times the two events occur and ignoring the rate of occurrence of each event. The empirical testing of relationships controls for this bias. Although the user may be unduly influenced to hypothesize a relationship, the knowledge acquisition routines are not influenced to accept the validity of the relationship.

Estimating conservatively.

The failure to revise estimates by incorporating new information is called conservatism. The system estimates exactly, within the context of a least-squares criteria. It must be admitted, however, that the level of user agreement (supplied by the user) may be conservative.

Being influenced by the way information is presented.

The impact of summarized data may be much greater than the same data presented in detail. This is a bias that must be of concern in the design of all computer-based systems. This design has attempted to incorporate features that reflect the results of prior research (Tversky & Kahneman, 1974, 1981) regarding the ways humans react to modes of presentation. The results have been mixed: Some users have found the SmartSLIM interface acceptable, some have offered suggestions for change.

Being influenced by data presented first.

Decision makers often reach premature conclusions on the basis of too small a sample of information. The system does not perform any function in which the order of alternatives plays a role. Where multiple alternatives are presented, as in the case of the path analysis, the alternatives are synthesized into an overall effect. This bias is controlled by the system.

Desiring self-fulfilling prophecies.

Decision makers value certain outcomes. Again, SmartSLIM's use of empirical tests to substantiate hypotheses obviates this bias. This assumes, of course, that the one desiring the prophecies to be filled is not in a position to alter the events which provide data to the database.

Being influenced by the ease of recall of a piece of information.

Data which can be easily recalled or accessed will influence the perception of the likelihood of the event that generates the data. Several features not discussed in this paper are specifically aimed at this issue, making all of the system knowledge readily accessible. This bias is clearly controlled. Confusing strong opinion with fact. Strongly held values may often be regarded and presented as facts. The system's empirical testing again addresses this issue. Regardless of the user's opinions, the statistical support for relationships plays a major role in its inclusion into the knowledge base.

Assuming that the unexpected occurrence of a "run" of some events "enhances" the probability of an event that has not occurred.

Sometimes known as the gambler's fallacy, this bias is exhibited when persons believe, for example, that if a fair coin is tossed and lands heads three consecutive times, then the probability that it will land tails on the next toss is greater than one-half. Because SMartSLIM calculates exact estimates, this bias is controlled.

Remembering events which are irrelevant.

Decision makers are often unable to think objectively if they receive information that an outcome has occurred and they are told to ignore this information. The system controls this bias by manipulating only variables that have explicit relationships to the problem at hand. The design of the system makes it difficult to construct relationships that are irrelevant, if the user does not try to subvert the system.

Believing that two independent events covary.

A mistaken belief that two events covary when they do not covary is called the illusion of correlation. The system clearly controls this bias by using empirical methods to protect specifically against it. In fact, a minor enhancement to the system was the inclusion of a command to calculate and display correlations.

Being unable to evaluate the impacts of choices not selected or hypotheses not tested.

Poor results may be accepted as good because of an inability to test alternative hypotheses. SmartSLIM provides commands to construct and test (possibly new) models for validity. This is an area where a specific knowledge source could be constructed to enhance this capability. For example, this knowledge source could possibly direct the discovery process in specific areas such as production, marketing, or finance.

Being influenced by data redundance.

Sage (1981) states: "The more redundancy in the data, the more confidence people often have in their predictions, although this over-confidence is usually unwarranted" (p. 648). SmartSLIM makes an effort to synthesize the redundance that occurs into a single interpretation using techniques from structural modeling. Hence, one may claim that the system is indeed influenced by data redundance.

Being influenced by the number of stimuli based on prior experience.

Reactions to stimuli are interpreted in accordance with previous expectations. This bias is controlled because each model constructed, whether as a result of a hypothesis or the discovery process, is tested anew. Hence, prior results do not influence the system.

Choosing an alternative which is desired to be associated with a given event.

The preference of the decision maker for particular outcomes and particular decisions can lead to the choice of an alternative that the decision maker would like to have associated with a given event. Again, the empirical testing of alternative relationships can address this bias, but the system cannot force a particular course of action. Therefore, the system is helpless if the user decides to manipulate variables in his control that have no relationship (as determined by the system) to the problem at hand.

BIASES NOT ADDRESSED BY SMARTSLIM

The biases not addressed by SmartSLIM fall into two categories. First, some of the biases result from a lack of specialized knowledge in statistics. Proper interpretation of the implications of sample size is an example. Efforts are underway to incorporate this type of specialized knowledge. The second type of uncontrolled biases result from SmartSLIM's dependence on user-supplied information. The agreement levels input to SmartSLIM are an example. Consequently, a bias such as "attributing higher validity to data which confirms expectations" is not addressed.

SUMMARY

This paper has argued that problem formulation is a critical aspect of the decision-making process, but one that has been neglected by DSS researchers. It has been further argued that human biases result in incorrect problem formulations and costly, decision-making errors.

SmartSLIM is a DSS designed to obviate human biases during the problem formulation process. Causal modeling and path analysis are used as fundamental tools to examine user-proposed relationships between variables. The objective is to control user biases through the use of empirical, objective observations. Many of Sage's 27 biases are addressed in this manner.

SmartSLIM's ability to determine relationships and construct models has also been compared with human subjects. In an evaluation based on a questionnaire administered to subjects regarding relationships between variables in SmartSLIM's database, the system's performance compared favorably with the human's abilities.

The research has shown that a system that incorporates causal modeling is a viable approach to the construction of an expert system for problem formulation in the business domain. Although some shortcomings in the approach have been identified, this design also provides a workable structure of the general business problem domain. This feature is particularly important, as it provides a basis for future research into the design and development of more sophisticated systems.

REFERENCES

Ackoff, R.L. (1979). The future of operational research is past. *Journal of the Operations Research Society, 30*, 93–104.

Ahituv, N., & Neumann, S. (1982). *Principles of information systems for management.* Dubuque, IA: William C. Brown.

Asher, H.B. (1983). Causal modeling. Beverly Hills, CA: Sage Publications.

Blanning, R.W. (1984). Management applications of expert systems. *Information and management, 7*, 311–316.

Bonczek, R.H., Holsapple, C.W. & Whinston, A.B. (1981). *Foundations of decision support systems.* New York, NY: Academic.

Courtney, J.F., & Jensen, R.L. (1981). *SLIM user's manual.* Dallas, TX: Business Publications.

Duncker, K. (1945). On problem solving. *Psychological Monographs, 58.*

Hora, S.C. (1985, April) Learning rates in supervised and unsupervised intelligent systems. Paper presented at the Workshop on Artificial Intelligence and Statistics, AT&T Bell Laboratories, Murray Hill, NJ.

Jensen, R.L., & Cherrington, M.L. (1977). *BML participant's manual.* Dallas, TX: Business Publications.

Johnson, W. (1946). *People in quandaries: The semantics of personal adjustment.* New York, NY: Harper Bros.

Judson, A.J., & Cofer, C.N. (1956). Reasoning as an associative process: I. direction in a simple verbal problem. *Psychological Reports, 2*, 469–473.

Kasper, G.M. (1985). The effect of user-developed DSS applications on forecasting decision-making performance in an experimental setting. *Journal of Management Information Systems, 2*, 26–39.

Kasper, G.M., & Cerveny, R.P. (1985). A laboratory study of user haracteristics and decision-making performance in end-user computing. *Information and Management, 9*, 87–96.

Libby, R. (1983). *Accounting and human information processing: Theory and applications.* Englewood Cliffs, NJ: Prentice Hall.

Loy, S.L. (1986). *An experimental investigation of a graphical problem-structuring aid and nominal group technique for group decision support systems.* Unpublished doctoral dissertation, Texas Tech University, Lubbock.

McLean, M. & Shepherd, P. (1976). The importance of model structure. *Futures, 8*, 40–51.

Mintzberg, H., Raisinghani, D., & Theoret, A. (1976). The structure of 'unstructured' decision processes. *Administrative Science Quarterly, 21*, 246–275.

Mitroff, I.I., Emshoff,J.R., & Kilmann, R.H. (1979). Assumptional analysis: A methodology for strategic problem solving. *Management Science, 25*, 583–593.

Newell, A., & Simon, H.A. (1972). *Human problem solving.* Englewood Cliffs, NJ:

Prentice-Hall.

Pounds, W.F. (1969). The process of problem finding. *Industrial Management Review, 11,* 1–19.

Pracht, W.E. (1984). *An experimental investigation of a graphical interactive structural modeling aid for decision support systems.* Unpublished doctoral dissertation, Texas Tech University, Lubbock.

Raiffa, H. (1968). *Decision analysis.* Reading, MA: Addison Wesley.

Reitman, W.R. (1964). Heuristic decision procedures, open constraints, and the structure of ill-defined problems. *Human Judgments and Optimality.* In M.W. Shelly,II & G.L. Bryan (Eds.), New York, NY: Wiley, pp. 282–315.

Rowe, A.J. (1977). How do senior managers make decisions? *Business and Economics,* 17–20.

Sage, A.P. (1981). Behavioral and organizational considerations in the design of information systems and processes for planning and decision support. *IEEE Transactions on Systems, Man, and Cybernetics, 11,* 640–678.

Simon, H.A. (1960). *The new science of management decisions.* New York, NY: Harper and Row.

Sprague, R.H. & Carlson, E.D. (1982). *Building effective decision support systems.* Englewood Cliffs, NJ: Prentice Hall.

Taylor, I.A. (1975). A retrospective view of creativity investigation. In I.A. Taylor & J.W. Getzels (Eds.), *Perspectives in creativity* (pp. 1–36), Chicago, IL: Aldine.

Tversky, A. (1972). Elimination by aspects: A theory of choice. *Psychological Review, 79,* 281–299.

Tversky, A., & Kahneman,D. Judgement under uncertainty: Heuristics and biases. *Science, 184,* 1124–1131.

Tversky, A., & Kahneman, D. (1981). The framing of decisions and the psychology of choice. *Science, 211,* 453–458.

Volkema, R.J. (1983). Problem formulation in planning and design. *Management Science, 29,* 639–652.

Wang, M.S., & Courtney, J.F. (1982). A conceptual architecture for generalized decision support software. *IEEE Transactions on Systems, Man, and Cybernetics, 24,* 701–710.

SECTION III

User Interface Specification Tools

Various tools have been developed to aid in the design of the user interface. Some of these tools serve as design aids for any computer program modules and are viewed primarily as structured techniques. These tools include data flow diagrams, Warnier-Orr diagrams, Nassi-Shneiderman diagrams, decision tables, and hierarchical charts. These are all portable, off-line tools which provide a framework for the designer but offer no guarantee that the resultant interface will adhere to human factors guidelines. The primary goal of this category of tool is to ensure cohesive modules which are loosely coupled and follow a logical hierarchical structure, thus resulting in efficient systems which perform correctly.

All of these tools are graphic rather than verbal. They are designed to fit onto one page of paper and allow the systems development team to walk through the system with the user and solicit feedback. Soliciting feedback from the user was a difficult, if not impossible, task when the traditional technical specification was verbal, lengthy, and filled with technical jargon. It is much easier to develop a system which satisfies the user when the user can be actively involved in the entire development process.

Other tools which enhance the level of user involvement and decrease the programming effort required to meet resultant user requests fall under the general category of prototype development tools. A prototype is a system shell which presents the user interfaces, both screen and hard copy, to the user. The prototyping tools allow rapid development of the interfaces and rapid changes via user feedback. They are application generators in the sense that very little hard coding is required on the part of the development team. Instead, programmers merely specify particular parameters, and the menus, input/output screens, and reports are generated by the prototype tool automatically. Prototyping tools reduce development time and also allow heavy user involvement in the development process which should, in turn, increase user satisfaction.

There are some negative aspects to prototyping tools, however. Prototypes shells, at best are incomplete systems which do not have the full data and calculations behind them. They tend to create false expectations on the users' part for early system delivery. Also, it is tempting for the analyst/designer to jump into prototyping before adequate analysis and design have been completed. The resultant systems may be user facile but not functional.

A wise system designer who understands these drawbacks can prepare the user psychologically for the time it takes to develop a successful system and spend adequate time on the analysis and design phases before beginning the prototype process. If these guidelines are adhered to, the system developer who uses prototyping has a powerful tool for ensuring a satisfactory user interface.

The two selections included in this section are "Applying Software Engineering Principles to the User Application Interface" by James A. Sena of Texas A&M University, Department of Business Analysis and Research and L. Murphy Smith of Texas A&M University, Department of Accounting, and "FORMFLEX: A User Interface Tool for Forms Definition and Management" by Joobin Choobineh of Texas A&M University, Department of Business Analysis and Research.

The Sena-Smith paper provides human factors guidelines for designing the user interface in a business data entry system. The Choobineh paper presents "FORMFLEX," which is a forms prototype development tool.

CHAPTER 6

Applying Software Engineering Principles to the User Application Interface

James A. Sena
and
L. Murphy Smith
Texas A&M University

This paper presents a standard procedure, using DBASE III, for entry to be used in general applications such as order entry, purchasing, and so forth. Any application which has a base set and an indefinite number of detail items fits this procedure. A novel inclusion is the associated dictionary file containing acceptable values for all data entries.

INTRODUCTION

Many experienced programmers and new users of micro systems are implementing proprietary applications on the microcomputer. Rather than use traditional procedural languages, such as COBOL or BASIC, to implement the application, these developers are employing micro database managers, such as DBase II or RBase 5000. Because the microcomputer is of a personal nature, the emphasis on user-friendly software is important. "Friendly", according to an article in *Computer Decisions* (Whieldon, 1980), means that "terminals are relatively easy and comfortable to use and that their features are designed with the needs of the operator in mind" or, even more aptly, "informative and forgiving" (p. 36). This paper focuses on the online entry of data for a typical business application and suggests a model for data-entry design.

DIRECTIONS

Several concepts of user identification and software engineering need to be considered to ensure that good system practices are employed in the development of online-interactive systems in a fashion similar to main-frame and minicomputer systems. Ramsey and Atwood (1979) specified some user characteristics that affect system design;

Naive users

Large, heterogeneous group
Benefit from and prefer computer
Requires more tutorial features

Managerial users

Highly variable information needs
Often believe that computer systems are too inflexible
Very low systems "impedance" required to capture managers as users
If dissatisfied, tend to make "distant use" of the system (placing an operator between himself and computer) or, at best, partial use

Scientific-Technical Users

Majority is dissatisfied with available computer-based tools
Dissatisfied users often respond by building their own systems

The classification of users according to their experience can determine the optimal system design and operation. For business-applications data entry, the users are a combination of seminaive and management-staff. Scientific and technical users are not true candidates for such application systems. Users prefer computer-directed dialogue for a specific application, according to Walther and O'Neill (1974). Feedback and built-in documentation are necessary ingredients. Micro application developers can learn from past experiences on mainframe-mini software development.

SOFTWARE ENGINEERING

Walther and O'Neill (1974) maintained that the user interface needed to be "programmed with the capability for making differential responses to a variety of users under a wide range of conditions" (p. 379).

Hansen (1971) cited eight user engineering principles formulating the ingredients of data-entry interaction to facilitate flexibility. These principles still apply today. The first principle was to build a PROFILE of the INTENDED USER in order to make specific design decision. The design had to be user considerate. All users share two common traits—they forget and they make mistakes.

According to Hansen, "because the user forgets the computer must augment the user's memory." One important way this can be accomplished is to observe the principle SELECTION NOT ENTRY. Provision of choices to users allows them to enter data quicker by selection.

Another principle is PREDICTABLE BEHAVIOR. By remembering a few characteristics and a few exceptions, the user can workout the details of any operation. The next principle deals with OPTIMIZING OPERATIONS. The modes and speeds of interaction and the sequence of user actions needed to invoke specific facilities can put stress on the physical appearance of the system. The guiding principle is that the system should be as unobtrusive as possible. In responding to user's request, the system needs to observe the principle of DISPLAY INERTIA. That is, the display should change as little as necessary to carry out the request. Another means of reducing user-interaction effort is to design the system so that the user can operate via MUSCLE POWER. Muscle power means depressing a function key or single key in response to a computer request. An entry should have few state-dependent meanings. A designated response must be available to ensure FAIL SAFE exits from any strange or unwanted state.

The system needs to protect users from both the system and themselves. Another principle is error engineering to provide GOOD ERROR MESSAGES. An error on entry or in modification can affect data-file integrity. To protect the user, the system must provide REVERSIBLE ACTIONS. These software engineering principles are summarized below. These principles are not an all-inclusive list. They constitute one basis for data entry design.

Software Engineering Principles

1. Profile the intended user
2. Selection not entry
3. Predictable behavior
4. Optimizing operations
5. Display inertia
6. Muscle power
7. Good error messages
8. Reversible actions

ASSUMPTIONS

The design of data entry and dialogue is constrained by the microcomputer hardware configuration. Design assumptions can be generalized to a broad set of devices. The assumptions made for this paper relate to the majority of contemporary micro systems. The microcomputer consists of an IBM/PC or PC compatible system capable of running DBase III. The keyboard is in the IBM PC format—CTRL, ALT, and 10 function keys. The monitor is an 80-column, 24-line screen with full-address capability. The monitor does not have to have color graphics capability.

The typical application is accessed using a menu-driven system. Figure 1 presents an example of such a menu. An order entry application will be used as an example throughout this paper. Most application systems today are integrated with other applications (e.g., accounts payable and receivable with general ledger). This integration centers about a set of database or common file structures. These structures operate using key-driven network or relational frameworks. Maintenance has several facets: data-entry, update, maintenance, and reporting. The primary areas of user interface are the data entry input and the reporting operation. Frequently, reporting is supplemented by user inquiry and database browsing. This browsing activity can be very

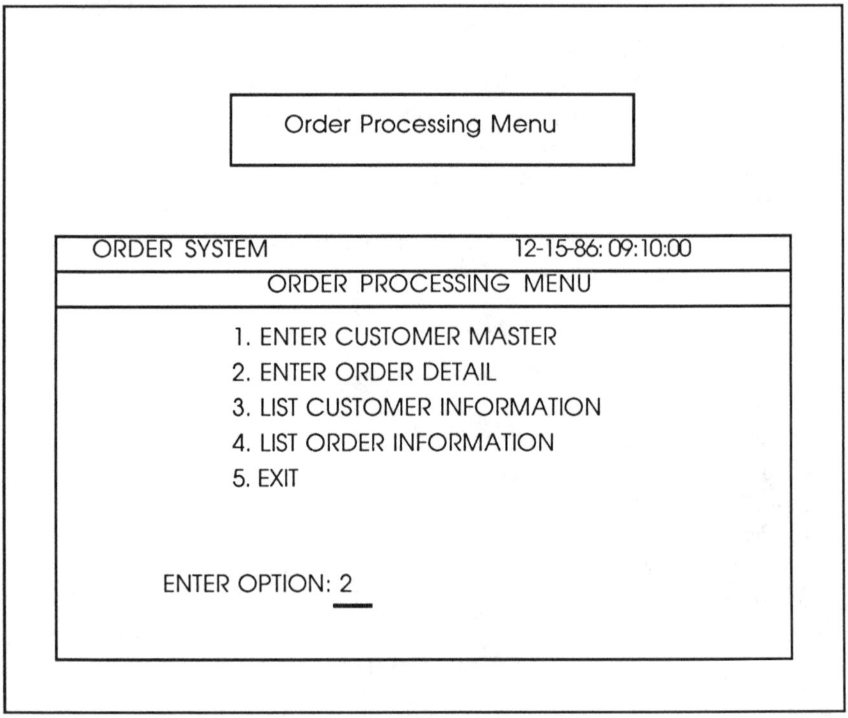

Figure 1.

user/machine intensive. The technique described in this paper does not address the query-browse operation, only the data entry area.

Data entry can be performed by a range of users parametric, staff, or management. The parametric user's primary task is application data entry responding to a sequence of parameters. They need not be familiar with application requirements because data is entered in a prescribed form (application dependent).

The parametric user needs control and guidance to ensure fluid data entry. On the other hand, staff or management personnel may not be as facile with microcomputer operation but are quite familiar with the application features and functions. In all cases, the person entering the data uses the same equipment and entry procedures.

SCREEN ENTRY FORMAT

In the operation of a typical application, selection is menu driven (SELECTION NOT ENTRY). Following appropriate selection, the designated procedure is activated. An indication of the desired selection is displayed. This display provides feedback to the user in order to verify proper selection. This verification is presented in the title area.

Data entry consists of two or three parts, depending on the application. The first part is the general or fixed data, such as customer number or name, date, invoice number, and the like. The second part is the variable or detail area. Variable refers to the number of detail entries as opposed to the entries themselves. A detail line in this example could contain the quantity, part number and price of an item sold to a customer. Hypothetically, there could be an unlimited number of such entries for a given situation. A user-oriented data entry system needs to handle this unlimited entry without restricting the user (INTERFACE FLEXIBILITY).

The last area provides total entry data and other related closing entries (e.g., freight and tax). In a well-designed system these last entries need not be actual entries. Instead, the system could perform the computations and display the results. The user verifies the display (PREDICTABLE BEHAVIOR). The system computes the total for the user, where applicable.

The general placement of screen entries is shown in Figure 2. There are four main areas: title section, reference or general area, detail line area, and the closing entry section. On the display, each section has a clear separation. This separation is accomplished through the use of solid or dotted lines.

```
┌─────────────────────────────────────────────────────────┐
│                                                           │
│        ┌──────────────────────────────────────┐          │
│        │    SCREEN FORMAT FOR ORDER ENTRY      │          │
│        └──────────────────────────────────────┘          │
│                                                           │
│   ┌───────────────────────────────────────────────────┐  │
│   │  ┌─────────────┐                                   │  │
│   │  │ TITLE LINES │      ───────────   ──────         │  │
│   │  └─────────────┘                                   │  │
│   │  ┌──────────────────────┐                          │  │
│   │  │GENERAL REFERENCE DATA│   ──────────             │  │
│   │  └──────────────────────┘   ──────────             │  │
│   │  ┌─────────────────────┐    ──────────   ────      │  │
│   │  │   DETAIL LINES      │    ──────────            │  │
│   │  │  ┌────────────┐     │                          │  │
│   │  │  │ TOTAL LINE │     │                          │  │
│   │  └──┴────────────┴─────┘                          │  │
│   │  ┌──────────────────────────────────────────┐    │  │
│   │  │   ENTRY LINE                             │    │  │
│   │  └──────────────────────────────────────────┘    │  │
│   └───────────────────────────────────────────────────┘  │
│                                                           │
└─────────────────────────────────────────────────────────┘
```

Figure 2.

TITLE SECTION

The title section contains one or more lines indicating the generating procedure for the data entry screen. The first entry on the title line is the procedure name. This procedure name is used as bridge between the user and the system developer. Through reference to this name, the user can communicate problems that may arise for the system developer.

An appropriate user title can consist of one or more lines to indicate the major function or purpose of this data-entry procedure. Usually, this title is tied to the menu selection. For example, the title could be "Customer Order." This title should be meaningful to the user of the application system.

Finally, the date and time are fed back to the user. This feedback has two purposes: The date is usually the date that will be stored for transaction entry; the time gives the user an indication of when the routine was entered. Depending on the micro, the time can be continually displayed.

GENERAL REFERENCE DATA

Typical application data entries in the general reference section relate to the particular application. Such applications as order entry, accounts payable, and accounts receivable, purchasing, and so forth all have similar reference fields that are entered. There is an identifier, such as order number. Given the identifier entry, the system responds with appropriate customer name, vendor name, or work description to assure users that they have entered the correct number.

Other entries include dates and associated or related identifiers. The dates refer to times other than the current date. A transaction can occur but not be entered at the time of occurrence. The other identifiers refer to subsystem or connected application files. For example, an invoice is usually associated with a particular vendor and a customer number is associated with a customer. The purpose of these entries is to support the user by providing feedback concerning supporting data elements.

DETAIL LINE AREA

The detail line area is the central focus of the data entry procedure. A single detail item, such as a sale item or a parts order, is entered on a single line. Subsequent detail entries are placed on following lines. The system needs to accommodate these entries in several ways:

1. A facility for unlimited detail entry (INTERFACE FLEXIBILITY) is required.
2. Each entry has a reenter option at the end of the entry line (PREDICTABLE BEHAVIOR).
3. Entries should be stored on a temporary data array (OPTIMIZING OPERATION).

A sale or purchase order can have an indefinite number of detail entries. Placing a limit on the number of entries is not good design. Because there can be an indefinite number of entries, the line entries can exceed the screen capacity. The screen design needs to accommodate line entries in a circular fashion. After the screen area is filled, the next entry "pushes up" or scrolls the detail area such that the first line is no longer visible. This process continues for all entries in the detail section. Figure 3 illustrates this process.

Correction of a single line item on a data-entry line follows directly after entry. If correction takes place on an entry-by-entry basis, the

```
                ORDER ENTRY SUBSYSTEM
  ORDER ENTRY                    08/08/87              18:06:49

  ORDER #: 10123                      ORDER DATE: 11/27/87
  SALESMAN #: 119                     CUSTOMER #: 4092
  SALESMAN NAME: DON MCMURTY          CUSTOMER NAME: DAMCRO OIL CO.

  LINE#  QUANTITY   PART #   PART DESCRIPTION     UNIT COST  TOTAL COST
    6       1       2109310  FLANGE 6.5             15.91      15.91
    7       2       4021131  BEAM 4X4X3             12.00      24.00
    8       4       4221341  BEAM 3X3X1.5            9.41      37.64
    9       3       4221341  BEAM 3X3X1.5            9.41      28.23
   10       2       8113341  PIPE 14X1.5X21         12.50      63.00
   11       1       5113210  BAR 4X5X11             31.50      12.50

  TOTAL                                           $$$  181.28

  Continue to ADD, (Y)es or (N)o?  Y

  Line 15 has been ADDED
```

Following return, the screen is pushed up. Quantity & Part Number from the previous line are displayed to assist entry.

```
                ORDER ENTRY SUBSYSTEM
  ORDER ENTRY                    08/08/87              18:06:49

  ORDER #: 10123                      ORDER DATE: 11/27/87
  SALESMAN #: 119                     CUSTOMER #: 4092
  SALESMAN NAME: DON MCMURTY          CUSTOMER NAME: DAMCRO OIL CO.

  LINE#  QUANTITY   PART #   PART DESCRIPTION     UNIT COST  TOTAL COST
    7       2       4021131  BEAM 4X4X3             12.00      24.00
    8       4       4221341  BEAM 3X3X1.5            9.41      37.64
    9       3       4221341  BEAM 3X3X1.5            9.41      28.23
   10       2       8113341  PIPE 14X1.5X21         12.50      63.00
   11       1       5113210  BAR 4X5X11             31.50      12.50

   12       1       6113121

  TOTAL                                           $$$  181.28
```

Figure 3. Detail line srcolling effect

process can be time consuming. Instead, a mechanism to query the user after all entries for a detail line have been made is more efficient. If the line has not been entered correctly, the data line is erased and the user reenters from the start of the line.

DATA ENTRY

To ensure consistency and display inertia, the data entry is made in a top-down, right-to-left fashion and the area of data entry follows behind or below the appropriate header display. The area for entry is highlighted. The exact format and acceptable range of values is displayed on the 23rd screen line. The last, or 24th, screen line is used to display error messages.

The data entry sequence is a form of dialogue. The user is prompted with appropriate questions for data entry—part number, quantity, and the like. Each entry is validated based on user specified criteria in the system design. The validation information is placed in an associated dictionary file and is accessed when the data element is to be entered. As each data element is entered, the validated data is placed in its proper position of the current detail line or section of the screen. When all entries for a line item have been completed, the user is queried to determine if the line entries are correct. If they are not correct, the line is erased and the process is repeated.

In certain situations, the user may encounter an irregularity on entry of the data document. To accommodate the modification process, a suspense data array is used to collect the entries and write them at document entry completions. Once the user is satisfied with the complete document entry, the results are used to update the application's master database structure. Figure 4 illustrates this process.

After all data elements have been entered, the user indicates that the document detail entry is complete. At that point, the user may elect (optionally) to review and selectively change the detail entries. At the end of this period of reexamination, the user can accept or reject the document entries. This correction/approval process is in two stages. The first stage deals with individual detail entries; the second stage addresses the composite set of all entries.

TOTAL LINES

As detail lines are entered, accumulations and calculation are made. Following indication that all detail lines have been entered, the total

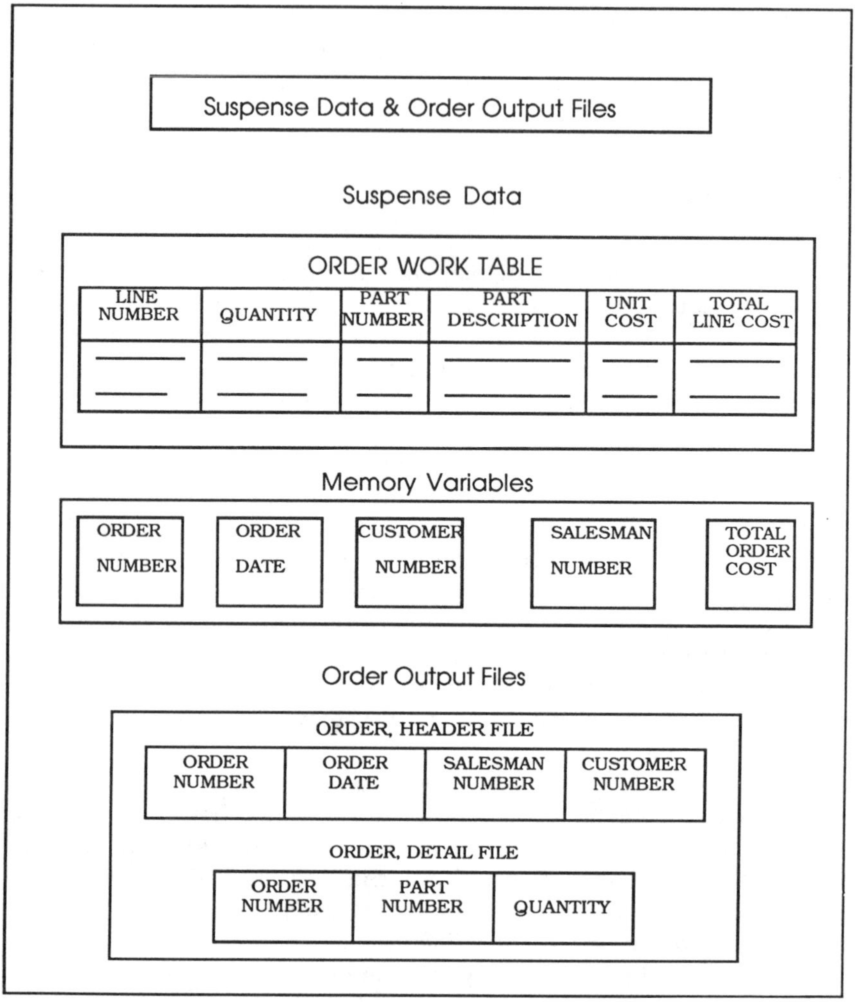

Figure 4.

lines are displayed. Depending on the application, the user enters additional lines such as freight charges and discount factors. These entries are rather straight forward and do not impact the general design.

There are several options available at the query point.

1. line is correct;
2. line is not correct;
3. terminate processing of program; or
4. restart entry of data.

Termination of processing (which can be generated on any item entry) causes a program exit without recording the entries for this document, for example, order data. Restart causes the program to erase the current array as well as reference data and start entry at the beginning of the document.

If the line is correct, the data elements are stored into the data array. The user signals the end of the detail line entries by indicating the END option. This is not the same as termination or restart.

CHECKING PHASE

After all detail data have been entered, the user has the option of reviewing and modifying the detail lines before releasing them for recording. In the checking phase the options include:

Review detail lines;

Modify detail lines; or

Accept detail lines.

REVIEW DETAIL LINES

In the review of detail lines, the user can scroll the detail area of the screen forward and backward to examine the lines that were entered and saved in the data array. Each entry contains a line number to be used in case a detail line is to be modified or deleted.

MODIFY DETAIL LINES

Using the line numbers from the review process, the user can change or delete a detail line. New detail lines are added at the back of the data array. Additions can be made at any time in the checking phase.

If a line is deleted, an array operation takes place. The deleted line is physically removed from the data array. Subsequent lines are renumbered. This can constitute a problem where several lines are to be modified or deleted. To ensure that the proper line is being deleted, the line is displayed and the user then must indicate again to delete this line via a prompt and response.

```
ORDER ENTRY SUBSYSTEM
ORDER ENTRY                        08/08/87                      18:06:49

ORDER #: 10123                          ORDER DATE: 11/27/87
SALESMAN #: 119                         CUSTOMER #: 4092
SALESMAN NAME: DON MCMURTY              CUSTOMER NAME: DAMCRO OIL CO.

LINE#  QUANTITY   PART #   PART DESCRIPTION        UNIT COST   TOTAL COST
  6       1       2109310  FLANGE 6.5                15.61       15.91
  7       2       4021131  BEAM 4X4X3               12.00        24.00
  8       4       4221341  BEAM 3X3X1.5              9.41        37.64
  9       3       4221341  BEAM 3X3X1.5              9.41        28.23
 10       2       8113341  PIPE 14X1.5X21           12.50        63.00
 11       1       5113210  BAR 4X5X11               31.50        12.50

TOTAL                                               $$$  181.28


Type  (A)dd,  (R)eview,  (I)nsert,  (M)odify,  (D)elete,  (E)xit:
```

```
┌─────────────────────────────────────────────┐
│        After Entry of (E)xit, the User is     │
│    Prompted to determine if the order entries │
│    are to be written to the Order File from the│
│              Order Work Area                   │
└─────────────────────────────────────────────┘
```

```
ORDER ENTRY SUBSYSTEM
ORDER ENTRY                        08/08/87                      18:06:49

ORDER #: 10123                          ORDER DATE: 11/27/87
SALESMAN #: 119                         CUSTOMER #: 4092
SALESMAN NAME: DON MCMURTY              CUSTOMER NAME: DAMCRO OIL CO.

LINE#  QUANTITY   PART #   PART DESCRIPTION        UNIT COST   TOTAL COST
  7       2       4021131  BEAM 4X4X3               12.00        24.00
  8       4       4221341  BEAM 3X3X1.5              9.41        37.64
  9       3       4221341  BEAM 3X3X1.5              9.41        28.23
 10       2       8113341  PIPE 14X1.5X21           12.50        63.00
 11       1       5113210  BAR 4X5X11               31.50        12.50


TOTAL                                               $$$  181.28

STORE these ORDER ENTRIES to permanent files?  (Y)es or (N)o?  Y
```

Figure 5. Order ending process

ACCEPT DETAIL LINE

Once the user is satisfied with the detail line entries the user is queried to verify that the document should be recorded. Figure 5 presents this process. There are several physical records types: header, detail, and total. The header and total are combined into one group. The detail records, being an indefinite number, are associated with the header record by key values.

To support a relational file system, the placement of the detail data onto direct access storage media is required so that document-entry access capabilities are maintained.

SUMMARY

This paper presents a standard procedure, using DBASE III, for detail entry to be used in general applications such as order entry, purchasing, and the like. Any application which has a base set and an indefinite number of detail items fits this procedure. A novel inclusion is the associated dictionary file containing acceptable values for all data entries.

The process is delimited to the IBM/PC or a compatible microcomputer. Where packaged software entry systems and application generators are used, the need for the procedures discussed in this paper still exist.

REFERENCES

Hansen, W. (1971). User engineering principles for interactive systems, *American Federation Information Processing Societies*, 523–540.

Ramsey, R., & Atwood, M. (1979). Human factors in computer systems: A review of the Literature, *Science Applications*, 13.

Walther, G., & O'Neill, H. (1974). OnLine user-computer interface—the effects of interface flexibility, terminal type, and experience on performance, *National Computer Conference*, 379.

Whieldon, D. (1980). How to pick 'friendly terminals', *Computer Decisions*, 12, 38.

CHAPTER 7

FORMFLEX: A User Interface Tool for Forms Definition and Management

Joobin Choobineh
Texas A&M University

Screen form as a medium of user interface is analyzed and discussed. A form model is described which captures the semantics of most everyday business forms. Based on this model FORMFLEX is developed. Three components of the FORMFLEX the Form Definition, the Form Manipulation, and the Rule Definition are described. These components aid the user in, respectively, defining form objects; manipulating form instances; and specifying integrity constraints, triggers, and alerters for a forms application.

INTRODUCTION

The existing computer technology supports character-oriented man-machine interfaces. A user enters a character string via keyboard which triggers a reaction by the machine which in turn is communicated by character strings to the user. The most popular character-oriented interfaces are (a) command languages, (b) menu selections, (c) question/answering (extensions of which are natural language interfaces), and (d) forms filling and reporting.

In this paper, a system is presented which employs a combination of these interfaces to manage business functions. The cornerstone of the system's interface is a collection of forms which are recognized to be the most important end-user interface in a business setting (Lefkovitz, 1979).

People in the work force are familiar with handling and filling out preprinted, structured forms. Most organizations use business forms to carry out their day-to-day operations, to communicate internally within the organization and externally to customers, suppliers, government agencies, and other entities.

A form is a standardized screen input/output which is used for data gathering, display, and update. Figures 1 and 2, respectively, depict a sales order and a shipment form of a hypothetical company which sells parts to customers.

Advantages of forms-oriented user interfaces consist of

1. *Popularity*. Forms are the most popular means of gathering data;
2. *Familiarity*. Most everyone is familiar with the process of filling out, reading, and interpreting the contents of a form;

SALES ORDER

SALE'S DATE	12-11-86	SALE'S ORDER NUMBER	153

BILL TO:

| NAME | ABC Headquarters |
| ADDRESS | Main Street Houston, Tx 70000 |

SHIP TO:

| NAME | ABC Store Branch |
| ADDRESS | Any Street New York, NY 20000 |

CUSTOMER ORDER #	1100077853	ORDER DATE	12-11-86

PRODUCT NAME	PRICE/UNIT	QUANTITY	AMOUNT
NUTS	15.00	40	600.00
BOLTS	12.00	25	300.00
TOTAL BEFORE TAX ---------->			900.00
TAX (5%) -------------------->			45.00
TOTAL---------------------->			945.00

CUSTOMER TYPE

[X] RETAIL   [ ] WHOLESALE

[ ] INSTITUTIONAL   [ ] INDIVIDUAL

SALESPERSON GOODSALESPERSON

Figure 1. An instance of the sales order form

```
+--------------------------------------------------------------+
|                          SHIPMENT                            |
+--------------------------------------------------------------+
| DATE OF                     INVOICE                          |
| AUTHORIZATION  [12-12-86]     NO        [580]                |
|                                                              |
| SHIP TO:                                                     |
|   NAME     [ ABC STORES - BANCH 1                 ]          |
|                                                              |
|            [ ANY  STREET                          ]          |
|   ADDRESS  [ NEW YORK, N.Y. 20000                 ]          |
|                                                              |
|   CUSTOMER [                                      ]          |
|   ORDER NO                                                   |
|                                                              |
|   SALES ORDER[ 153     ]    SHIPPING  [ TUC ]               |
|   NO                        POINT                            |
+--------------------------------------------------------------+
```

	WAREHOUSE			
PRODUCT-NO	LOCATION	BIN-NO	QUANTITY	WEIGHT
P10	TUC	2	18	180
		3	8	80
P20	TUC	8	10	50
	PHE	4	10	50
		8	5	25
TOTAL	--------------------------------->			385

```
| AUTHORIZED                  CARRIER                          |
| BY          [ SHIPPING CLK ]        [ ACME        ]         |
+--------------------------------------------------------------+
```

Figure 2.   An instance of the shipment form

3. *Applicability*. The concept of a form as a structured object is applicable to varying types of applications;
4. *Formality*. Being structured objects, forms can easily be formalized;
5. *Completeness of functionality*. A form is functionally self-contained;
6. *Stability*. Once designed, forms remain stable over time. Changes, if any, will be minor and infrequent;

7. *Productivity.* As a consequence of ease of use (see 2 above) and repeated use over time (see 6 above), user productivity will increase.

A SURVEY OF FORMS-ORIENTED SYSTEMS

In its 1979 report, the Conference on Data Systems Languages (CODASYL) End User Facility Committee (EUFC) recommended the forms-oriented approach as the most important medium for user interface (Lefkovitz, 1979). Following the EUFC recommendation, there have been a number of implementations of forms-oriented systems. The report was a result of the recognition by the committee members of some ongoing research efforts and a need for further research in the forms-oriented interface area.

One of the earliest reported systems on forms management was the Business Definition Language (BDL) (Hammer, 1977). A BDL program used four types of objects: documents, steps, paths, and files. A document is a form template which is used by a user as a logical unit of input/output. A step is the procedural attachment to a document. A path connects two or more steps together by piping an output document from one step to an input document of another step. Files are used to save documents.

In that same year, the System for Business Automation (SBA) was reported in Zloof (1977b). This system was later extended and reported in Dejong (1980) and in Zloof (1981). SBA was built on the Query By Example (QBE) (Zloof, 1977a). The building blocks of SBA are boxes which can represent data, programs, people, locations, or any other object. These objects are not predefined by SBA. Each box has a name, input and output section, and a body. The body of an SBA box is used to define the display of the box and to map from the objects shown on the box to a database. Querying and data manipulation is performed in a manner almost identical to that found in QBE.

The QBE concept was so appealing that a number of other researchers developed form management systems based on that idea. Among them were Forms Operations By Example (FOBE) by Luo (1981) and the Forms Pattern Language by Larson (1984). In Luo (1981), various representations of forms were discussed and a BNF specification for form properties was given. An interesting idea of Larson (1984) was the nesting of one or more forms in another form. It claimed that the forms can be nested to an arbitrary depth.

A number of other attempts have been made to formalize the form model. One of the most comprehensive and generalized form models is that of Tsichritzis (1982). In this work, a formal distinction is made between form type, form instance, and form templates. Form-type definitions include a set of operations procedures on the forms in addition to the description of the properties of the fields of the forms. A novel idea of this work is the generalization of the form template to any medium of communication. For instance, given the existence of the proper technology, a voice template may be defined for a form so that an instance of it can materialize as voice. This work was an extension of Tsichritzis (1980) and Ladd (1980).

As an example of an attempt at formalizing the form management system as a programming language, the reader is referred to Studer (1984). The VDM formalism (Bjorner, 1978) is used to specify forms and operations on them nonprocedurally.

FORMANAGER (Yao, 1984) is a comprehensive form management system which is tightly coupled to a relational DBMS. Forms are modeled as hierarchical data structures and are mapped to/from the flat structures of the relational model. The form management system, therefore, takes advantage of the already built in data management capabilities of the DBMS. The form processing is menu-driven and the forms are controlled procedurally.

Embley (1984) proposed the Forms Programming System (FPS) to model business operations. The association of forms to programming languages, functional dependencies, and databases is discussed in order to achieve a coherent form definition and management system. The computational relationships among the form fields are analyzed, and the database retrieval and update through forms are discussed.

Among the more recent systems are FORMAL, which is an extension of Shu (1982) and reported in Shu (1985), and FILLIN, reported in Wartik and Penedo (1986). FORMAL is an attempt to aid the end user visually in defining form applications. The form is used to both represent the data objects and program structure. FORMAL is not a freeform-painting user interface. Instead, a form is a data object whose columns represent data names and whose rows specify the attributes of the data, including the procedures that operate on them. The data (columns) can be represented in a hierarchical fashion. On the other hand, the FILLIN system is not capable of handling hierarchical data. In FILLIN, the specification of the form properties and processes is done by a programmer. The end user of the FILLIN is assumed to be computer literate.

There is almost unanimous agreement that a form can be abstracted as a hierarchical data structure. Different approaches to forms management have been taken. Some systems tightly bind a forms management to a DBMS, whereas others provide and manage separate files for each form type. From the human factors standpoint, a user should be able to specify the forms properties and the procedures without the aid of programmers or manuals. FORMFLEX is an attempt in this direction.

FORM MODEL

A form model consists of three parts. A collection of form types, each of which consists of one or more form fields, operations on those fields and some associated integrity and security constraints. The operations and the constraints may involve form fields from several forms. For each form type, there is one or more form templates. Each template is a particular representation of the form fields which is understandable by a human user. The templates are medium dependent. For instance, one may represent the same forms on paper or screen. Special consideration must be made to display forms that do not fit on a single screen. One may also envision form templates stored as audio signals which will be presented to the user once they are filled with (voice) data and triggered. This paper addresses only screen templates.

A form instance is created by, or presented to, the user upon request. When a form template is filled out with data, it becomes an instance of that form type. The user can create, update, delete, or retrieve an instance of a form type through a template.

Components of Form Templates

A screen form template consists of a title, text fragments, and separators such as vertical or horizontal lines. The title is normally the name of the form type, such as "Sales Order" or "Shipment". Some of the blank spaces on the form template are used for entering and/or displaying the form field values.

Properties of Form Types

A form type consists of one or more form fields. Each form field has a number of characteristics. Following are properties of form types and fields:

Display properties are mappings from a form field to a particular template. For instance, in a screen template, it is the coordinates of the form field on the screen and some other properties, such as color or font, depending on the capabilities of the medium of the template.

Flow properties are:

1. "Form flow," which designates the routing (R) of a form (F) by an agent (A) from a station (S1) to another station (S2). Each routing, therefore, is a quadruple R (F, A, S1, S2) which is triggered by an event, (E). An agent is either a human user who initiates the routing upon perceived occurrence of the event (E), or it may be a process which is triggered by some event and it in turn triggers the routing of the form. Using this model, a chain of form flow triggers can be constructed in order to automate office procedures.

2. "Form field flows" specify the origin and the sources of the form fields. A form field draws its value from one of the six sources. Table 1 lists the sources of the values for the form fields.

Hierarchical properties of the form represent a hierarchical abstraction of the association between the form fields of one form type. It is a one-to-many mapping from one group of the form fields to another. For instance, on the sales order form, there is a one-to-many mapping for the group of single valued form fields such as sales date and sales order number, to the multivalued form fields such as product name and price/unit. The hierarchy is not necessarily limited to two levels as might be implied by this example.

Static constraints on the form fields of a form type are of two fundamental kinds. The *intra*form constraints are imposed on the form fields of one form. The *inter*form constraints are imposed on the association of the form fields of two forms. Table 2 summarizes these constraints. (Dynamic constraints will be discussed below.)

To be successful, a forms management system needs to provide a facility to define, manipulate, and control forms. This facility is described in the next section.

TABLE 1. ORIGINATION TAXONOMY OF FORM FIELDS

ORIGIN - TYPE	SYMBOL	SOURCE
USER-TRIGGERED	"U"	USER ENTERS VALUES
SYSTEM-TRIGGERED	"S"	SYSTEM ENTERS VALUES WITHOUT
		REFERENCING ANY VALUE ON THE FORM
COMPUTATION-TRIGGERED	"C"	VALUE IS COMPUTED FROM ONE OR
		MORE FORMS
FORM-TRIGGERED	"F"	VALUE IS IDENTICALLY TRANSFERRED
		FROM ONE FORM TO ANOTHER
VALUE-TRIGGERED	"V"	VALUE DISPLAYED BECAUSE OF A VALUE
		OF A FIELD IN A CURRENT FORM
FORM-VALUE-TRIGGERED	"FV"	VALUE DISPLAYED BECAUSE OF A
		VALUE OF A FIELD IN ANOTHER FORM

TABLE 2. CONSTRAINTS ON THE FORM FIELD

INTRA-FORM CONSTRAINTS

* UNIQUENESS (OF THE REPEATING FIELDS, I.E. KEYNESS)
* NULLNESS (IS NULL ALLOWED FOR THE FIELD?)
* DATA TYPE
  * PRIMITIVE (NUMERIC, REAL, DOLLAR, TEXT, DATE, TIME)
  * USER-DEFINED (I.E. ENUMERATED TYPE. A SET OF VALUES WHOSE PRIMITIVE TYPE IS ONE OF THE ABOVE)
* LENGTH (MAXIMUM LENGTH OF THE FIELD)
* RANGE (LOWER AND UPPER BOUNDS ON THE SET OF ACCEPTABLE VALUES)
* DEFAULT (WHEN THE FIELD IS NOT FILLED IN WITH ANY VALUE FROM ANY OTHER SOURCE)
* EXISTENCE (THE EXISTENCE OF THE FORM FIELD FF1 IN FORM F1, IS DEPENDENT ON THE EXISTENCE OF FF2 IN FORM F1)

INTER-FORM CONSTRAINTS

* SCALE (WHEN THE SCALE OF A FORM FIELD CHANGES UPON BEING ROUTED TO ANOTHER FORM. APPLIES ONLY TO FORM FIELDS OF ORIGIN "F")
* EXISTENCE (THE EXISTENCE OF THE FORM FIELD FF2 IN FORM F2, IS DEPENDENT ON THE EXISTENCE OF FF1 IN FORM F1)

DESCRIPTION OF THE FORMFLEX

FORMFLEX is an integrated form definition and management system. It allows users to design and edit screen form templates, name the form fields for each form, specify their characteristics, formulate constraints, and manipulate instances of forms.

Several human factors are considered in the design and implementation of FORMFLEX:

1. allowing the user to back out and unbind a decision made earlier;
2. a help screen for each prompt;
3. minimization of keystrokes;
4. minimization of the demand on the user's memory by providing keywords and domain objects on the screen;
5. matching the system to the user's skill level; and,

6. elimination of syntax and spelling errors by providing all that is needed on the screen.

Figure 3 depicts the architecture of FORMFLEX. Through the Form Definition Interface, users define the form schemas for a collection of an enterprise's forms. From the form schemas and through a conversation with a human database designer, the Expert DataBase Design System builds a database schema for the set of the forms. In order to preserve the integrity of the data, users can define and save rules with the aid of the Rule Definition Interface. The Form Manipulation Interface allows the user to display, insert, delete, and update instances of forms as long as the operation does not violate the saved rules and other constraints stored in the Form Schema Base. Queries may also be saved in the Query Base for further recall execution. Form Definition, Rule Definition, and Form Manipulation Interfaces are described here. Expert Database Design System is reported elsewhere (Mannino, 1984), (Choobineh, 1986a, 1986b).

Form Definition Interface (FDI).

The process of form definition in FORMFLEX consists of two distinct phases of creating (CREATE) a screen form template with the associated form fields, and of precisely defining (DEFINE) the properties of those form fields.

In the CREATE phase, the user paints the form on the screen with the aid of the cursor movement keys and the keyboard. When painting is finished, the system requests the allocation of form field areas on the painted form. The allocation process consists of naming the form fields and specifying their length.

In the DEFINE phase, the user specifies the properties of the form fields which were named in the CREATE phase. (Most of these properties were described in the previous section.)

FDI accommodates two levels of user experience. The "novice" level is for users who have had experience with the system. This level is menu driven and the communication with the user is either through menus or conducted by a dialogue. The "expert" level is for users who are familiar with the process of designing a form in FORMFLEX. This level is command driven and prompts are words or sentence fragments.

At any given point in time, the user can switch between the expert and the novice levels. This allows gradual and painless evolvement from novice to expert for a frequent user. On the other hand, experienced users who are regularly using commands do not have to know all of

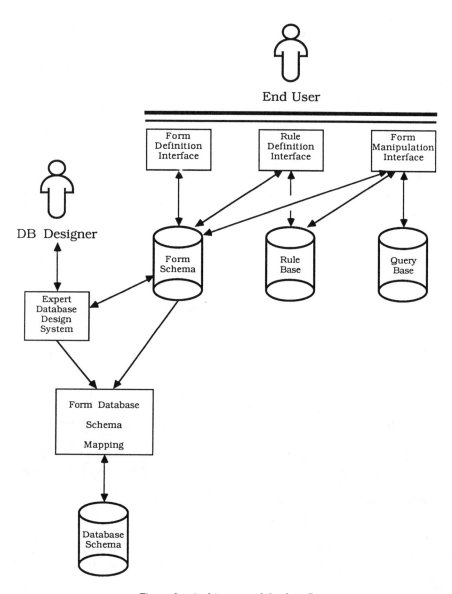

Figure 3.   Architecture of the formflex

them simultaneously. If desired, they can switch to the menu at any point in the session.

Experience with other systems indicates that menu-driven systems, although easy to learn and use, become both boring and inefficient when the user becomes rather familiar with the menus. On the other hand, although the command-driven systems are not easy to master in a short time, once learned, they are very efficient and desirable.

Of particular interest at this stage of interface design is the ability of the FDI to

1. switch back and forth between the menu and the command modes;
2. switch directions from forward to backward and vice versa;
3. provide detailed help screen (upon user request) for each of its prompts; and
4. remember its state of conversation with the user when it is restarted at a later time.

Point 2. needs further clarification. FDI logs its conversation with the user. The user can browse backward through his or her conversation in order to review and possibly revise a decision made earlier. There are two commands (PRIOR and NEXT) which enable the user to change directions while in the DEFINE mode. They enable the user to browse through the conversation backward or forward.

Computational aspects of the form fields are also specified at the form definition stage. Examples are aggregate fields, such as the value of the field TOTAL being the sum of the values of the repeating field AMOUNT on the sales order form. In particular, the user can specify:

1. aggregates; COUNT, SUM, AVERAGE, MAX, MIN;
2. arithmetics: *, /, +, -; and,
3. increments (decrements) with start, increment (decrement), and finish arguments.

This last capability enables the user to generate unique sequential identifiers for each form type.

Rule Definition Interface (RDI).

The static constraints (consisting of data type, uniqueness, nullness, range, and format) were captured at the form definition time. This section discusses the dynamic type of constraints which include integrity constraints, triggers, and alerters. In this paper, these are collectively called "rules." This notion of rules is more general than the traditional IF-THEN rules.

Figure 4 depicts the Rule Definition screen. The screen window is divided into seven panes. VERBS, CONNECTIVES, META OBJECTS, SYSTEM, and FUNCTIONS are menu panes from which the user can assemble rules at the bottom pane. The top pane is the title of the screen which includes the name of the application, in this case, "Order Processing."

Meta objects consist of FORMS, PEOPLE, and STATIONS. The contents of each can be obtained by a pull-down menu. Figure 5 depicts the screen where the meta object FORMS for the order processing application is pulled down.

The FUNCTIONS pane lists the user-defined functions and the saved rules. For instance, the Julian function depicted in Figure 4 converts DATE in the form of MM-DD-YY to Julian date. The user can scroll vertically through this pane if the list of the functions and rules are long.

Rules are assembled by using VERBS, CONNECTIVES, OBJECTS, and FUNCTIONS. Through the SYSTEM menu pane (see Column 3, Figure 4), the assembled rules may be SAVEd, RETRIEVEd, DELETEd,

FORM MANIPULATION, Order Processing			
VERBS	CONNECTIVES	META OBJECTS	FUNCTIONS
PRINT GET SEND DELETE INSERT RECEIVE DO DOWHILE SET BEGIN END	WHERE, WHEN TO, OF AND, OR, NOT >, <, = BEFORE, AFTER NEW, (,) EXISTS, ANY IF, THEN, ELSE +, -, *, / SUM, AVG. MAX, COUNT	FORMS PEOPLE STATIONS	JULIAN (DATE)
		SYSTEM	
		DELETE QUERY SAVE QUERY RETRIEVE QUERY EDIT QUERY EXECUTE, EXIT	

Figure 4. Rule definition screen

FORM MANIPULATION, Order Processing			
VERBS	CONNECTIVES	META OBJECTS	FUNCTIONS
PRINT GET SEND DELETE INSERT RECEIVE DO DOWHILE SET BEGIN END	WHERE, WHEN TO, OF AND, OR, NOT >, <, = BEFORE, AFTER NEW, (,) EXISTS, ANY IF, THEN, ELSE +, -, *, / SUM, AVG. MAX, COUNT	FORMS PEOPLE STATIONS SYSTEM DELETE QUERY SAVE QUERY RETRIEVE QUERY EDIT QUERY EXECUTE, EXIT	JULIAN (DATE)
DO NOT DELETE SALES-ORDER IF EXISTS SHIPMENT WHERE ORDER-NO OF SALES-ORDER = ORDER-NO OF SHIIPMENT			

Figure 5.   Forms menu is pulled-down and the user has assembled a rule

or EDITed as needed. The "EDIT RULE" choice increases user productivity when the user creates new rules from similar ones which have been saved.

To pull down a menu, the user places the cursor on the symbol and presses the return key. To retract it, the cursor is placed on the higher level object (in this case, the META OBJECTS box). Similarly, a form type with its associated form field names can be "popped up" for user's recall and review of the form field names. Figure 6 depicts the sales order form with its associated form field names. Notice that the form field blanks are filled with the form field names.

An example of an integrity constraint is "Do not delete a sales order form if a shipment form has been executed." Figure 5 also shows how such a constraint is assembled using the symbols in the menu panes.

The passive type of trigger where a form field triggers filling out of another form field in another form was discussed earlier (see "Form Model"). An example of an active type of trigger is "Prepare a purchase order form and send it to the purchasing clerk for further processing, when the quantity of product p1 becomes less than 20 units." Using the symbols of the menu panes, form names, and form field names, this trigger can be expressed as

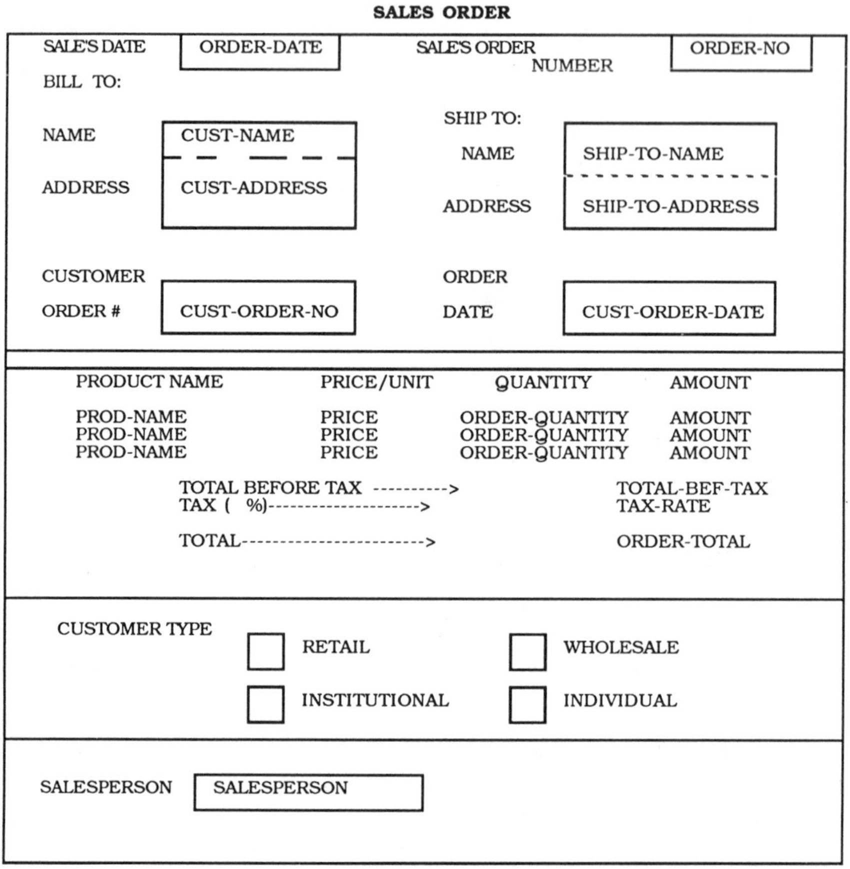

SALES ORDER

SALE'S DATE	ORDER-DATE	SALE'S ORDER NUMBER	ORDER-NO

BILL TO:

SHIP TO:

NAME	CUST-NAME	NAME	SHIP-TO-NAME
ADDRESS	CUST-ADDRESS	ADDRESS	SHIP-TO-ADDRESS

CUSTOMER ORDER #	CUST-ORDER-NO	ORDER DATE	CUST-ORDER-DATE

PRODUCT NAME	PRICE/UNIT	QUANTITY	AMOUNT
PROD-NAME	PRICE	ORDER-QUANTITY	AMOUNT
PROD-NAME	PRICE	ORDER-QUANTITY	AMOUNT
PROD-NAME	PRICE	ORDER-QUANTITY	AMOUNT

TOTAL BEFORE TAX ----------> TOTAL-BEF-TAX
TAX (%)--------------------> TAX-RATE

TOTAL----------------------> ORDER-TOTAL

CUSTOMER TYPE

☐ RETAIL   ☐ WHOLESALE

☐ INSTITUTIONAL ☐ INDIVIDUAL

SALESPERSON | SALESPERSON |

Figure 6. Sales order form with its associated form field names

SET PRODUCT-NO OF NEW PURCHASE-ORDER TO P1 AND

SEND PURCHASE-ORDER TO PURCHASE-CLERK

WHEN QUANTITY OF PRODUCT P1 < 20

An alerter is a statement such as "Alert the credit manager of the new sales order form if the customer is more than 30 days late on his previous payment. It can be expressed as

AFTER RECEIVE OF SALES-ORDER

IF EXISTS IN INVOICE CUSTOMER-NAME OF SALES-ORDER AND

BALANCE O AND JULIAN (SYSTEM–DATE) JULIAN (INVOICE-DATE) 30

THEN SET CUSTOMER-NAME OF LATE-PAYMENT TO

CUSTOMER-NAME OF SALES-ORDER AND

SEND SALES-ORDER TO CREDIT-MANAGER AND

SEND LATE-PAYMENT TO CREDIT-MANAGER

The last rule assumes that there is an invoice form which has the customer name, invoice number, amount of the invoice, and the balance due on it. Also shown is the use of the function displayed in the FUNCTIONS pane of this application.

Form Manipulation Interface (FMI).

The objects of interest at the Form Manipulation Interface are instances of form types just as they were form types and form templates in the Form and Rule Definition Interfaces.

Figure 7 shows the Form Manipulation screen. The screen is almost identical to the Rule Definition screen. The PRINT verb is added here which can replace the GET when a hard copy of the result of a query is desired. The SYSTEM pane contains the QUERY commands instead of the RULE commands. In addition, it contains the EXECUTE command to run the query. The FUNCTIONS pane lists the functions and the saved queries instead of the functions and the rules.

Figure 7 also shows a query which is assembled by the user from the symbols of different panes. The query asks for all the sales orders which do not have any corresponding shipments (i.e., all outstanding orders).

To create a new form instance, the user issues the command "NEW", followed by the form type name, in the query pane. A form of the specified type is then popped up. A toggle key switches the screen from displaying form instance values to/from the form field names. The values of the form fields are displayed in regular video whereas the form field names are displayed in reverse video. This facility aids the user in associating the values on the form template to the form field names instantaneously when needed.

Changing the values of form fields of an instance of a form type is done directly by the user on the screen. The idea is similar to the manipulation of spreadsheets. Once a value is changed by the user on the form instance which is being processed, all other values on the form which are related or are dependent on it will also be automatically

FORM MANIPULATION, Order Processing			
VERBS	CONNECTIVES	META OBJECTS	FUNCTIONS
PRINT GET SEND DELETE INSERT RECEIVE DO DOWHILE SET BEGIN END	WHERE, WHEN TO, OF AND, OR, NOT >, <, = BEFORE, AFTER NEW, (,) EXISTS, ANY IF, THEN, ELSE +, -, *, / SUM, AVG. MAX, COUNT	FORMS PEOPLE STATIONS SYSTEM DELETE QUERY SAVE QUERY RETRIEVE QUERY EDIT QUERY EXECUTE, EXIT	JULIAN (DATE)
GET ORDER IF NOT EXISTS SHIPMENT WHERE ORDER-NO OF ORDER = ORDER-NO OF SHIPMENT			

Figure 7. The form manipulation screen with a query assembled by the user in the query pane

changed. Due to the existence of the interform constraints, values of the form fields of the other forms in the system may also be changed.

SUMMARY

This paper discussed the importance of the forms as a vehicle for user interface. The major reported forms-oriented systems were surveyed and their major contributions were highlighted. The form model, which was developed here, is an attempt to integrate many of the characteristics of forms systems. The FORMFLEX system is a proposed version of a forms definition and management system with the emphasis on theend users being able to specify their forms definition, management, and control requirements.

Presently, the Form Definition Interface of the FORMFLEX is implemented in Pascal and is fully operational under VAX VMS. The Rule Definition and the Form Manipulation Interfaces are under development. Future research includes human factor measurements to gauge user satisfaction with the system. As a result of these measurements, some fine tuning may become necessary.

ACKNOWLEDGMENT

Jeff Clancy and Craig Scott, while students at the University of Arizona, designed and developed the Form Definition Interface under the supervision of the author. The name *FORMFLEX* was their idea.

REFERENCES

Bjorner, D., & Jones, C.B. (1978). The Vienna development method: The meta-language, in G. Goos & J. Hartmanis (Eds.), *Lecture Notes in Computer Science*.

De Jong, P. (1977). System for business automation (SBA): A unified application development system, In S.H. Lavington (Ed.), *Proceedings of the IFIP Congress*, pp. 417–424, Amsterdam: North-Holland.

Embley, D.W. (1984). A forms-based programming system, in E.A. Unger, P.S. Fisher, & J. Slonim (Eds.), *Advances in data base management*, 2, 197–223.

Hammer, M. (1977). A very high level programming language for data processing applications, *Communications of the ACM*, 20, 832–840.

Ladd, I. & Tsichritzis, D. (1980). An office form flow model, *Proceedings of AFIPS National Computer Conference*, 533–539.

Larson, J. (1984). The forms pattern language, *Proceedings of the International Conference on Data Engineering*, 183–192.

Lefkovitz, H.C. (1979). A status report on the activities of the CODASYL End User Facilities Committee (EUFC), *SIGMOD Record*, 10, 2–3.

Luo, D., & Bing Yao, S. (1981). Form operation by example a language for office information processing, *Proceedings of ACM SIGMOD*, 212–233.

Mannino, M.V., & Choobineh, J. (1984). Research on form driven database design and global view design, *Database Engineering*, 7, 4.

Shu, N.C., Lum, V.Y., Tung, F.C., & Chang, C.L. (1982). Specification of forms processing and business procedures for office automation, *IEEE Transactions on Software Engineering*, 5, 499–511.

Shu, N.C. (1985). FORMAL: A forms-oriented, visual-directed application development system, *COMPUTER*, 18, 38–49.

Studer, R. (1984). Abstract models of dialog concepts, *IEEE Conference on Software Engineering*, 420–429.

Tsichritzis, D. (1980). OFS: An integrated form management system, *Proceedings of the Very Large Data Bases Conference*, 161–166.

Tsichritzis, D. (1982). Form management, *Communications of the ACM*, 25, 453–478.

Wartik, S.P., & Penedo, M.H. (1986). Fillin: A reusable tool for form-oriented software, *IEEE SOFTWARE*, 61–68.

Yao, S.B., Hevner, A.R., Shi, Z., & Luo, D. (1984). FORMANAGER: An office forms management system, *ACM Transactions on Office Information Systems*, 2, 235–262.

Zloof, M.M. (1977). Query-by-example: A data base language, *IBM Systems Journal*, 16, 4.

SECTION IV

The System Analyst

The second player in the human factors relational network is the analyst/ designer. This person is responsible for analysis, design, and often implementation of information systems. This player uses interface specification tools and guidelines for human factors to develop usable systems via user interfaces. Also, certain analyst attributes impact the overall development and analyst/user interaction process. These attributes include

1. User/analyst communication issues (i.e., common semantic base)
2. Analyst/designer training
3. Development team composition
4. Management of the software development process
5. Structured walkthrough
6. Analyst/designer expertise
7. Analyst/designer power base
8. Analyst/designer cognitive styles

The role of the analyst/designer has changed over the years. At one time, this person spent most of his or her time involved in technical tasks, isolated from the user and other team members. With the advent of end-user computing and heavy user involvement in system development, the analyst/designer finds himself or herself spending a great deal of time involved in people-oriented, rather than technical, tasks. The attitude of the analyst towards the user and vice versa can have a great deal of impact on the success of the system being developed.

The selection which addresses some of the issues of analyst/designer attributes is "Cognitive Styles, Project Structure, and Project Attributes: Considerations in Project Team Design" by Kathy Brittain White of the University of North Carolina, Greensboro, Department of Information Systems and Operations Management. This paper focuses on the composition of the system development team in order to ensure both effective system design and user/analyst interaction.

CHAPTER 8

Cognitive Styles, Project Structure, and Project Attributes: Considerations in Project Team Design

Kathy Brittain White
University of North Carolina, Greensboro

The management information systems (MIS) literature supports the notion that many factors impact the successful design of systems. The factors include project structure, task structure, and the characteristics of the project team members. Research relating to each of these components has not been integrated. This paper provides a synthesis of research issues relating these factors and how these may impact team design and team performance. The paper specifically discusses the interaction among team-member characteristics, project structure, and project attributes in the successful development of information systems (IS).

INTRODUCTION

Many factors impact the successful development of information systems (IS). The management information system (MIS) literature suggests that these components include the technical components (hardware and software), project structure (McFarlan & McKenney, 1984), the characteristics of the project team members (Kaiser & Bostrom, 1982; White & Leifer, 1986), the nature of the task (White, 1984) and the organizational culture (Mason & Mitroff, 1977). Benjamin, Rockart, Scott Morton, & Wyman (1982), Zmud (1979), and others support the belief that a multiplicity of factors impact information systems development successes and failures.

With so many project variations possible, McFarlan & McKenney (1983) view project management in IS as highly dependent on the system to be developed. Although there might be a general-purpose set of tools, the contribution each device can make to planning and controlling the project varies widely according to the project's characteristics. Different types of projects require different strategies and must be assessed as the specific requirements needed for project success.

One of the critical factors in any project development activity is the selection of the project team. Despite the documented importance of the project team members' characteristics to the ultimate success of the project, little research specifically addresses project team design issues. Although there has been research dealing with project success and team composition (Kaiser & Bostrom, 1982; White, 1984), such research has treated project development as a unidimensional task, failing to consider the realities of the systems requirements and changing nature of the project phases. Some research has looked at the impact of homogeneous and heterogeneous team design and their success in solving structured and unstructured IS tasks (Aamodt & Kimbrough, 1982; White, 1984). An expanded study conducted by White (1986) surveyed project team participants attempting to identify the process and technical characteristics desired from project team members during the various phases of the systems development cycle. Heretofore, there has been no synthesis of these research studies on project team design and the affects on project team performance and systems development success. The purpose of this paper is to discuss the interaction among team members' characteristics, project structure, and project attributes in the successful development of IS. Project structure as discussed by McFarlan and McKenney (1983) will first be examined. The relationship of the overall project structure to the various phases of the systems development cycle will be reviewed. Personality characteristics as categorized by the Jungian framework will be related to the successful development of IS. In summary, the implications of these various components for project assessment and team design will be discussed.

PROJECT STRUCTURE

McFarlan and McKenney (1983) identify three dimensions influencing the risk inherent in a project development. The first is project size. The second is the experience of the systems-development team with the technology involved in the project. The third dimension is the structure of the project, whether it is highly structured with outputs clearly defined or has very little structure. Based on these dimensions, four distinct categories of projects are: (a) high-structure/low-technology (b) high-structure/high-technology, (c) low-structure/low-technology, and (d) low-structure/high-technology.

In a high-structure/low-technology project, the project presents familiar technical problems with clearly defined outputs. Such a project is one of the easiest to manage and can be defined as a low-risk project.

In a project defined as high-structure/high-technology, the technology is vastly more complex than the first type but the system continues to have clearly defined outputs. Both of these types of projects are structured with only the technology varying. It can also be suggested that these types of projects constituted, by far, the majority of traditional IS when the environment was off-line and batch.

The last two project classifications have low project structure in that the outputs are not clearly defined. In a low-structure/low-technology project, there is much interaction with users, although the technology is not complex. Low-structure/high-technology projects carry high organizational risk, are quite complex, and also require much communication with users in the organization. Success in such low-structure projects requires external integration tools which include organizational and other communication devices that link the project team's work to the users at both the managerial and the lower levels (McFarlan & McKenney, 1984).

The four types of project could be found under development in most major organizations. However, in the quest to gain a competitive advantage by using information systems, many IS projects could be categorized as low-structure/ high-technology classification.

SYSTEM DEVELOPMENT PHASES

In further decomposing project characteristics, Berrisford and Wetherbe (1979) suggest that the systems development cycle is composed of roughly four stages or what might be thought of as tasks: (a) analyze problems/ opportunities, (b) design system, (c) develop and test system, (d)implement ,operate, and maintain system, and perform post audit (p.12).

In linking the above discussion on project structure and technology to the various phases, White and Leifer (1986) found the "analyze problems/ opportunities" and "implementation" phases to have low structure due to the external people involved during this time. In addition, because managers and end users are often not part of the systems design team, external project team participants viewed these phases as having more uncertainty as to the expected outcomes than the other phases. The "systems development" and "test" phases as well as "system operation and maintenance" were identified as having high structure because there are many guidelines and procedures developed to assist people in accomplishing these tasks.

Based on these works, evidence is offered that overall project characteristics vary as to structure and technology requirements. Further, the systems development phases within the project can be further delineated as to the structure and technology requirements.

McFarlan and McKenney (1983), in addressing the characteristics of systems projects, relate these differences to the management tools required in the different project environment. To extend their line of reasoning, the overall project characteristics also impact the types of individuals who would be most successful on the project. The next section presents relevant literature concerning task/team design issues.

TASK/TEAM CONSIDERATIONS

Task/team design is composed of the relationships between task requirements and work group structure. Because it is beyond the scope of this paper to cover all of these issues adequately, this section will be limited to those issues relating to how the tasks of the unit are divided up and how those tasks are coordinated. Chervany and Dickson (1978) indicate that behavior appears to be determined to a large degree by the characteristics of the task in which the individual or group is involved. Teams successful at an unstructured task were not necessarily as successful at a structured one, whereas teams that performed best on a structured task were less successful on an unstructured one (Aamodt and Kimbrough, 1982; Kilmann, 1977; White, 1984). In addition, it follows that if the tasks associated with systems development change in the course of the systems design process, then the way the team is structured should vary concomitantly. Leifer and White (1985) suggest that characteristics of team members would be most differentially effective in various phases of the system life cycle. Project team members who could communicate and interact effectively with others would be more important where interaction with people was necessary, than in the design phases where more logical and analytical types would be more effective.

The variances in project requirements and the variances in the phases of systems development would be expected to influence the kinds of characteristics team members should possess to complete the tasks. A review of the literature on these individual characteristics will be discussed in order to draw a linkage between task characteristics and the design of the project team.

COGNITIVE STYLES

One cognitive style that has been extensively studied in the IS literature is that of the Jungian typology (Jung, 1968). Personality characteristics of IS project team members have been examined in light of this typology in several research studies (Kaiser and Bostrom, 1982; White, 1984). Personality characteristics as described by the Jungian dimensions (Mitroff & Kilmann, 1976) are included as Figure 1.

In applying the Jungian typology to an analysis of the success and failure of systems development project teams, Kaiser and Bostrom found that the more effective project teams had a balance of the four Jungian types, whereas unsuccessful teams had one or two predominant types. White (1984) further substantiated their findings that heter-

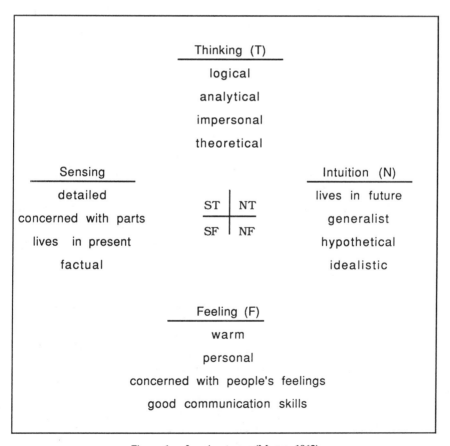

Figure 1.   Jungian types (Myers, 1962)

ogeneous teams (as defined by the Jungian typology) are best on the projects that were examined in these studies. A critical finding in both of these studies was the lack of intuitive/feeling (NF) and sensing/feeling (SF) types in the MIS area (Kaiser & Bostrom, 1982; White, 1984). The studies also suggest that, without an appreciation of the cognitive requirements of the project or of the various tasks contained within the project, it is not likely that an appropriate team match will be made.

Further support for the need for project team members to possess characteristics identified with SF and NF cognitive styles is provided by White and Leifer (1986). In identifying team member characteristics critical to systems development success at various phases of the project, project team participants ranked a mixture of technical and behavioral characteristics. These technical and behavioral characteristics differed, depending upon the phase of the systems development project. Good communication skills and ability to interact with people effectively were top ranked in two of the systems development phases. These two skills are specifically identified with the SF and NF Jungian styles.

A component that was not considered in the four previously mentioned studies were overall project categorization as defined by McFarlan and McKenney (1983). The following section discusses the project categorization schema in relationship with Jungian cognitive styles.

JUNGIAN FRAMEWORK AND PROJECT CATEGORIZATION

Kilmann (1977) has combined the Jungian framework with a number of organizational activities. He makes the argument that each of the four cognitive styles would tend to be engaged in specific activities within the organization. The sensing/thinking (ST) type would be drawn to activities involving detailed impersonal facts and impersonal analytical reasoning and would be best matched when involved in such organizational activities as analyzing cost of goods sold and inventory costs. This ST component within the organization is labeled internal technology. The thinking/intuiting (NT) type would be likely to maximize their effectiveness through synthesis and impersonal analytical reasoning and would be best matched in such organization activities as determining the cost of capital or developing new products. The NT component is termed external technology. The SF type would approach effectiveness through detailed facts and personal value judgments. They might very well be found in activities such as training or the human resource area. The NF type would approach effectiveness through synthesis and personal value judgments and is referred to as external people. The activities identified here would include evaluation of customer demand for products and the ability to identify new problems and/or opportunities. The argument can be made that the activities related to the four styles in Kilmann's model are critical for organizational success. In keeping with Jungian theory, all activities related to the four styles are valued and a balance is needed for an organization to maintain a healthy posture. As the IS area is a microcosm of the total organization, it seems appropriate to apply Kilmann's framework specifically to the information systems area. In the external technology quadrant identified with the NT cognitive style, activities in the IS area might include hardware acquisition, disaster recovery, and networking. The internal technology quadrant associated with the ST cognitive style might encompass such IS activities as backups and optimizing response time. The internal people quadrant identified with SF cognitive style could include activities such as employee training and employee turnover issues. The external people quadrant identified with NF cognitive style might include such information systems activities as end-user computing, information center, and executive support. This quadrant with the corresponding IS activities, is shown in Figure 2.

In linking the project structure work of McFarlan and McKenney (1983) with the extension of Kilmann's (1977) model, the activities included under both external technology (NT) and internal technology (ST) require little interaction with other individuals. Systems development projects involving the activities included in either of the cells would tend to have high structure. In contrast, the activities included under the external people cell would have a high level of interaction with members of the organization and would seem to have much less structure than the other activities. Systems development projects involving these activities would tend to have low structure.

IMPLICATIONS FOR PROJECT ASSESSMENT AND TEAM DEVELOPMENT

What does all this mean for project team design and project development success? Basically, the argument is made that the traditional IS projects were marked by high structure and very much favored characteristics identified with ST/NT cognitive style. Both of these types are drawn to analytical and technical detail. Two studies (Kaiser & Bostrom, 1982; White, 1984) have found MIS departments skewed with an abundance of these two styles. When IS were operated in batch mode with little interaction with users, there was a congruence between the

INFORMATION SYSTEMS EFFECTIVENESS

EXTERNAL PEOPLE END-USER COMPUTING INFORMATION CENTER EXECUTIVE SUPPORT	**INTERNAL PEOPLE** EMPLOYEE TURNOVER EMPLOYEE ATTITUDES EMPLOYEE COMMITMENT
EXTERNAL TECHNOLOGY NETWORKING DISASTER RECOVERY CHARGE-BACK/RESOURCE ALLOCATION HARDWARE ACQUISITION	**INTERNAL TECHNOLOGY** BACK-UPS OPTIMIZING RESPONSE TIME SCHEDULING

Figure 2.

project structure and the characteristics of the individuals found in IS. Although these projects may require an in-depth knowledge of technology, there was a correlating high structure because users were not seen as integral parts of the systems development process.

As the IS area matured, user involvement, end-user computing, and other organizational concerns became an integral part of project development. The emphasis was on how to deal with the user effectively and how to develop systems more effectively to meet user specifications. These types of projects would be classified as low structure and requiring external integration tools.

In other words, the changing nature of IS projects requires more attention to the design of project teams. A project with low structure and high technology would require a very different set of team members than a project with high structure and either high or low technology. The nature of the current MIS projects requires skills identified with NF/SF individuals and MIS designs to be integrated with ST/NT designs.

A real concern is that many current systems projects may require characteristics that IS personnel have not possessed in the past. If, as Kaiser and Bostrom (1982) suggest, there are voids of the SF/NF cognitive styles, it provides a challenge to project management to ensure that individuals with the needed communication and behavioral skills are represented on projects having low structure and high technology.

SUMMARY

This research synthesis suggests that the nature of the project bears directly on the personality requirements needed by team members. Further, as the system development cycle progresses, the team member characteristics may change, suggesting that one core team may not be appropriate for all stages of a project. It also suggests the need to define the overall project characteristics as well as the stages of the project to make a better project/team match. An explanation is offered for the failures of many project teams. A team that worked well on one project or in one stage of a project can dissolve into conflict, dissent, and inertia on another project or at a different project stage, simply because the team member characteristics are no longer in congruence with the current project requirements.

The implication is that project team design is as multidimensional and complex as is project management and is critical to support the expanded mission of the MIS area. It is suggested that project characteristics as well as the systems phases involved with the overall project development activity should be evaluated in light of required team member characteristics. It further offers the Jungian typology as one method to define many of the team member characteristics desired for project success.

REFERENCES

Aamodt, M.G., & Kimbrough, W.W. (1982). Effect of group heterogeneity on quality of task solution, *Psychological Reports, 50*, 171-174.

Benjamin, R., Rockart, J., Scott Morton, M.S., & Wyman, J. (1984). Information technology: A strategic opportunity, *Sloan Management Review, 25,* 3–10.

Berrisford, T., & Wetherbe, J. (1979). Heuristic development: A redesign of systems design, *MIS Quarterly, 3,* 11–19.

Chervany, N.L., & Dickson, G.H. (1978). On the validity of the analytic-heuristic instrument utilized in 'The Minnesota Experiments': A reply, *Management Science, 24,* 1091–1092.

Jung, C.D. (1968). *Psychological types,* New York: Pantheon Books.

Kaiser, K.M., & Bostrom, R.P. (1982). Personality characteristics of MIS project teams: An empirical study and action-research design, *MIS Quarterly, 6,* 43–60.

Kilmann, R.H. (1977). *Social Systems Design,* p. 36, Amsterdam: North-Holland.

Leifer, R., & White, K.B. (1985). Designing information systems task teams, *Proceedings of the ACM-SIGBDP Conference End-User Computing: The Changing Role of the Systems Professional and End User,* Duluth: University of Minnesota.

Mason, R., & Mitroff, I. (1973). A program for research on management information systems, *Management Science, 19,* 475–487.

McFarlan, F.W., & McKenney, J. (1983). Corporate information systems management, pp. 117–134, Homewood, IL: Irwin.

Mitroff, I.I., & Kilmann, R. (1976). Qualitative versus quantitative analysis for management science: Difference forms for different psychological types, *Interfaces, 6,* 17–27.

White, K.B. (1984). MIS project teams: An investigation of cognitive style implications, *MIS Quarterly, 8,* 95–101.

White, K.B., and Leifler, R. (1986). A preliminary investigation of informationystems development success: Perspectives from project team participants, *MIS Quarterly, 10,* 215–224.

Zmud, R. (1979). Individual differences and MIS success: A review of the empirical literature, *Management Science, 25,* 966–979.

SECTION V

Information Presentation

Information has many attributes, including scope (level of detail), mode of presentation, timeliness, accuracy, value, sufficiency (overload/underload), horizon (time frame), and others. The focus of this section is upon information presentation. There are several modes of information presentation, including audible, tactile, and both visual hard copy and soft copy (visual display terminal). Information which is presented in any of these modes or media can also be categorized as tabular, graphic, numeric, and alphanumeric.

There have been a great number of studies comparing paper versus online presentation of information. The results of these studies are mixed. Performance is task specific and situational. For example, data entry is a task which is particularly enhanced by online presentation. Data entry on paper is slower and less accurate than online. However, some decision-making situations, which require a great deal of data browsing, seem to be hindered by the temporary nature of online presentations and limitations in comparison which are easy when a decision maker has hard copies of the information before him or her. Other variables, such as environment, user characteristics, and expertise interact with the mode of presentation variable. User characteristics are numerous, often complex, and lack good instruments of measure. Some user characteristics include cognitive information-processing style, locus of control, and attitude towards the information system and task.

Results of research on information presentation should impact the design of the user interface. Other information-presentation issues are the amount of white space to include around information, the amount of information to place on one screen, use of color, use of highlighting, blinking, audible signals, and so forth.

The selection included in this section is entitled "Factors Affecting Opinion and Knowledge Responses to Paper and Online Presentations of Questionnaires" by Peter J. Newsted of the University of Calgary, Faculty of Management.

CHAPTER 9

Factors Affecting Opinion and Knowledge: Responses to Paper and Online Presentation of Questionnaires

Peter R. Newsted
University of Calgary

In order to characterize the differences between manual and computerized responses to knowledge and opinion questions, exhibit-effectiveness data from a Canadian National Parks Visitor Center survey are presented and reanalyzed. Respondents to a manually administered questionnaire were compared to those answering the same questions at a computer terminal. Though respondents are seen to differ in both age and education level, knowledge differences are present only for certain types of exhibits especially those involving sound as well as a major visual component where the computer group scored higher. The computer and manual groups were similar in their indication of how easy they felt most exhibits were to understand. However, the computer group indicated they saw significantly fewer major exhibits than did the manual group. It was also found that the use of computerized surveying was well received by both visitors and staff. Respondents in the computer group particularly preferred this approach over paper-and-pencil questionnaires. As it has already been shown that when computerized and noncomputerized situations are made very similar, there are no knowledge-performance differences, it is concluded that the slight performance differences seen in the current study do not invalidate the increasing trend toward more computerized testing and surveying though further studies are needed to determine the effects of other levels of the identified variables.

INTRODUCTION

With the advent of inexpensive and readily available microcomputer equipment, it is appropriate to consider such technology as a means of

149

improving the efficiency and reducing the cost of administering opinion and knowledge surveys. Certainly, their relatively low fixed costs and almost nonstop availability suggests that they may be an appropriate adjunct to already scarce manpower in many surveying situations. However, it must be ascertained whether the data which such devices can collect is comparable to a typical manual survey.

As there now exists a continuum of studies with varied presentation contexts, it is useful to try to organize and extend what is now known about what causes response differences between textual material presented on paper or on some form of display screen. Nearly a decade ago, it was suggested that computer conferencing could be used for opinion research (cf. Hiltz, 1979). And though Hiltz was not confronted with the current plethora of entry devices and many people using them, she did note that there were certainly some populations (such as experts who already had terminals) who would more readily take to such surveying than others, thus immediately presenting situations where responses must be carefully considered before they are generalized to other situations. More recently, presentation contexts have been varied in precisely controlled settings (e.g., Switchenko, 1984; Trollip & Sales, 1986; Cushman, 1986) which have shown that when the presentation formats are made virtually identical in terms of contrast, color, lines per inch, justification, duration, and page size, that no response differences are to be seen when subjects are queried about the content of the material presented.

Unfortunately, these rigid settings however necessary to determine the specific effects of presentation variables do not represent normal situations which maximize the typical advantages of each situation. For example, books can be easily browsed and carried, whereas texts and questions presented by computers can be methodically scanned and organized for appropriate presentation formats and branching to relevant questions.

When practical situations are examined, however, only a few differences have been seen. Referees of scholarly papers, while giving similar reviews, were only slightly slowed down in a computer context compared to a typed presentation (Wright & Lickorish, 1984). This is similar to the findings of Muter, Latremouille, Treurniet, & Brown (1982) who found no comprehension differences in a 2 hour reading of paper or TV text (though the reading at a screen was, again, slower). In marketing survey situations (*Marketing News*, 1985a, 1985b), where a polling "pole" containing a computer-controlled entry keyboard was used to survey people in a wide variety of contexts, from students on campuses to customers in department stores, ASK Associates (the developers of this system) claim that they have developed special techniques to yield "reliable samples." But the difficulty, of course, and the commercial advantage, of such proprietary techniques is that all methods and data have not been released for impartial evaluation. To try to quantify and illustrate differences which may be present, as well as to suggest methods for obtaining such reliability, data collected in parallel in a manual survey and computerized survey in an operating visitor center in a Canadian National Park can be examined.

This approach differs from all such previous studies identified (such as Rushinek, Rushinek, & Stutz, 1983) which carefully selected the respondents for the computer setting. It also differs from an experiment which allowed subjects to self-select themselves but in which subjects were given both a manual and a computerized survey (Erdman, Klein, & Grist, 1983). It is reasonable to expect there will be a difference between systematically selected individuals and those who self-select themselves to use only a computer to answer questions. For example, it might be anticipated that a younger population of mostly males might be attracted to a microcomputer, given its similarity to an arcade, whereas this group would be less represented in a random sample. A study such as Erdman et al.'s cannot determine this, as their interest was specifically in the single subpopulation of high school students in the first place. It is interesting to note that these investigators did find that their computer questioning was so popular that more subjects returned for a second session with it than could be accommodated. Furthermore, the case that computer use of any kind may be frowned upon by a broader population, particularly in the natural setting of a national park.

As it is difficult to get people to use a computer in any kind of random fashion corresponding to typical surveying procedures, it is appropriate to compare results from these procedures to identify similarities and differences which may be postulated to be common over similar surveying contexts.

PROCEDURES FOLLOWED

Sampling Details

The manual survey was started on August 21, 1983 and run in parallel with the computerized survey from August 25 to September 18, 1983 at the Icefield Visitor Center (IVC) in Jasper National Park. The computerized survey was delayed because of program errors which were rectified by August 25th.

The target population for both types of surveying was daytime visitors of all ages and sexes to the IVC (whether they had been there previously or not). For the manual survey, the sampling frame included all visitors present in the central hall of the IVC during any of the selected sampling periods (to be described below). Staff administering the manual survey were instructed to try to approach people as they were leaving, rather than entering, in order to maximize their exposure to exhibits. Typically, staff had up to three visitors filling out a questionnaire at one time and approached new visitors as these forms were collected. The frame for the computer collection method was "all visitors present at any time." A sign was attached to the computer encouraging visitors to explore the center before responding, again, in an attempt to maximize their exposure to exhibits.

In the manual survey, respondents were asked to complete a four-page typed questionnaire. Those who responded at the computer answered the same questions but, instead of using paper and pencil, they pushed buttons on the computer keyboard to correspond to their choice of answer, which was displayed along with a question on the adjacent screen. All irrelevant keys were screened from visitor use.

Questions Asked

Both surveys asked the same questions about the eight major exhibits at the IVC, which are defined in the exhibit legend in the Appendix. Demographic questions requested age, sex, and education information (and whether this was a repeat visit to the microcomputer for the computer group). Orientation questions asked if a given exhibit had been seen. Affective questions were included to query visitors about computer acceptability and whether they felt exhibits were easy to understand. The bulk of the questions were cognitive or knowledge questions about the factual content of the exhibits. The cognitive questions were generated in direct proportion to the amount of knowledge which each exhibit attempted to convey (as determined by the IVC staff). Thus, high-information exhibits such as the slide show had ten cognitive questions while the smaller area activities exhibit had only two. Special questions were also devised for children under the age of 12. These included the same demographic, orientation, and affective questions as the adults received, but had only those cognitives which the Parks staff viewed as easy enough for children. Further, children were not asked about the naturalist or area activities because it was felt that to do so would overburden them with questions, particularly about those two exhibits with detailed format in which they would probably have little interest.

As this request for information from both children and adults presented more questions than a single respondent could handle, subsets were devised for rotating presentation six to adults and three to children. Each of the subset formats consisted of three initial demographic questions, followed by orientation/affective/cognitive sets for three different exhibits. The first such "set" asked four cognitive questions and the last two sets each asked two. After the third of these sets was asked, three final affective questions were asked: (a) the respondent's favorite exhibit; (b) his or her preference for manual or computerized surveying; and (c) whether the computer had been used (for the manual group) or how easy it was to use (for the computer group). As already mentioned, the child formats had only those cognitives which were judged easiest, and, further, each of the three orientation/affective/cognitive sets for the children had only two cognitives – not four, two, and two.

The subsets for the computer group were designed to be the same as the manual format (though this was not always the case, as people not staying to answer all questions caused the questions to get out of order an undetermined number of times, something which could clearly be prevented in future computerized surveying attempts). The computer group was shown, also, the correct answer for any question that was missed. The question-asking program was written in PASCAL and run under MS/DOS 1.25 on a Victor 9000 microcomputer.

Administration Procedures

The IVC staff were given detailed instructions to guide them in the use of both surveying methods. In total, 11 different staff members administered manual questionnaires for 36 1-hr sampling periods. Though 40 hr of staff time were originally allocated for this sampling, 2 assigned hours were accidentally missed by the staff and 2 hours had to be cancelled when it was realized that the opening hours of 9 a.m. to 7 p.m. were changed after Labor Day to 9 a.m. to 5 p.m. after the interviewing schedule had been set.

The sampling periods were randomly assigned in direct proportion to the hourly visitor arrival rate. Thus, as 12% of the daily visitors arrived between 2 and 3 p.m., this translated to 12% of 40 available hr which rounded to 5 hr. The staff was able to do the daily start-up and back-up procedures at the computer without apparent incident. Each procedure required approximately 10 to 15 min. All staff expressed the belief that the instructions were easy to understand and expected they would have little or no difficulty in following them. This was, in fact, the case as both forms of collection were completed without major problems. Only 4 of 597 manual forms were spoiled and unusable (because child forms were given to adults); the data from a 5th and part of a 6th respondent at the computer were unusable because of electrical power problems and/or obvious "playing the computer" (evidenced by entering a "99" for age with no indication of having seen any exhibits). Further inspection of the computer data revealed 34 apparently erroneous ages of 1, 2, or 99 which were clearly not typical of the age distribution; hence, these ages were deleted for these respondents, though the rest of their data was kept as it appeared reasonable. This left 989 respondents, 237 of whom were not analyzed as they indicated they were repeat users of the computer. No complaints were received by the staff about the computer other than to point out typographical errors or discuss the correctness of answers.

Data Handling

In order to compare the computer with the manual data, each respondent was scored as to the percentage of cognitives which he or she got right (based on the number which were administered). To evaluate exhibit effectiveness, this percentage was computed separately for exhibits which visitors had seen and had not seen (as determined by the orientation question for each exhibit).

As "no response" was not possible at the computer, all questions received some response (unless a respondent terminated his session by walking away). On the manual survey, however, "no response" to a cognitive question was possible and consequently was scored as one-fourth correct to make it comparable to the one-in-four chance of correct guessing at the computer.

RESULTS

Respondent Characteristics

The manual and computer respondents were different in a number of ways:

1. The median age was 34 years for the manual group but only 26 for the computer group. This is accounted for both by more people between the ages of 11 and 20 and by a greater proportion of people in the 21 to 30 age group who used the computer. As can be seen by examining the age distributions in Table 1, people of all age groups used both methods, though there are significant differences in these distributions.
2. Significantly more males were sampled by both procedures. How-

Table 1

Age Distributions of Respondents in the Computer and Manual Groups

AGE RANGE IN YEARS	COMPUTER GROUP (734 RESPONDENTS) PERCENTAGE	MANUAL GROUP (585 RESPONDENTS) PERCENTAGE
1–10	10	2
11–20	20	8
21–30	39	31
31–40	16	16
41–50	4	12
52–60	6	14
61–70	4	13
71–80	1	2
81–90	0	0

Note. The two age distributions differ from each other beyond the 1% level of significance (as determined by the chi-square test).

ever, there was no significant difference in the proportion of males in the two groups (see Table 2).

3. Table 3 gives the education distributions of the two groups and, again, these distributions are significantly different with the computer group having a much higher percentage of people with only a Grade-8 or less education.

Exhibit Effectiveness

Over all exhibits, Table 4 shows that people got more cognitive questions correct if they had seen an exhibit, thus indicating the effectiveness of exhibits in communicating factual knowledge about the Icefield. These differences are significant in both the manual and computer

Table 2

Sex Distributions of Respondents in the Manual Groups

EDUCATION	COMPUTER GROUP (752 RESPONDENTS) PERCENTAGE	MANUAL GROUP (591 RESPONDENTS) PERCENTAGE
Male	59	57
Female	41	43

Note. The percentage of males in both groups is greater beyond the 1% level of significance (as determined by the binomial test). Using the chi-square test, there is no significant difference between the groups as to sex distributions.

Table 3

Education Distributions of Respondents in the Computer and Manual Groups

EDUCATION	COMPUTER GROUP (752 RESPONDENTS) PERCENTAGE	MANUAL GROUP (587 RESPONDENTS) PERCENTAGE
Grade 8 or less	22	7
Finish high school	14	18
Some college or university	18	26
University degree	25	21
Some graduate work	7	11
Completed a master's degree	10	8
Completed a doctoral degree	4	7

Note. The two education distributions are different from each other beyond the 1% level of significance (as determined by the chi-square test).

groups. This table also shows that the computer group got significantly more correct answers over all exhibits.

Given the overall significance of correctness scores, based on whether an exhibit was seen or not and whether a visitor was questioned manually or by computer, it is appropriate to analyze these scores exhibit by exhibit. As the seen/unseen dimension bears directly on the effectiveness of an exhibit, it will be addressed in this section while the presentation method will be left to the next section. Table 5 clearly shows (with few exceptions) that having seen an exhibit appears to promote greater knowledge about Icefield features. This is particularly true for the manual group where only the model is seen as not significantly effective. (This is probably an anomaly of the data as only a very low 6% of the visitors indicated they did not see it.) The exhibits

Table 4

Percentage of Cognitive Questions Answered Correctly Over All Seen and Unseen Exhibits for the Computer and Manual Groups.
(Numbers in Parentheses Represent Numbers in Each Cell and Standard Deviation of Mean Perecentage, Respectively.)

	COMPUTER GROUP PERCENTAGE	MANUAL GROUP PERCENTAGE
Seen	74 (596, 22)	67 (543, 23)
Unseen	69 (386, 25)	61 (363, 26)

Note. With the exception of 67% versus 69%, each of the four percentages is different from each other beyond the 1% level of significance (as determined by two-tailed *t*-tests which are appropriate in this context because of large sample sizes, even with some skewed data.)

seem less effective for the computers users. This may be due to their overall greater knowledge of Icefield features in the first place.

Manual Versus Computer Responses

The responses of the manual group and computer group have been compared in a number of ways.

1. Across most of the eight exhibits, the computer group got more cognitive questions correct on both those exhibits they saw and those they did not see (see Table 6). Interestingly, only 4 of these 16 differences are individually significant. If one discounts the last two minor exhibits (for which there are fewer respondents and only two questions), the computer group scored significantly higher only on seen exhibits which had a sound, instead of text, component (i.e., the slide show and the model). To compare further the two groups on these questions about factual knowledge, the pattern of answers to these questions was examined. The response patterns to alternatives for each cognitive question are quite similar even if the overall correctness is greater for the computer group. This means that the most frequently chosen alternative (and the second, third, and fourth choices) were commonly the same, whether measured manually or by computer. Only the absolute value of the percentages varied. On the "favorite exhibit

Table 5
Percentage of Cognitive Questions Answered Correctly for Seen and Unseen Exchibits by Computer and Manual Groups.
(Numbers in Parentheses Represent Number of Questions Tried.)

EXHIBIT	COMPUTER GROUP		MANUAL GROUP	
	SEEN PERCENTAGE	UNSEEN PERCENTAGE	SEEN PERCENTAGE	UNSEEN PERCENTAGE
Slides	85 (650)	69 (332)[a]	77 (562)	62 (316)[a]
Time	65 (752)	56 (310)[a]	63 (668)	51 (208)[a]
Anatomy	74 (614)	62 (247)[a]	76 (535)	64 (172)[a]
Model	73 (560)	65 (69)	54 (612)	58 (36)
Man	59 (332)	55 (236)	60 (358)	47 (256)[a]
Signs	82 (190)	72 (212)[a]	78 (221)	65 (200)
Naturalist activities	80 (74)	66 (114)	65 (100)	50 (120)[a]
Area activities	54 (92)	51 (57)	63 (128)	46 (96)[a]

[a]Percentages correct within each group which are different from each other at or beyond the 5% level of significance (as determined by the chi-square test).

Table 6
Percentage of Cognitive Questions Answered Correctly by Manual and Computer Groups for Seen and Unseen Exhibits. (Numbers in Parentheses Represent Number of Questions Tried.)

EXHIBIT	SEEN			UNSEEN		
	MANUAL PERCENTAGE	COMPUTER PERCENTAGE	RATIO	MANUAL PERCENTAGE	COMPUTER PERCENTAGE	RATIO
Slides	77 (562)	85 (650)[a]	0.90	62 (316)	69 (332)	0.90
Time	63 (668)	65 (752)	0.97	51 (208)	56 (310)	0.91
Anatomy	76 (535)	74 (614)	1.03	64 (172)	62 (247)	1.03
Model	54 (612)	73 (560)[a]	0.74	58 (158)	65 (69)	0.89
Man	60 (358)	59 (332)	1.02	47 (256)	55 (236)	0.85
Signs	78 (221)	82 (190)	0.95	65 (200)	72 (212)	0.90
Naturalist activiyties	65 (100)	80 (74)[a]	0.81	50 (120)	66 (114)[a]	0.76
Area activities	63 (128)	54 (92)	1.17	46 (96)	51 (57)	0.90

[a]Percetnages correct for each pair which are different from each other at or beyond the 5% level of significance (as determined by the chi-square test).

question," a similar ranking or pattern of answers was also found, as the slides and model exhibits were indicated as the overwhelming favorite two exhibits by each group (though not in the same order in each group).

2. With respect to the percentage of each group which saw the eight exhibits, the computer group said they saw less (in six out of eight exhibits) but still scored higher (see Table 7). It should be noted that these differences are significant only for the first four major exhibits.

3. In considering how easy each group found the exhibits to understand, examination was made of the median affective understanding scores (from the 5 point easy/hard scale where "1" indicated an exhibit was "very easy" to understand to "5" indicating an exhibit to be "very hard" to understand). On seven of the eight exhibits there were no significant differences between these scores (see Table 8).

Responses Compared to Demographic Data

1. There were inconsistent changes in performance with different ages and a fairly clear but small improvement with increased education, particularly for those who had seen exhibits; however, no Kendall tau correlations exceeded .20. Using the more powerful Pearson correlation in a multiple regression to predict correctness scores, R^2 did not exceed .03 (or 3% of variance explained) for the independent variables of age and education).

2. Males did better than females at almost all points; however, only

Table 7
Percentage of Respondents Who Said They Saw An Exhibit.
("No Answer," Scored as Not Seen in Manual Group, Was Not Possible
To Score in Computer Group. Numbers in Parentheses Represent
Number of Respondents.)

EXHIBIT	COMPUTER GROUP	MANUAL GROUP
Slides[a]	60 (305)	69 (285)
Time[a]	64 (350)	80 (285)
Anatomy[a]	64 (371)	79 (289)
Model[a]	85 (210)	96 (192)
Man	57 (303)	58 (288)
Signs	46 (239)	52 (191)
Naturalist activities	43 (117)	39 (97)
Area activities	64 (108)	52 (94)

[a]Percentages seen for each group which are different from each other at or beyond the 5% level of significance (as determined by the chi-square test).

Table 8
Median Understanding Scores for the Eight Exhibits
(1 = Very Easy to Understand to 5 = Very Hard to Understand).
Number in Parentheses Represent Number of Respondents to Each
Understanding Question.)

EXHIBIT	COMPUTER GROUP	MANUAL GROUP
Slides	1.3 (121)	1.5 (194)
Time	2.2 (93)	1.9 (229)
Anatomy	2.0 (98)	1.9 (232)
Model	1.5 (124)	1.4 (185)
Man	1.8 (105)	1.6 (168)
Signs[a]	2.2 (36)	1.6 (102)
Naturalist activities	1.5 (16)	1.9 (45)
Area activities	1.6 (44)	1.9 (47)

[a]The median understanding scores for the computer gorup on this exhibit is different from the score median of the manual group beyond the 1% level of significance as determined by the median test.

the performance-by-sex tau correlation of .07 in the computer group is significant beyond the 5% level.

Computer Use

Computer users much prefer the computer over paper and pencil, rating it 1.3 on a 5-point preference scale (where "5" indicated that respondents "much prefer paper and pencil"). The manual group's median for this computer preference scale was 3.2 (different from the computer group beyond the 1% level of significance using the Kolmogorov-Smirnov test).

As "3" on this scale means "no preference," this should not be taken as an aversion to the computer by the manual group but, rather an indication that the average visitor probably has no inclination either for or against the computer and may even possibly favor the computer if the average over both presentation methods is considered. This overall preference score was 2.2, indicating a positive preference for the computer. However, one problem in this respect was that because 40% of the manual respondents indicated that they had not seen the first couple of days of the survey period, it probably would have met with an even more favorable response had it been more prominently displayed.

The favorable response that computer questioning received in this study confirms similar findings by Griest, Van Cura, & Kneppreth (1973) who used a computer to interview emergency room patients and by Slack, Hicks, Reed, & Van Cura (1966) who used it to take medical histories. The computer users also found that the computer was quite easy to use, giving it a 1.2 rating on a 5-point easy/hard scale (where "1" equals "very easy to use" to "5" equals "very hard to use"). It is particularly noteworthy that 76% of the computer users rated it "very easy" to use. Less than 4% of the group using the computer found it either "hard" or "very hard to use." No relationships of note were seen between computer preference and the demographic variables.

DISCUSSION

In comparing the results of the manual group with the results of the computer group, it can be assumed that, for major exhibits (i.e., the first six), there is no difference in the groups except for the two exhibits with sound (the slides and the model). The manual correctness scores of cognitive questions on these two exhibits are approximately 85% of the computer scores. An explanation for the computer group scoring higher in general and in particular on the slides and model may be that people who self-select for testing may be better prepared than those who are chosen randomly. As the computer group actually saw proportionately fewer exhibits (cf. Table 7), it may also be that they already knew more about glaciers and the Icefield in the first place (given that these respondents can be believed when they indicate that they are not repeat users). This result in the computer group is also supported by the fewer significant differences in correctness scores between those having seen and those not having seen given exhibits (cf. Table 5).

With the computer uniformly available during all IVC hours, the more avid, and, perhaps, therefore more knowledgeable, visitors at nonpeak hours (which consisted of a higher proportion of hikers and climbers) may also account for the higher scores by the computer group. (Unfortunately, the current computer group data does not allow determination of when a given response was made.) A further possibility that the generally younger respondents with less education in the computer group might account for the improvement by this group on the primarily sound exhibits is discounted by the general improvement with education or no consistent change in performance when the groups are matched on age and education levels. It should not be forgotten, however, that the computer attracted a significantly younger sample than random surveying did and, with other kinds of exhibits or questions about other topics (such as politics), other significant differences might well appear.

An additional correspondence in results between the current computerized surveying technique and the manual one is the high similarity in respondents' opinions of their understanding. As indicated in Table 8, the median level of perceived understanding which is determined by each technique is quite close for seven out of eight of the exhibits.

As more data is obtained, clearer trends may emerge, and it may be possible to confirm further or reject the theory that computer users tend to do better on exhibits with spoken, rather than textual, explanation. For example, it may be found that the computer users actually do better on popular exhibits (which in this study also happened to be those with sound). Further experimentation may also indicate an interaction between education, age, and use of sound as, intuitively, it seems that younger respondents with less well-developed reading skills might absorb more information from such auditory exhibits. Testing of exhibits with and without visual content may also yield interesting interactions when more conceptual questions are asked, such as those in market surveys or political opinion polls. In the meantime, all such computer-collected data should be used cautiously, with the anomalies of this study carefully kept in mind.

CONCLUSION

There is no doubt that a younger population of both sexes is attracted to a computer-input device than is typically surveyed in a random fashion. It is also the case that respondents to a computer-input device also have a lower education level, though a bimodal distribution exists with a second peak at the university education level (as well as at the Grade-8 or less level). Likely confounded with age and education level is a better performance by the computer sample on those displays which involved sound in addition to visual material. When exhibits contained text without sound, no significant knowledge differences were found, though there is a trend toward better performance by the computer group at all levels. Thus, in returning to the initial question of what factors affect response differences in computer and manual presentation of material, one is left with the somewhat puzzling conclusion that the populations differ as to age and sex but, in the current context, this does not seem to matter either in terms of knowledge or opinions about exhibits, though the computer respondents while sometimes seeming to know more, do say they observed less! What does matter is the character of the material queried as to its presentation medium. But, with the consistency of the computer data (in terms of response patterns to alternative answers and choices) even for exhibits with sound, at least a baseline is available for determining the effects of changing exhibits for the population it attracts. Do new exhibits explain more than old ones?

Does a changed exhibit now communicate more than it did? Have exhibit preferences changed? Are there different patterns in different seasons? All of these questions can be answered with computer surveying by comparing computer-collected baseline data with later data which is also collected by computer.

It is also likely that age and education interactions will be seen with other formats and with other questions. Hence, as a preliminary conclusion, the factors (i.e., independent variables) in Table 9 from this and the other studies cited can be listed as having potential affects on manual/computer responses differences. This list can be viewed as an adjunct to the Beard and Peterson (in press) taxonomy.

Overall, for the ranges of these variables which have been studied, it seems clear that presentation format has a small but significant effect on performance, usually to the determent of computer users. The type of task makes a difference only when there are long bodies of information presented on a screen rather than on paper, with the response at the screen being slower. Aural presentation also improves performance at a computer, though comparative response time has not been measured. And the type of subject has little effect other than that volunteers at screens differ demographically from randomly selected respondents.

REFERENCES

Beard, J.W., & Peterson, T.O. (in press) A taxonomy for the study of human factors in management information systems, In J.M. Carey (Ed.), *Human factors in management information systems* (this volume pp.) Norwood, NJ: Ablex.

Cushman, W.H. (1986). Reading from microfiche, a VDT, and the printed page: Subjective fatigue and performance, *Human Factors, 28,* 63–73.

Erdman, H., Klein, M.H., & Griest, J.H. (1983). The reliability of a computer interview for drug use/abuse information, *Behavioral Research Methods and Instrumentation, 15,* 66–68.

Griest, J.H., Van Cura, L.J., & Kneppreth, N.P.A. (1973). A computer interview for emergency room patients, *Computers and Biomedical Research, 6,* 257–265.

Hiltz, S.R. (1979). Computerized conferencing for opinion research, *Public Opinion Quarterly, 43,* 562–571.

Muter, P., Latremouille, S. A., Treurniet, W. C., & Beam, P. (1982). Extended reading of continuous text on television screens, *Human Factors, 24,* 501–508.

Newsted, P.R. (1985). Paper versus online presentations of subjective questionnaires, *International Journal of Man-Machine Studies, 23,* 231–247.

Rushinek, A., Rushinek, S., & Stutz, J. (1983). An empirical analysis of the computerization of interactive software systems, *Information and Management, 6,* 281–287.

Slack, W.V., Hicks, G.P., Reed, C.E., & Van Cura, L.J.A. (1966). A computer based medical history system, *New England Journal of Medicine, 274,* 194–198.

Staff. (1985a, January 4). Polling pole polls people, *Marketing News,* 44.

Staff. (1985b, May 24). Stores, campuses use poles for polls, *Marketing News,* 25–32.

Switchenko, D.M. (1984). Reading from CRT versus paper: the CRT-disadvantage hypothesis re-examined, *Proceedings of the 28th annual meeting of the Human Factors Society*, 429–430.

Trollip, S.R., & Sales, G. (1986). Readability of computer generated fill-justified test, *Human Factors, 28*, 159–163.

Wright, P., & Lickorish, A. (1984). Investigating referee's requirements in an electronic medium, *Visible Language, 18*, 186–205.

APPENDIX

Exhibit Legend

Slides:	Slide show in the theatre
Time:	Large, green wall exhibit titled "Glaciers through Time"
Anatomy:	Large, blue and white wall painting titled "Anatomy of a Glacier"
Model:	Large model of the Columbia Icefield located in the center of the main exhibit wall with explanatory sound track
Man:	The exhibit called "Glaciers and Man," located across from the information desk
Signs:	Grey metal signs located just outside the windows of the main exhibit room
Naturalist activities:	The exhibit on naturalist activities located in the hallway
Area activities:	The area activities board in the hallway

SECTION VI

System User Documentation

Effective use of a management information system (MIS) depends not only on the interface design, but on the documentation which facilitates the initial and continued use of the system. Once the MIS is in place, and the training period is over, the user must rely on support mechanisms which guide routine and advanced processing. This support can take on many forms both offline and system resident. These forms include operation manuals, system messages, user's guides, online help facilities, information centers, online tutorials, and embedded training.

User documentation serves many purposes:

1. to aid the user in task completion;
2. to help train the user;
3. to allow the user to explore the advanced capabilities of the system;
4. to help troubleshoot system use problems;
5. to help undo user mistakes; and
6. to help the user understand the underlying structure of the system.

The creation of adequate user documentation has often been neglected by system developers. Creating user documentation is tedious, time consuming, and primarily a verbally oriented task. Often, it is left until the end of a development project and allocated inadequate time and money.

The documentation should be altered whenever the system is altered.

Because there is usually no direct link between offline documentation and program code, the documentation of the system changes often is left undone. This can be very frustrating for the user.

Researchers are working on automated documentation techniques where the program code generates documentation automatically. They are also directing efforts toward natural-language specification techniques which automatically generate code (application generators). Both of these efforts should move MIS environments toward more effective end-user documentation and computing.

The selection for this section on end user documentation is entitled "Theories of Explanation: Expert Systems and Simulations" by David H. Helman and Jeffrey Bennett of Case Western Reserve University.

This paper presents an explanation facility for complex systems. These explanation facilities are intended to aid in the understanding of both the final output generated by the system and the manner in which the system solved the problem.

CHAPTER 10

Theories of Explanation: Expert Systems and Simulation

David H. Helman
Jeffrey L. Bennett
Case Western Reserve University

Explanation facilities provide a useful interface between users and expert system programs or computer simulations. In this paper, we focus on artificial intelligence techniques for writing explanation facilities and the theories of explanation associated with them. We describe conceptions of explanation as trace explanation, inference modeling, script-based explanation, and as envisioning. We show how these conceptions and the techniques that are associated with them can be applied to explanation facilities for computer simulations. We describe our own taxonomy of explanations and show how this taxonomy has been implemented in an explanation facility (NATURALIST) for an inventory-control simulation. We hypothesize that the taxonomy that underlies NATURALIST is quite general, and that it will provide guidelines for the design of simulation explanation facilities in a variety of problem domains.

INTRODUCTION

Rule-based expert systems, on the one hand, simulate the symbolic reasoning of experts concerning one or another problem domain. Classical simulations, on the other hand, are sets of numerical functions which are supposed to represent one or another mechanism or system. Rule-based expert system programs trace a path through AND/OR graphs as they receive the responses of the user to system queries. Simulation programs generally require input only at the beginning, when the user must supply initial variable values.

To a naive user, neither the behavior of a rule-based expert system (symbolic inferences) nor the behavior of a simulation (numerical computations) is usually transparent. The user often will not understand why an expert system program asks particular questions. This kind of misunderstanding may be alleviated, to some extent, if the rules of the expert system program are available to the user. If the if-then rules of the expert system are available to the user, these may, nevertheless, appear arbitrary and unjustified. The ordering of the rules in an expert system can also be a problem: If the strategy of the expert system programmer is not apparent to the user of the program, then he or she may not understand or believe the conclusions of the system. An explanation facility for an expert system program, therefore, should justify to the user both the rules of a system and their ordering so that the inferential behavior of the system is transparent.

The problem of explaining computer simulations is very similar (see Helman, 1986). Computer simulations may produce an overwhelming amount of numerical information; information overload may make it difficult for the simulation user to understand where or how his or her questions are being answered. The functions that constitute the simulation may be difficult to understand. A more fundamental problem is that a user may not understand the relationship between the simulation functions and the domain that is being modeled by the simulation. A simulation explanation facility should make clear the behavior of the simulation program as well as its meaning (i.e., its function as a model of the problem domain).

Artificial intelligence researchers have written a number of programs which provide explanations for rule-based and causal expert systems. In this paper, we focus upon four significant research programs pertaining to explanation in artificial intelligence and consider the possibilities for the applications of this research to explanation facilities for computer simulations. We describe how we have integrated some of these techniques into a simulation explanation facility (NATURALIST). NATURALIST attaches to a specific inventory control simulation (Gaither, 1982). We hypothesize, however, that the taxonomy of explanations that underlies NATURALIST is quite general, and that this taxonomy will provide guidelines for the design of simulation explanation facilities in a variety of problem domains.

EXPLANATION AND TRACE

The classical explanation facilities for rule-based expert systems provide explanations by generating a trace of the symbolic reasoning of the system (Winograd, 1972; Shortliffe, 1976). A symbolic trace facility can provide How?, Why?, and Why not? explanations of the reasoning of a system through a restatement of the rules that are, or could be, used in arriving at a specific conclusion. How? explanations can be provided by tracing through all the rules that must be applied in order to achieve the goal to be explained. Why? explanations can be produced by supplying all the goals which call the given goal-to-be explained as a subgoal (i.e., by furnishing a trace from the present goal to the root goal in the AND/OR tree defined by the rules of the expert system). A Why not? explanation can be given by pinpointing possible sources of failure to establish the goal in question (e.g., missing information, low confidence values associated with statements).

A problem with a simple symbolic trace facility is that it is limited to reexpounding the rules of the expert system. A simple example illustrates the consequences of this limitation. Suppose that one has an expert system which is designed to determine on what shelf in the oven to cook a given piece of food. A user inputs to the system the data (pie, small) and the system returns (top shelf). In response to a How? query (i.e., "How did you conclude 'top shelf'"), the system returns the domain rule "If x is a small dish, then x is placed on the top shelf." To what extent does this provide explanatory information to the user? The user, in particular, will not understand how the rule 'If X is a small dish, then x is placed on the top shelf' is justified. Is this rule an arbitrary convention? Is the rule dictated by the engineering of the oven?

We have found that trace mechanisms are useful in simulation explanation facilities for the explanation of numerical calculations. That is, the user may wish to know how a system derived a given output. The answer to this question, in NATURALIST, is given by tracing the simulation calculations for that output and accompanying these calculations with text that describes the calculations (see Section VIII below). A trace through the simulation equations cannot give us any sort of deep knowledge about the problem domain being modeled (see Chandrasekaran & Mittal, 1982). If we are interested in understanding the simulation as a model of a real-world system or mechanism, then a mere restatement of the simulation calculation will be of little help.

EXPLANATION BY INFERENCE MODELING

Expert systems are supposed to simulate the perspectives and reasoning of experts concerning real-world problem domain. A simple trace through the AND/OR graph defined by the rules of an expert system, as noted above, will often fail to simulate the perspectives of an expert because it does not justify the rules themselves or their ordering. An interesting and relatively successful approach to this problem has been to place each expert system rule in its context. That is, the sort of problem that is typically suited for the application of an expert system involves a number of solution stages. If the expert system can make clear to the user the kinds of inferences or reasoning involved at each stage of the problem solution, then the user of the expert system has a better chance of achieving a coherent and unified understanding of the problem domain. In practice, expert system designers have clarified the overall structure of problem domains by dividing the rules of their expert systems into a number of inference classes and then providing a distinct type of explanation for each class of inference (Weiner, 1980; Swartout, 1981; Clancey, 1983; Chandrasekaran, 1985).

One particularly interesting taxonomy classifies rules into distinct types based on their strategic role within a system (Hasling, 1984). From a strategic point of view, some rules are, for example, used to establish a hypothesis space, others are designed to collect information, others are supposed to test hypotheses, and so on. If we place each rule within a strategic context, then we can give the user an overall sense of what we are trying to accomplish at any given point in an expert system program. In NEOMYCIN, we can ask the system, at any point, to place the present expert system query in a strategic context. The following example illustrates the kind of strategic information which NEOMYCIN can supply:

NEOMYCIN-Has Mary been hospitalized recently?
USER-WHY (i.e., WHY is it important to determine whether Mary has been hospitalized recently?)
NEOMYCIN-We are trying to round out the diagnostic information by looking generally into past medical history and by reviewing systems.

There are unasked general questions that can help us with the diagnosis (from Hasling, 1984).

Inference modeling represents a promising but unexplored area in the development of simulation explanation facilities. One can distinguish, from a semantic point of view, various tasks that are performed by groups of simulations within a simulation model. In the Gaither inventory control model, for example, some functions compute the optimal safety stock, whereas others model acquisition costs. One could supply information which clarifies the individual modules in the Gaither model as well as information which isolates the role of those modules in the overall model.

Chandrasekaran (1985) has made a convincing case that the classes of inferences or strategic tasks in expert systems are, to a significant extent, domain independent. One will, for example, find in virtually any expert system components that narrow down the possibilities (i.e., components which perform the task of classification). If there is one kind of explanation that is appropriate for each domain-independent class of inference or strategic task, then one can hope to write a (partially) domain-independent explanation facility. Much research remains to be done in classifying types of simulations and their modules before a similar effort will be possible with regard to simulation explanation facilities.

SCRIPT-BASED EXPLANATION

Scripts are a linked list of procedures which constitute a stereotypical action, event, or process (Schank & Abelson, 1977). For example, a script for eating at a restaurant might consist of the following: "Sit down at table. Order from menu. Eat meal. Receive check. Pay bill." Scripts can provide useful data structures in the design of explanation systems for expert systems. Suppose an expert system asks the user about a given lab test. The user may want to know the scenarios that are typically associated with a lab result that is both positive and unusual for the age group of the person being tested. A script-based explanation facility can supply these scenarios on one or another level of abstraction (e.g., the user may want to know merely what to expect given any positive lab result of this kind) or for one or another level of user expertise. A script-based explanation facility is also modular and easily modified. If the user of an expert system notices that part of a common scenario is not stored by a system, he can easily alter a script or add a new script. It is also possible for script-based information systems to be modified automatically. An interesting area of research concerns the automatic modification of parts of a script-based abstraction hierarchy, given explicit alterations in some particular script (see Schank, 1982).

The causal explanation module in our explanation facility for the Gaither simulation (see below) is equivalent to a script-based system. In our causal explanation facility, we have attached scripts (in the form of AND/OR trees) to explain changes in simulation variable values from one year to the next. If the results of our experiment with the Gaither model are typical, the notion of scripts (as well as the recent algorithms of Schank for modifying script-based memories) has great utility for simulation explanation facilities.

ENVISIONING

Envisioning is a form of qualitative reasoning which is capable of producing causal explanations of device behavior. The process of envisioning was developed by de Kleer and Brown (1982a,1982b) in their investigations into the construction of explanation facilities for qualitative simulations of physical devices (i.e., causal expert systems).

In order to understand de Kleer and Brown's theory of envisioning and how this process is used in the production of causal explanations, it is first necessary to define the four various concepts employed by de Kleer and Brown in their theory of qualitative reasoning: (a) device topology, (b) envisioning, (c) causal model and (d) running. *Device topology* is defined as a representation of the physical organization of a system, depicting its various components and the interconnections between them. *Envisioning* is the reasoning process by which 'the function of a device is inferred from its topology, given the knowledge that the system has of qualitative physical laws. A *causal* model describes the behavior of a device as a product of the causal interactions of its various components. A *running* of the causal model produces a specific behavior by generating a determinate causal chain of events.

According to de Kleer and Brown (1982b), explanations are produced in qualitative reasoning at the level of envisioning. At this domain level, explanations can be thought to serve three primary purposes: (a) to provide an account of how a system responds to disturbances from its resting state, (b) to generate a description of the function of a novel device based on its component models, and (c) to aid in the redefinition of primitive models by identifying embedded implicit assumptions and making them explicit in new idiosyncratic component models. Although all three functions are of interest in the development of a complete explanation facility, we shall consider only the first in examining the potential of envisioning in explanation facilities for computer simulations.

De Kleer and Brown (1984) make it quite explicit in the description of their system that causal explanations are concerned not with how a physical system reaches a given resting state or why it remains in that given state, but rather with how a series of effects on components in the system are propagated through time. That is, in the theory of de Kleer and Brown, all causal explanations are strictly expressed in the form C1 causes C2....Cn. Applying this format to a physical system, such as a pressure regulator, produces the following explanation for a closing of a valve: An increase in source flow causes the sensed pressure to increase which causes the diaphragm to move downward against the force of the spring causing the valve to close (de Kleer & Brown, 1984).

What is noteworthy about the kinds of explanations generated by the envisioning process is not their informational content, but that their derivation from qualitative reasoning has, therefore, enormous implications for robotics, for qualitative reasoning techniques could obviate the need for laborious reprogramming of robots. Qualitative reasoning is also useful in domains, such as medicine, where inexact or fuzzy reasoning about physical systems is necessary (see Widman, in press).

Much research remains to be done, however, concerning the application of qualitative reasoning techniques to existing numerical simulations. Experts examining large amounts of numerical information derived from a simulation do explicate that information with reference to qualitative general laws. For example, a systems engineer might note that a simulation of pressure in a flexible pipe is returning relatively constant values for, although fluid flow is increasing, so is pipe volume. It is extremely difficult however, to write a domain-independent program that will extract and condense numerical information using qualitative general laws. The alternative (domain-specific) approach is merely to encode the correlations between numerical and symbolic information (e.g., references to qualitative laws) with reference to a particular knowledge base.

AN EXPLANATION FACILITY FOR A QUANTITATIVE SIMULATION

NATURALIST is a system designed to provide explanations for a quantitative simulation of inventory control. Gaither (1982) has developed a computer simulation model for inventory control that determines the optimal order point and order quantity for a given item by minimizing the total annual material costs associated with that item. The basic design for the model of Gaither (see Figure 1) is as follows:

Variable Definitions

Q = fixed order quantity in units per order.
C = carrying costs per unit in dollars per unit per year.
D = annual demand in units per year.
S = ordering or setup cost in dollars per order.
ac = acquisition costs in dollars per unit.
r = incoming transportation costs in dollars per unit.
SS = level of safety stock in units.
A = probability of stockout in each reorder cycle.
S' = Stockout, reorder costs, et., in dollars per stockout.

Simulations are run on a given set of six input values (we will call such a set an INPUTSET) which determine the variables C,D, S, ac, r, and S'. At the beginning of a simulation run, an initial estimate of the optimal

$$TMC = \frac{Q}{2} C + \frac{D}{2} S + ac(D) + r(D) + (SS)C + A(S') \frac{D}{Q}$$

Total Annual Material Costs	= Annual Carrying Costs
	+ Annual Ordering Costs
	+ Annual Acquisition Costs
	+ Annual Incomming Transpostation Costs
	+ Annual Carrying Costs for Safety Stock
	+ Annual Expected Stockout Costs

Figure 1. Basic Gaither Model

order quantity Q is made by use of the formula QO = 1/2 2D(S)/C. Beginning with the INPUTSET and initial value of Q0 and proceeding iteratively for each incremented value of Q, the simulation calculates the level of safety stock (SS) that minimizes both the annual carrying costs for safety stock and the annual expected stockout costs. The simulation will then determine the total annual material costs associated with the given value of Q. At the conclusion of the simulation, the system returns the value of each component of total annual material costs associated with the optimum order quantity (we will call such a set an OUTPUTSET). The results from part of a simulation run are shown in Table 1:

The goal of the naturalist explanation facility is to provide a set of functions and texts which better enable a user to understand the equations of the simulation, the relationship between a given INPUTSET and OUTPUTSET, and the particular domain one is using the Gaither simulation to model. The design of NATURALIST is based upon an extensive literature in the history and philosophy of science that is concerned with the structure of explanatory activity in the natural and social sciences. We have implemented modules that provide four

Table 1.

Inventory Control Simulation for 1986   Simulation 1   Page 2

Order Quantity (units)	Service Level (1-alpha)	Safety Stock (units)	Annual Ordering Cost	Annual Carrying Cost	Annual incoming Transportation Cost	--Annual safety Stock Cost-- Expected Carrying Cost	Stockout Cost	Total Cost	Annual Acquisition Cost	Total Annual Material Costs
794	0.9821	136	882.62	932.95	4280.00	319.60	55.30	374.90	268275.00	274665
802	0.9821	136	873.82	942.35	4220.00	319.60	54.74	374.34	268275.00	274666
910	0.9821	136	865.19	951.75	4200.00	319.60	54.20	373.80	268275.00	274666
818	0.9821	136	856.72	961.15	4050.00	319.60	53.67	373.27	268275.00	274516
826	0.9821	136	848.43	970.55	4050.00	319.60	53.15	372.75	268275.00	274517
834	0.9821	136	840.29	979.95	4050.00	319.60	52.64	372.24	268275.00	274517
842	0.9821	136	832.30	989.35	4050.00	319.60	52.14	371.74	268275.00	274518
850	0.9821	136	824.47	998.75	3900.00	319.60	51.65	371.25	268275.00	274369
858	0.9772	130	816.78	1008.15	3900.00	305.50	65.18	370.68	268275.00	274369
866	0.9772	130	809.24	1017.55	3900.00	305.50	64.58	370.08	268275.00	274372
874	0.9772	130	801.83	1025.95	3900.00	305.50	63.99	369.49	268275.00	274373
882	0.9772	130	794.56	1035.35	3750.00	305.50	63.41	368.91	268275.00	274225
890	0.9772	130	787.42	1045.75	3750.00	305.50	62.84	368.34	268275.00	274227
898	0.9772	130	780.40	1055.15	3750.00	305.50	62.28	367.78	268275.00	274228
826	0.9772	130	773.51	1064.55	3750.00	305.50	61.73	367.23	268275.00	274230
914	0.9772	130	756.74	1073.95	3600.00	305.50	61.19	366.69	268275.00	274082
922	0.9772	130	750.39	1083.35	3600.00	305.50	60.65	366.15	268275.00	274085
930	0.9772	130	753.55	1092.75	3600.00	305.50	60.13	365.63	268275.00	274089
939	0.9772	130	747.12	1102.15	3600.00	305.50	59.62	365.12	268275.00	274092
946	0.9772	130	740.80	1111.55	3600.00	305.50	59.12	364.62	268275.00	273945
954	0.9772	130	734.59	1120.95	3450.00	305.50	58.62	364.12	268275.00	273947

distinct types of explanations described in this literature: (a) what-if explanations, (b) genetic explanations, (c) functional explanations, and (d) causal explanations. An additional module for the production of how-possibly explanations is presently under development.

A how-possibly explanation explains an event by describing the presuppositions or principles that, if known, would have led a person to expect the event (Dray, 1957; Hempel, 1965). In the context of a computer simulation, a how-possibly explanation facility will describe the implicit assumptions that are made in the simulation model. That is, a how-possibly explanation facility will indicate to the user the conditions under which an set of equations does and does not adequately model a problem domain. The design principles for, and limitations of, the four explanation modules have already been implemented in NATURALIST.

WHAT-IF EXPLANATIONS

The basic idea behind what-if explanations is that a simulation, as well as the problem domain it models, is better understood when we can see what will happen under hypothetical contrasting conditions (what-if explanations can, therefore, be provided by spreadsheet software). NATURALIST provides what-if explanations by computing the real and percentage changes in values in the OUTPUTSET produced by user-prompted changes to the INPUTSET and to the functions of the simulation equation. For example, we can, with regard to the sample simulation run shown in Table 1, change the input variables for demand and acquisition costs per unit. We can also alter transportation costs from a discontinuous function of order quantity to a constant function for unit transportation costs, total transportation costs will raise price 5 %, total material costs will rise 5 %, annual expected stockout costs will rise 3 %, and so on. The graphical display in Figure 2 indicates these changes.

This example indicates the capabilities of the what-if explanation module in NATURALIST. In practice, the user should only change one variable value or function at a time and make such changes incrementally. In any problem domain, furthermore, only certain what-if changes

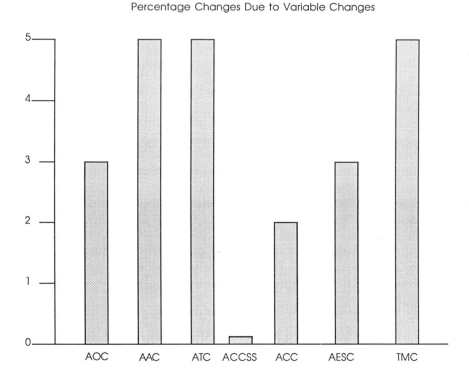

Figure 2. Percentage changes of components total material costs

make sense. It would be valuable for a novice user of a simulation to know the rules that constrain the correct use of a what-if facility. There are a number of interesting research problems pertaining to the representation of such constraints that remain to be investigated.

GENETIC EXPLANATIONS

A genetic explanation explicates the occurrence of a given event through a historical description (Dray, 1957). Such explanations are paradigmatic in historical studies and are oftentimes used by scientists when a reference to general laws would require communicating unnecessary details. The building of a genetic explanation facility into NATURALIST reflects our fundamental (cognitive) hypothesis regarding explanation: There are a variety of types of explanatory activity that are important in nearly all problem domains. In biology, for example, one would like a causal explanation, but as biologists communicate with one another, they often will rely upon what-if or genetic or how-possibly explanations. An adequate computer explanation facility must supply as many kinds of information as experts would supply in explaining the given problem domain. From an informational point of view, we cannot assume that one type of explanation is fundamental.

For the concept of genetic explanation to apply to the Gaither simulation, we must suppose that the simulation is run over an extended period of time, and that we have a record of the actual, as well as the expected, variable values. Graphing changes in variable values provides some useful information, but such graphs will not tell us what to expect in the present time period or why significant changes occurred when they did in past time periods. In our present explanation facility, we record some of this information, because we ask the user to input text that explains variable values that diverge significantly from the values in the time period immediately past.

We are presently working on methods for constraining the texts that users may supply to the genetic facility. Constraining the symbolic information supplied by users to the genetic data base allows the causal explanation module to access historical information (see below).

FUNCTIONAL EXPLANATION

A functional explanation elucidates an event or a device by placing it in the context of the larger system of which it is a part (see Hempel, 1965). The functional explanation facility in NATURALIST answers the question, "What caused the simulation to arrive at value V for quantity Q?" This question is answered by (qualitative) traces of the computation that led to the calculation of V for Q. We illustrate a qualitative trace for a calculation of acquisition costs in Figure 3:

CAUSAL EXPLANATION

The causal explanation facility in NATURALIST answers the question, "Why did the optimal value for total material costs (TMC) change in the way it did from one year to the next?" Our first step towards answering this question is to calculate numerically the effect of changes in component variable values on change in total material costs (TMC) (the technique is similar to partial differentiation — see Kosy & Wise, 1984).

Functional Trace of Acquisition Costs

	Annual Carrying Cost
+	Annual Ordering Cost
+	Annual Acquisition Cost
+	Annual Incomming Transportation Cost
+	Annual Carrying Cost for Safety Stock
+	Annual Expected Stockout Cost
=	Total Annual Material Costs

Acquisition Costs Contributes to Annual Acquisition costs
Annual Acquisition Costs = Acquisition Cost * Demand

Δ Acquisition Costs	= 2%
Δ Demand	= 4%
Δ Annual Acquisition Costs	= 6%

This change in Annual Acquisition Costs made a linear contribution to the rise of Total Material Costs (TMC)

Figure 3. Illustration of the qualitative trace provided by NATURALIST for a calculation of acqusition costs

We can, for example, after this calculation, conclude that changes in acquisition costs, on their own, would have accounted for half of the total change in TMC. Why, however, did acquisition costs change as they did?

In our causal explanation module, we use a backtracking, rule-based reasoning program to determine the causes of changes in variable values (e.g., some top-level goals in the program are the possible causes of acquisition cost increases). What is perhaps more interesting about this module is that we have interleaved the symbolic reasoning program with information derived from the Gaither simulation. In most symbolic reasoning programs, conclusions are reached by (a) deduction, or (b) asking the user a question. We can, however, use the simulation and the simulation explanation facility as a kind of oracle for a symbolic reasoning mechanism. Rising inflation, for example, might account for rising acquisition costs, if these costs have, in the last years, tracked inflation.

FUTURE DIRECTIONS

We have recently initiated two projects which extend the research described in this paper. First, we are transferring the causal explanation module of our present explanation system to a PROLOG-based explanation shell (see Sterling, 1985). Second, we would like to test our theory of explanations empirically. We have, in conjunction with Professor Elizabeth Short of the Case Western Reserve Department of Psychology, designed several experiments to explore the relationship between increased understanding of simulation models and the use of one or another module (e.g., causal, what-if) in a simulation explanation facility.

ACKNOWLEDGMENTS

We thank Drs. Yoh-han Pao, Elizabeth Short, Leon Sterling, and Lawrence E. Widman. We also thank Anthony W. Foster, who programmed the version of the NATURALIST explanation facility described in this paper.

REFERENCES

Chandrasekaran, B. (1985). *Generic tasks in expert system design and their roles in explanation of problem solving*. (Tech. Rep.). Columbus: Ohio State University, Laboratory for Artificial Intelligence Research.

Chandrasekaran, B., & Mittal, S. (1982). Deep versus compiled knowledge approaches to diagnostic problem solving. *Proceedings of the National Conference on Artificial Intelligence*, 349–354.

Clancey, W. (1982). The epistemology of a rule-based expert system – A framework for explanation. *Artificial Intelligence, 20*, 215–251.

de Kleer, J., & Brown, J.S. (1982a). Foundations of envisioning. *Proceedings of the National Conference on Artificial Intelligence*, 434–437.

de Kleer, J., & Brown, J.S. (1982b). Assumptions and ambiguities in mechanistic mental models. In D. Gentner & A.S. Stevens (Eds.), *Mental Models*, Hillsdale, NJ: Erlbaum.

de Kleer, J., & Brown, J.S. (1984). A qualitative physics based on confluences. In D. Bobrow (Ed.), Qualitative Reasoning about Physical Systems. Cambridge, MA: M.I.T. Press.

Dray, W. (1957). *Laws and Explanation in History*. Oxford, England: Oxford University Press.

Gaither, N. (1982). Using computer simulation to develop optimal inventory policies. *Simulation, 39*, 81–87.

Hasling, D.W., Clancey, W.J., & Rennels, G. (1984). Strategic explanations for a diagnostic consultation system. *International Journal of Man-Machine Studies, 20*, 3–19.

Helman, D. (1986). Symbolic explanation facilities for computer Simulations. *(Tech. Rep. 102–86)*. Cleveland, OH: Case Western Reserve University, Center for Automation and Intelligent Systems.

Helman, D., Bennett, J., & Foster, A. (in press). Simulations and symbolic explanations. *Proceedings of the International Symposium on Methodologies for Intelligent Systems*, ACM Sigart Press.

Hempel, C.G. (1965). *Aspects of scientific explanation*. New York: MacMillan Press.

Kosy, D.W., & Wise, B.D. (1984). Self-explanatory financial planning models. *Proceedings of the National Conference on Artificial Intelligence*, 176–181.

Schank, R., & Abelson, R. (1977). *Scripts, Plans, Goals, and Understanding*. Hillsdale, NJ: Erlbaum.

Schank, R. (1982). *Dynamic Memory*. Cambridge, England: Cambridge University Press.

Shortliffe, E. (1976). *Computer-based Medical Consultations: MYCIN*. New York: Elsevier.

Sterling, L. (1985). Explaining explanations clearly. *(Tech. Rep. 124–85)*. Cleveland, OH: Case Western Reserve, Center for Automation and Intelligent Systems Research.

Swartout, W.R. (1981). Explaining and justifying expert consulting programs. *Proceedings of the International Conference on Artificial Intelligence*, 815–822.

Weiner, J.L. (1980). BLAH, a system which explains its reasoning. *Artificial Intelligence, 15*, 19–48.

Widman, L. (in press). Representation method for synamic causal knowledge using semi-quantitative simulation. *Proceedings of MEDINFO '86*.

Winograd, T. (1972). *Understanding Natural Language*. New York: Academic Press.

SECTION VII

End User Involvement

The degree to which the end user is involved in all phases of system development has increased over the years. This involvement increases both the likelihood that the resultant system will be satisfactory to users and the amount of time necessary to complete the development task.

There are several techniques, such as graphic system design aids, structured walkthroughs, and rapid prototyping, which facilitate end user involvement. User representatives are often assigned to a system development project on a fulltime basis throughout the duration of a project.

These types of involvement are voluntary in nature and the level of involvement can be determined by the organization. There is also required user involvement during the needs requirements determination at the beginning of the project. When the system is implemented and in production, the user is necessarily involved in the end use and ongoing production of the system. Issues which focus on end user involvement at the system production level include

1. End user training;
2. User resistance to change;
3. User feedback for system evaluation; and
4. User acceptance of the system.

All of these issues impact on the success of the information system. Research in these behaviorally driven areas can have significant impact on user acceptance and system performance. A system which is technically adequate or even superior may fail when the behavioral reactions of the users are not anticipated and ameliorated. Once a system is in place, evaluation of performance is important in order to enhance current system usability and also to gain feedback for future system design.

Before a management information system (MIS) can be implemented, the end users must be trained to use the system. Training effectiveness, in turn, is dependent on the understanding of how people learn. "End User Computing: A Research Framework for Investigating the Training/Learning Process" by Robert P. Bostrom, Lorne Olfman, and Maung Sein, of Indiana University, Department of Operations and Systems Management addresses the training/learning issues and provides a research framework for investigation.

Also included in this end user involvement section is "The Darkside of Office Automation: How People Resist the Introduction of Office Automation Technology" by Claudette Peterson, Texas A&M University, department of Business Analysis and Research and Tim O. Peterson, Texas A&M University, department of Management and "Understanding Resistance to System Change: An Empirical Study" by Jane M. Carey, Texas A&M University, Department of Business Analysis and Research. These two papers explore user resistance to change and methods of combating the resistance to change in order to ensure system acceptance and successful implementation.

"A Plan for Evaluating Usability of Software Products" by Eileen Kopp and JoAnn Timmer of IBM Corporation focuses on techniques for evaluating competitive software from a usability standpoint.

CHAPTER 11

The Darkside of Office Automation: How People Resist the Introduction of Office Automation Technology

Claudette M. Peterson
Tim O. Peterson
Texas A&M University

Office automation holds out the hope of increasing the productivity of the largest information-processing unit within all organizations—the office. Although it holds the greatest promise for future productivity improvements, it also will cause many dramatic changes to occur within the offices of today. These changes will arouse individuals' attitudes and feelings which may lead to resistance of this new technology. Organizational factors will also cause resistance to the change. This paper examines the attitudinal factors and organizational factors which lead to resistance of change of office automation technology. It presents five dysfunctional behaviors which result from these factors and concludes with some suggestions for dealing with these dysfunctional behaviors.

INTRODUCTION

Many theorists have proposed that organizations should be thought of as information-processing systems (e.g., Galbraith, 1977; O'Reilly & Pondy, 1980; Simon, 1973; Tushman, 1979). Certainly, the major information processing center in any organization is the office. Kofer (1984) identified the office as the "place where people deal with information handling tasks." The office staff creates, captures, processes, stores (files), retrieves, and disseminates information to all parts of the organization (Greenwood & Greenwood, 1984:54). Office personnel spend most of their time performing five basic functions:

1. *information capture*: the process of creating, collecting, organizing, and entering data into some usable form;

183

2. *information processing*: storing the information in some form of filing system for later use;
3. *information storage*: storing the information in some form of filing system for later use;
4. *information retrieval*: accessing the filed information when it is needed (Danzin, 1983); and
5. *information dissemination*: providing information to other parts of the organization in a usable form.

The cost to American corporations annually to perform these tasks is about $1 trillion. This accounts for between 30% and 50% of the total overhead costs of most organizations (Greenwood & Greenwood, 1984). Even a small improvement in office productivity would then provide for a major financial saving and a significant increase in office workers' productivity. A study published in, 1982 by the American Productivity Center reports that 99 large companies (considered to be leaders in the field of office productivity) averaged gains of 9.5% from their office productivity improvement programs (White-Collar Productivity, 1982). From this, one can estimate that American corporations could potentially save $95 billion per year by putting productivity improvements to work in their offices. Those productivity improvements come in the form of office automation. Office automation uses electronic and computer-based technology to perform the functions identified earlier. In a way, office automation is a specialized application of computerized information systems methods and technology.

New office technology provides six major improvements:

1. improved data capture
2. improved data manipulation
3. improved data editing
4. improved data storage
5. improved data access
6. improved information exchange

Although office automation seems to be the change that is needed by American business in order to increase the office worker's productivity, the new technology will also cause dramatic changes to occur in both the jobs and design of the office of the future. Little attention has been paid to the social redesign of the office, which will be necessary to make the best use of new office equipment (Driscoll, 1979). These changes have caused people to fear being replaced, "just as they feared the electric typewriter when it entered the office scene" (Quible & Hammer, 1984, p. 25). Surely the introduction of office automation equipment into the office will also cause uncertainty and anxiety to occur among the office personnel. Otway and Peltu (1984) comment on the effect of office automation this way:

> News of an impending reorganization heralds the start of an agonizing period of uncertainty in organizational life. There is a pervasive fear of the unknown: some managers will emerge as winners, others will be losers; power balances will change; long standing work relationships may be disrupted; new communication channels will open, others will close; the context of jobs and work practices will be different. New office technology implicitly brings with it these kinds of far reaching changes (p. 1).

The introduction of computer-based office automation systems can lead to complex organizational changes. New procedures and information flows may require fundamental changes in task design and social interactions. The organization may be altered. This, alone, may cause problems while the new power relationships are established.

The fears and anxieties caused by the introduction of an office information system technology are of many different types. Galitz (1984) identified nine fears or attitudes people experience because of the introduction of a new office information system. These are summarized in Table 1. Quible and Hammer (1984) believe that the reasons office employees resist include (a) they fear being replaced by the new sophisticated, more efficient equipment and (b) they experience anxiety when confronted with having to learn to use new, sophisticated, technical equipment. For whatever reason, these fears and feelings of uncertainty generally cause individuals to resist changes. Greenberger (1968) says that an "explanation of human inertia would cite man's tendency to resist the new and espouse the old, his need for security and his fondness for familiar objects even while exploring the unfamiliar."(p. 304).

In addition to attitudinal factors, organizational factors can also cause people to resist change. Dickson and Simmon (1970) identified four organizational factors which they believed lead to the resistance of newly installed management information systems (MIS). These four factors are summarized in Table 2.

In that same article, Dickson and Simmon examined three dysfunctional behaviors which were the outcome of these four organizational factors and personal characteristics of people reacting to the installation of an MIS. In their paper, Dickson and Simmon say that, to reap the benefits of an MIS, it is often more important to solve behavioral problems than technical problems. They found, from a series of interviews with 17 firms associated with the University of Minnesota's

Table 1

Attitudinal Factors Which Cause Individuals to Resist Change

FACTOR	DESCRIPTION
Feelings of change	Change often threaten one's self-esteem or image in the eyes of others. Often, low self-images are brought to work and confrontation with machines threatens to reveal a person's own worst fear of incompetence.
Fear of being replaced by a machine	The computer may be perceived as an instrument that actually replaces the worker. One's own value in the workplace may be totally undermined with disastrous monetary and psychological consequences.
Fear of failure	Many workers have spent years developing the skills that have made them proficient at their jobs. Why change? If they do change, what will happen to them if they cannot perform the new task or with the new equipment?
Fear of the unknown	People need to be able to predict what they will face in the future. Established patterns are known factors, whereas new systems pose the threat of ambiguity and uncertainty.
Psychological habit	Established rules, policies, and procedures frequently become habits, and people rely on them for both guidance and protection. These habits are their security blankets. Changes frequently disrupt this security by making established habits inapplicable.
Loss of control	Computers are frequently perceived as a threat to one's power or influence. Computer systems are also commonly perceived as things over which one has no control.
Changes in interpersonal relationships	People have a strong need to interact with others. Changes that disturb existing social patterns or result in isolation are unbearable. Change can also disturb worker relationships with superiors.
Lack of understanding	Resistance to change is likely if workers don't understand its purpose.
Lack of identification	A system should not be perceived as imposed. If the change is not initially sought by workers and if the consequences of the consequence of the change do not appear directly beneficial to them, their resistance is likely.

Management Information System Research Center, that these firms were more concerned with topics involving people problems during installation than with any of the more technical topics suggested by the interviewer.

From this finding, Dickson and Simmon (1970) go on to identify three specific dysfunctional behaviors aggression, projection, and avoidance that may appear in organizational personnel once an MIS is installed. These same behaviors can be observed in the more specialized information system of office automation. It seems that the installation of a new, computerized information system causes feelings and attitudes to develop in individuals and these feelings and attitudes lead to the

Table 2
Organizational Factors Which Cause Individuals to Resist Change

FACTOR	DESCRIPTION
Departmental boundaries	Most complex organizations have definite departmental boundaraies. The introduction of information systems often causes changes in these boundaries or blurs their existence. Violation or elimination ofa these boundaries will cause individuals to fear loss of status and territory and cause resistance to occur.
Informal structures	All organizations develop an informal structure with a set of rules, a code of ethics, and a set of informal communication channels. New information systems threaten to change or eliminate the informal structures. For these reasons, people will resist new changes.
Organization's culture toward	All organizations have a culture. Part of that culture is the organization's attitude toward change. If top management's overall attitude toward change is positive and communicated with a spirit of cooperation, the change has a better change of success. If change is viewed by top management with distrust and anxiety, then a new system faces problems.
Method of introducing	Considerable research has been done on different methods of introducing change into organizationai settings which indicates that how the change is introduced plays a pertinent role in whether or not the change is accepted.

dysfunctional behaviors. In addition, organizational factors also play a role in causing dysfunctional behaviors to occur. This idea is conceptualized in Figure 1.

But, even before the system is installed, it must be proposed. It is during this stage that the same feelings, fears, and attitudes are aroused. These inner states of turmoil may lead to other dysfunctional behaviors. These behaviors may have the result of slowing down the proposal process, reducing the benefits that could be realized or even completely halting the project. It seems that the behaviors at the proposal stage must be considered and dealt with, even before those identified by Dickson and Simmon (1970) at the installation stage. This modified approach is shown in Figure 2. The modified model would suggest that information system analysts, as well as office automation change agents must first be aware of the behaviors which manifest themselves when the new system is proposed.

DYSFUNCTIONAL BEHAVIOR

When a new information system is proposed, a number of dysfunctional behaviors are possible. It should be noted that the three dysfunctional

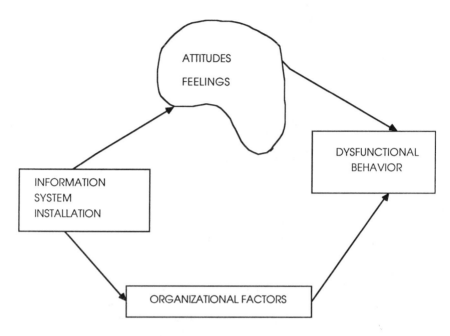

Figure 1. A framework for the Dickson and Simmons' MIS installation and dysfunctional behavior relationship

behaviors identified by Dickson and Simmon (1970) – projection, aggression, and avoidance – are possible at all stages of the office automation system life cycle. Description of these dysfunctional behaviors are summarized in Table 3.

A case of projection is the frequently expressed concern over data security when a new office automation system is being proposed or implemented. Office personnel express concern about the confidentiality of letters and documents that are stored electronically. They blame

Table 3
Dickson & Simmon's Dysfunctional Behaviors (1970)

BEHAVIORS	DEFINITIONS
Aggression	Behavior in which an individual attacks (either physically or nonphysically) the object causing the problem. The intention is to damage the object of the attack.
Projection	This exists when people blame the system for causing difficulties that are, in fact, caused entirely by something else.
Avoidance	When people withdraw from frustrating or stressful situations.

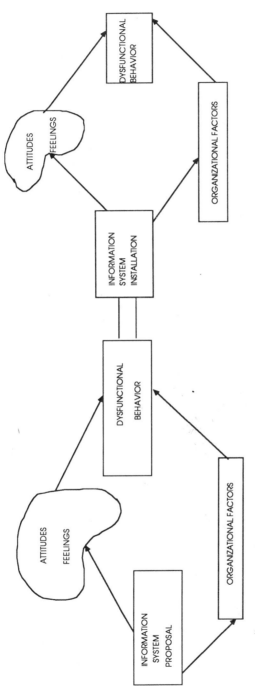

Figure 2. A modified framework for the information system life cycle and dysfunctional behavior relationship

189

the system for problems they themselves cause by taping their password on their work stations or by leaving a confidential letter displayed on their terminal while they leave the area to perform other tasks.

A manager may tell his clerical staff to pad the activity reports (a form of indirect aggression) so that his unit doesn't lose clerical staff members or to justify additional equipment above what his unit actually needs. In one such study, a manager was reported to have checked the daily typing activity log personally. He then made additions to the log for fear of losing his personal secretary.

In addition, one of the authors has seen normally rational managers become incensed and threaten "to never use the system" (an example of avoidance) at the mere talk of automating their offices. This resistance to change seems to be the result of managers' realization that their jobs and their interaction patterns with members of the organization will undergo significant changes because of the new office information system (Argyris, 1970).

During one office automation project, one of the authors observed that one of the clerical staff members was not turning in her daily typing activity logs. When approached about this, her response was that she was too busy with the day-to-day work to keep track of all this additional information. This is an excellent example of avoidance in the hopes that the new proposed system will go away. Later, when this individual was told that she had to turn in these daily reports, she grudgingly agreed. When the summary calculations were produced for her work station, the statistics reported that she worked on the average of 60 hr a week just typing. Through an unobtrusive measure, it was verified that the individual rarely worked more than 12 hr a week on typing activities. What this example illustrates is that when one dysfunctional behavior is denied, others will be attempted in order to achieve the same end. The information change agent should be aware of this important point.

In addition to the dysfunctional behaviors identified by Dickson and Simmon (1970), we have identified two others which seem to be very prevalent during the early stages of a new office information system consideration: defensive planning and chronic skepticism.

Defensive planning is the type of planning that is done under duress or as a reaction to some external environmental factor. It is usually done with great reluctance. This method of planning does not produce new work units which reap the total benefits of the new work methods. Instead, it produces maladapted work units which are usually less effective and efficient than before the new work methods or technology was introduced. According to Goodman, Bazerman, and Conlon (1980) this happens because the new form of work is not congruent with the existing organizational structure and so does not become institutionalized into the work unit.

According to Odiorne (1981) defensive planning is the result of an antiplanning mentality possessed by many American corporations. Odiorne identifies two types of planning: implicit and explicit. Implicit planning is the kind that people do when they get up on Saturday morning and say "Let's go shopping!" and everyone piles into the car and heads out to the mall. They are not going shopping because they need something, but just for the fun of it. The goal is to have fun and half of the fun is getting there. This kind of planning is close to the "American way" according to Odiorne (1981, p. 4). This approach to planning is a freewheeling way of life. Those people who do not accept this approach to planning are considered party-poopers or wet blankets. In an office information environment, this type of planning can be observed when an office purchases a new office information system because the ABC corporation has one. Odiorne says that this is the way American corporations have been run throughout the 19th and 20th centuries. James (1984) says that "failing to plan" and "waiting to plan" are two of the most common reasons that office automation implementation fails. It seems that, in the past, success came so easily to American corporations that planning for it was unnecessary. But the complexity of organizations today, coupled with the cost and impact of new office information systems, make this form of planning outdated and unacceptable.

The other type of planning, explicit planning, isn't nearly as much fun. It requires effort and time. In fact, Bologna (1978) reports that the most frequent reason given by middle and upper managers for not planning is that it consumed too much time. It seems that it is for these reasons that many American managers have continued to hold on to an antiplanning mentality which leads to a defensive planning posture.

The second type of dysfunctional behavior we have identified is chronic skepticism. By constantly doubting, questioning, and disagreeing with the new proposed office information system, the chronic skeptic stymies or prevents changes from occurring. In many ways, the chronic skeptic sabotages the efforts of the explicit planner. Skeptics (Argyris, 1970) often express opposition to new office information systems in terms of two specific issues: (a) they don't understand the new information technology and (b) they don't believe it is wise to use such technology when it still hasn't proven itself. Although skeptics use these two issues as their foundation for continuous disagreement and doubts, they are usually the same people who, when offered information or training on the new information technology, are also the people who say they are too busy.

DEALING WITH DYSFUNCTIONAL BEHAVIOR

A number of authors (Dickson & Simmon, 1970; Cirillo, 1984; Faerstein, 1986; Bair, 1986) have provided suggestions on how to minimize the effect of dysfunctional behaviors. These suggestions are summarized in Table 4. Although these seem like valid suggestions to minimize the impact of the dysfunctional behaviors, the problem does not seem to be in knowing what to do,ut in actually doing it. During the proposal stage, all work groups have a vested interest in the proposed office information system, but none is greater than the technical staff's. When a work unit is intimately involved, the staff members are the champions of the new system. They know the advantages and benefits which can be realized from this new technology. From this vantage point, they may not see any reason for the resistance or see any need to employ the suggestions in Table 4. By failing to follow the suggestions, they may unwittingly defeat the proposal they are championing. The motto for office information system change agents should be, "Office Information Change Through Office Personnel Acceptance." This touchstone would help office information system change agents to be aware of the office

Table 4

Six Suggestions for Minimizing Dysfunctional Behaviors

---

1. *Supportive climate:* Examine the organization's climate for aceptance of a new information system, such as support from top management and conduciveness to risk taking (Dickson & Simmon, 1970; Cirillo, 1984; Bair, 1986).

2. *Open communication:* Clear and frank communication from top management about the philosophy behind the acquisition of the equipment and its purpose for the organization andthe individual employees is essential. This includes time spent clarifying and answering questions about the proposed system (Dickson & Simmon, 1970; Cirillo, 1984; Faerstein, 1986).

3. *Employees involvement:* Get the employees involved early in the decision to automate the office so that they feel as though the system belongs to them, rather than to the technical staff (Dickson & Simmon, 1970; Cirillo, 1984; Bair, 1986; Faerstein, 1986).

4. *Office automation planning:* Plan the scope of the new office information system, to determine what tasks and personnel will be affected (Dickson & Simmon, 1970).

5. *Meet users' needs:* Make the new system fulfill the needs of the user. Survey, interview, and meet with prospective users. Listen to, and act upon, their needs (Dickson & Simmon, 1970; Bair, 1986).

6. *Education and training:* Educate both managyers and end users on the philosophy and value of office automation. Provide training on specific skills (e.g., word processing, electronic mail, electronic filing, retrieval, etc.) so the complete power of the system can be used (Cirillo, 1984; Faerstein, 1986).

---

employees' anxieties, the organizational factors present, the dysfunctional behaviors possible, and the ways to minimize these behaviors when an office information system is proposed.

DYSFUNCTIONAL BEHAVIORS OF THE TECHNICAL STAFF

Dickson and Simmon (1970) state that the technical staff displays none of the dysfunctional behaviors they identified. The authors would argue that the technical staff often displays all three behaviors during the system development life cycle. Unlike the end users, who display these behaviors toward the automated system, the technical staff commonly directs aggression, avoidance, and projection toward the users.

Avoidance is demonstrated when the technical team makes decisions about the end users' needs without including the users in the design and development meetings. This can lead to surprises when the system is turned over to the users and the outputs do not meet their needs.

The technical staff sometimes displays aggression toward the organization and its members. They may use technical jargon or speak condescendingly to users to justify why a system they perceive as clean and efficient is the correct choice even if the users feel it will not meet their needs.

Argyris (1970) reports that, from his research experience, this seems to happen because "the MIS expert displays a combination of arrogant selling zeal and organizational defensiveness which does not make relations with suspicious managers any easier." Argyris (1970) describes a situation in which the MIS team

> ...tried to be diplomatic. Their diplomacy came in the form of translating their ideas into "simple" managerial language, by suppressing (they thought) their disrespect for the low intellectual caliber among the managers, and by not confronting the managers or any threatening issues. But their diplomacy didn't last long. When they met too much resistance they either withdrew or became aggressive and competitive in return. To make matters worse, their feelings of intellectual superiority were no longer concealed and they came across to their intended clients as arrogant (p. 25).

Just as users project undeserved blame on the office automation system, the technical staff projects blame on users. The authors have observed that when a user calls to report a system problem, the initial response of the technical staff is that the user has made an operating error. It is often necessary to ask the user several questions to determine how the problem occurred, but there is a tendency for the technical staff to ask these questions with the attitude that they will discover what the user did wrong. They resist the idea that there may be a real problem with the automated system.

From these observations, it appears that further research is needed to understand better the technical staff display of dysfunctional behaviors toward the end user. If technical personnel are displaying avoidance, aggression, and projection in their dealing with users, how can these change agents expect to minimize these same behaviors in the users?

REFERENCES

Argyris, C. (1970). Resistance to rational management systems. *Innovation, 10,* 28–35.

Bair, J.H. (1986). Listening to users is half the job in automation. *Government Computer News, 5,* 73.

Bologna, J. (1978). *Planning commandments.* Westfield, MA: MBO, Inc.

Cirillo, D.J. (1984). Helping middle managers manage office technology. *Personnel, 61,* 6–12.

Danzin, A. (1983). The nature of new office technology. In H.J.Otway & M. Peltu (Eds.), *New office technology: Human and organizational aspects.* Norwood, NJ: Ablex.

Dickson, G.W., & Simmon, J.K. (1970). The behavioral side of MIS. *Business Horizons, 13,* 39–71.

Driscoll, J.W. (1979). People and the automated office. *Datamation, 25,* 106–112.

Faerstein, P.H. (1986). Fighting computer anxiety. *Personnel, 63,* 12–17.

Galbraith, J. (1977) *Organizational design.* Reading, MA: Addison-Wesley.

Goodman, P.S., Bazerman, M., & Conlon, E. (1980). Institutionalization of planned organizational change. In B.M. Staw & L.L. Cummings (Eds.), *Research in organizational behavior.* Greenwich, CT: JAI.

Greenberger, M. (1968). The computer in organizations. In C.A. Walker (Ed.), *Technology, industry, and man,* (pp. 304–324). New York: McGraw-Hill.

Greenwood, F., & Greenwood, M. (1984). *Office technology: Principles of automation.* Reston, VA: Reston.

James, P.N. (1984). Avoiding the 10 common pitfalls in office automation. *Journal of Information Systems Management, 1,* 3–12.

Kofer, G.R. (1984). Future uses of future offices. In A. Monk (Ed.) *Fundamentals of human-computer interaction,* (pp. 181–192). New York: Academic.

Odiorne, G.S. (1981). *The change resisters.* Englewood Cliffs, NJ: Prentice Hall.

Otway, H.J., & Peltu, M. (1984). The challenge of new managerial roles. J.H. Otway & M. Peltu (Eds.), *The Managerial Challenge of New Office Technology.* London: Butterworths.

O'Reilly, C.A., & Pondy, L. (1980). Organizational communication, In S. Kerr (Ed.), *Organizational Behavior.* Columbus, OH: Grid.

Quible, Z., & Hammer, J.N. (1984). Office automation's impact on personnel. *Personnel Administrator, 29,* 25–32.

Simon, H.A. (1973). Applying information technology to organization design. *Public Administration Review,* 268–278.

Tushman, M.L. (1979). Impacts of perceived environmental variability on patterns of work related communications. *Academy of Management Journal, 22,* 482–500.

White-collar productivity: The national challenge. (1982). Houston, TX: The American Productivity Center.

CHAPTER 12

Understanding Resistance to System Change: An Empirical Study

Jane M. Carey
Texas A&M University

The introduction of change into an organization is examined in the context of management information systems (MIS). The results of a study of acceptance of major computer system change using a psychological and behavioral-driven model are reported. Among the variables tested, acceptance of change (attitude toward new system) is positively related to previous use, education, and current usage of the new system. The personality variable (behavioral rigidity), however, is not related to acceptance when examined across subpopulations of users. Managerial applications of study variables and findings are discussed.

INTRODUCTION

In the technical business world of today, change is the norm. This is especially true with respect to management information systems (MIS). The MIS manager must introduce change on a regular basis, often in the face of strong organizational resistance.

Resistance to change by individuals and organizations is a well-documented phenomenon (Thompson, 1967; Lawrence & Lorsch, 1967; Burns & Stalker, 1961). It has been noted that some organizations have resisted change even at the peril of eminent nonsurvival (Maniha & Perrow, 1965; Hedberg, 1979). The theoretical causes of such resistance are varied; avoidance of uncertainty (Carter, 1971), adherence to structured programs (March & Simon, 1958), isolation and refusal on the part of top management to obtain information based on reality (Hedberg,

Nystrom, & Starbuck, 1976), organizational paradigms (Sheldon, 1980), or an irreversible momentum or, more precisely, inertia (Miller & Friesen, 1980).

MIS introduction into an organization (or change from one system to another) is common in many organizations. It is a change which carries, in many cases, great impact on the daily routines of individuals within the organizations. Mansour and Watson (1980) conducted a study which validated the amount of resistance to change by organizational personnel as one of the several determinants of information system performance. Michael Wood (1985) suggests that fostering successful systems conversion requires a "common ground" approach between users and data processing (DP) staff. The crux of Wood's "common ground" approach is to utilize interview sessions in a neutral environment to encourage positive attitude toward change.

Daniel Robey (1979) also identifies a positive relationship between user attitude toward an information system and system use. The more positive the attitude of the user toward the system, the more the user will take advantage of the system's availability. As the amount of usage increases, the reported satisfaction level also increases. Several companies, such as Aetna Life and Casualty and Index Systems, recognize that human factors play a critical role in the success of new or changing MIS (EDP Analyzer, 1985). Developing a technically sound system does not ensure success if the system is not usable.

The stress that accompanies introduction of system change into an organization often frustrates DP and user staff. Power (1984) suggests that rather than focus on the negative aspects of change, user and DP management should look at the "dynamic opportunities" that change affords them. In order to take advantage of these opportunities, all participants must first understand the nature of change, make plans to combat resistance to change, and take advantage of the change process.

Hershey and Blanchard (1977) have developed a useful model for examining change. They view organizational change as the culmination of a hierarchy preceded by changes in individual behavior, attitudes, and knowledge (See Figure 1). At each higher level of the hierarchy, change is more difficult and time consuming to accomplish.

THE PRESENT STUDY

The installation of a new computer system at a major southern university afforded the researcher an opportunity to examine the change process in a MIS context. The computer system was changed from one DEC 10 system to two IBM 4341 systems. The user interfaces were quite

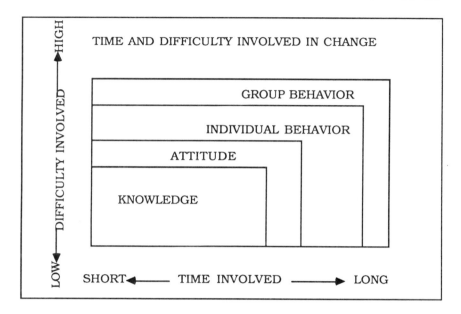

Figure 1. Participative change cycle (Hershey & Blanchard, 1977, p. 281)

different from one another and this required the users to relearn many tasks that had previously been learned on the old system. The changeover was phased in such a way that both systems were operable for some time, and many of the users had the option of choosing which system to use during this period. This provided the researcher with a built-in control group. Users who continued to utilize the old system could be compared to those who changed to the new system.

The purpose of the present study is to identify factors which could retard the successful introduction of a major MIS change. Specifically, the variables described in the Hershey and Blanchard model (1977) — (a) individual behavior, (b) attitude, and (c) knowledge, were examined.

Individual behavior was operationalized as a personality variable measured by Schaie's Tests of Behavioral Rigidity (TBR) (Schaie, 1960). Schaie defines rigidity as "a tendency to perseverate and resist change, to resist the acquisition of new patterns of behavior" (p. 11). The internal consistency of the instrument was validated by Langer and McCain (1964).

Attitude in Hershey and Blanchard's (1977) model was measured by two proxy variables. One was called 'commitment to the old system'. Three questions in the survey were designed to measure this commitment (see Figure 2).

The second attitude measure was the number of hours logged on the

---

    * Do you still use the DEC-10?

        ____ yes   ____ no

If you answered yes, complete the next two questions. If you answered no, skip them.

    * If you have a preference for either system, which do you prefer?

    ____ IBM 4341   ____ DEC-10   ____ No preference

    * How would you rate your attitude towards the DEC-10 in relation to the IBM 4341?

More Negative towards   More Positive towards
The DEC than the IBM   1   2   3   4   5   The DEC than IBM

Figure 2.

(DEC 10) system. Resistance to change may be more pronounced, the more entrenched an individual is in the status quo. New users who have never used any system may have a more positive attitude toward a new system than those users who have been using the status quo a long time.

Four aspects of knowledge are examined:

1. hours logged on the old system,
2. hours logged on the new system,
3. attendance at user seminars for the new system,
4. previous experience with the new system within a different organizational setting.

Based on this examination, the following hypotheses are presented.

Hypothesis I: Acceptance of the new system will be negatively correlated with:

1. behavioral rigidity,
2. commitment to the old system, and
3. hours logged on the old system.

Hypothesis II: Acceptance of the new system will be a positively correlated with knowledge of the new system as measured by:

1. hours logged on the new system,
2. new system seminar attendance, and
3. previous new system experience.

The Hypothesized model is:
  Acceptance of change =
  f(−individual rigidity
    − commitment to the status quo
    − knowledge of the status quo
    + exposure to change
    + preparation for change
    + previous experience with change)

METHODOLOGY

The overall design of the study is called an adaptive experiment (Lawler, 1977). Lawler suggests that by monitoring change in organizations, researchers are afforded excellent opportunities for such adaptive experiments.

The sampling technique is a stratified random sample. Six distinct user subpopulations were identified: faculty, computer center staff, graduate researchers, undergraduate accounting, business, and computer science majors. The overall response rate was 54% (179 out of 332).

Acceptance of the new system was measured by the use of eight semantic differential statements regarding the system reliability, ease of operation, friendly interface, logical interface, ease of understanding, concise interface, documentation, and overall attitude. Crombach's alpha is calculated to be .88989 and signifies that the eight questions measure the same underlying construct. Based on this value, the eight statements are additively combined and used as the dependent variable (acceptance of change for the new system) in a regression analysis.

Regressions were run with the following independent variables:

1. personality of the individual (TBR);
2. commitment to the status quo (preference for and continued use of the DEC-10);
3. knowledge of the status quo (length of time on the DEC-10);
4. exposure to change (length of time on IBM);
5. preparation for change (attendance of seminars); and
6. previous experience with change (prior exposure to an IBM system in a different setting).

RESULTS

Table 1 includes the R^2 and f values for regressions run with each of four subpopulations (faculty, computer center staff, computer science majors, graduate researchers). (Two subpopulations undergraduate business majors and undergraduate accounting majors were dropped from this analysis because the majority had no exposure to the status quo and could not make comparisons between the two systems.) The overall R^2 (.49635) and f value (10.29) indicates that this model is a good predictor of the acceptance of change. The subpopulation with the highest R^2 (.69147) and also the largest positive test of behavioral rigidity (TBR) beta weight is that of undergraduate computer science students who also have the most normal distribution for TBR scores.

The beta weights are summarized for the overall model in Table 2. The signs of the beta weights are as expected with one exception. The overall TBR has a negative beta weight. This is due to the faculty subpopulation whose distribution of TBR score is skewed to the flexible side and at the same time has a rather negative attitude towards the new system (change). Also, the graduate researchers, who have a slightly skewed distribution of the TBR to the rigid side, as a whole carry rather positive attitudes towards the new system (Table 3).

The variable with the largest beta weight is exposure to change (hours

TABLE 1

Acceptance of Change				
Subpopulation	R Square	f	Significance Level	DF
Faculty	.50765	2.41	.05	8, 30
Computer Center Staff	.44494	5.88	.01	8, 24
Graduate Researchers	.47613	14.70	.01	8, 29
Undergraduate - Computer Science	.69147	6.44	.01	8, 24
Total Sample	.49635	10.29	.01	8, 103

TABLE 2

Total Sample Beta Weights			
Variable	Beta	f	Significance
Behavioral Rigidity	-.11368	2.09	.05
Commitment			
1. Preference for Old System	-.02731	.12	--
2. Still use Old System	-.11679	1.09	--
Knowledge			
1. Hours Logged on New System	.59720	54.76	.000
2. Attendance of New System Seminars	.11307	2.12	.05
3. Previous Experience with New System	.12296	2.35	.05

logged on the new system). The longer the user spends on the new system, the more positive his or her attitude toward the system becomes. Other variables significant at the .05 level are behavioral rigidity (TBR), seminar attendance, and previous experience with the new system.

DISCUSSION

Both of the major hypotheses and all subhypotheses, with one exception, are accepted. The exception is the TBR which is not useful in predicting the acceptance of change. Interestingly, the more rigid a user's personality, the more likely he or she is to accept the new system. However, acceptance of the new system is negatively related to user commitment and experience with the old system. Previous experience,

TABLE 3

Subpopulation	TBR 0-89	TBR 90-137	% Below Ave. Flexibility
Rigidity and User Type			
Faculty	7	23	23.3%
Computer Center Staff	7	14	33.3%
Graduate Researchers	12	17	41.0%
Undergrad - Computer Science	5	19	20.8%
Undergrad - Accounting	9	7	56.25%
Undergrad - Business	36	23	61.0%

current usage, and seminar attendance are positively related to acceptance of the new system. These five relationships were hypothesized.

What implications does this model have for managers who are involved in MIS change and are charged with the task of acting as change agents? In the discussion that follows, each independent variable is examined with relationship to the level of managerial control and appropriate managerial action.

PERSONALITY

Personality is measured by the test of behavioral rigidity scores. This is a difficult variable to control since managers have other considerations when hiring personnel. The personality of the workforce is usually set prior to the introduction of the change. To offset this mindset, change could be introduced by stages (e.g., departmentally). The logical approach would be to measure the rigidity of all departments and introduce the change first into those departments whose flexibility (average TBR scores) is at a higher level than other departments in order to avoid high level of resistance. Once the change has been introduced to these departments, the acceptance level of the more rigid user (lower average TBR scores) may increase.

COMMITMENT

Commitment to status quo includes preference for the status quo over the change and continued use of the status quo when the change is available and encouraged for use. It may be advantageous to make the status quo unattractive in some manner. In the case of the computer system, reliability could be altered or some restrictions placed on use of the status quo system. At the same time, an effort might be undertaken to make the new system more attractive to users. By using techniques that enhance the image of the new system and increase the status of users of the new system, the commitment to the old system could be lessened.

KNOWLEDGE

Knowledge of the status quo includes length of time spent with the status quo and familiarity with the status-quo. There is little that the manager can do to alter this variable. He or she should be aware that the longer the status quo has been in force, the more resistance there will be to change. Understanding this relationship, can alert the change agent to the difficulties inherent in the change and allow the determination of a plan of action.

EXPOSURE TO CHANGE

The longer the user is exposed to the change, the more positive his or her attitude will be towards the change. The manager should make every effort to encourage adoption of the new system by users as soon as possible. Time and money incentives could be offered. Approaches, such as offering hands-on instruction or team exercises, could prove effective in giving users painless exposure to the change. This variable was the most important in the model (carried the largest beta weight).

Any effort to encourage early usage ought to have a large payoff in terms of making the transition smooth and moving from a stressful situation to a more relaxed one.

PREPARATION FOR CHANGE

Seminars may be utilized to train the user. An additional or alternative preparation could be psychological. The manager could attempt to break down the psychological barriers against the change by distributing positive literature and using media communications to promote the advantages of the change.

PREVIOUS EXPERIENCE WITH THE CHANGE

Exposure to the new system in a different setting prior to introduction has a positive relationship to acceptance of the new system. It might be possible to do some exchanging of employees to give the users an experience with the change prior to the actual implementation of the change.

CONCLUSION

This study identifies several key variables which contribute to the acceptance of change of an MIS by individuals. The variables are individual rigidity, commitment to the status quo, knowledge of the status quo, exposure to the new system, preparation for the new system, and previous experience with the new system in a different environment. The managerial change agent can alleviate resistance to change to a new MIS by understanding the relationships between these key variables and acceptance to change. Success of a new MIS can be influenced by these variables. A new MIS must be technically sound but it also must be accepted by the users or it will fail.

REFERENCES

Bass, Bernard M. (1960). *Leadership, psychology, and organizational behavior*, New York: Harper and Bros.
Burns, T., & Stalker, G. (1961). *The management of innovation*, London: Tavistock.
Carter, E. (1971). The behavioral theory of the firm and top-level corporate decisions, *Administrative Science Quarterly, 16*, 413–428.

EDP Analyzer. (1985). Manage the impact of systems on people, *23*, 1–12.

Hedberg, B. (1979). How companies can learn to handle change, *International Management, 34*, 33–34.

Hedberg, B., Nystrom, P., & Starbuck, W. (1976). Camping on seesaws, prescriptions for self-designing organizations, *Administrative Science Quarterly, 21*, 41–65.

Hershey, P., & Blanchard, K. (1977). *Management of Organizational Behavior,* pp. 280–284, Englewood Cliffs, NJ: Prentice-Hall.

Hershey, P., & Blanchard, K. (1980). Management of change, *Training and Development Journal, 34*, 80–84.

Hultman, K.E. (1980). Identifying and dealing with resistance to change, *Training and Developing Journal, 34*, 28–33.

Langer, P., & McCain, C. (1964). Rigidity and the SORT, *Journal of Clinical Psychology, 20*, 489–492.

Lawler, E.E. Adaptive Experiments An Approach to Organizational Behavior Research, *Academy of Management Review, 2*, 476–585.

Lawrence, P., & Lorsch, J. (1967). *Organization and environment,* Boston, MA: Harvard University Press.

Maniha, J., & Perrow, C. (1965). The reluctant organization and the aggressive environment, *Administrative Science Quarterly, 10*, 238–257.

Mansour, A.L., & Watson, H.J. (1980). The determinants of computer-based information system performance, *Academy of Management Journal, 23*, 521–533.

March, J., & Simon, H. (1958). *Organizations,* New York: Wiley.

Miller, D., & Friesen, P.H. (1980). Momentum and revolution in organization adaptation, *Academy of Management Journal, 23*, 591–614.

Miller, D., & Mintzberg, H. (1973). Strategy formulation in context, *California Management Review, 16*, 44–58.

Power, B.L. (1984). Change creates dynamic information systems opportunities, *Data Management, 23*, 20–23.

Robey, D. (1979). User attitudes and management information system use, *Academy of Management Journal, 22*, 527–538.

Schaie, W.R. (1958). Difference in some personal characteristics of 'rigid' and 'flexible' individuals, *Journal of Clinical Psychology, 14*, 11–14.

Sheldon, A. (1980). Organizational paradigms: A theory of organizational change, *Organizational Dynamics, 8*, 61–80.

Student, K.R. (1978). Managing change: A psychologist's perspective, *Business Horizons, 21*, 28–33.

Thompson, J. (1967). *Organizations in action,* New York: McGraw-Hill.

Wismer, J.N. (1979). Organizational change: How to understand it and deal with it, *Training, 16*, 27–31.

Wood, M. (1985). Converting systems requires a 'common ground' approach. *Data Management, 23*, 16–18.

CHAPTER 13

A Plan for Evaluating Usability of Software Products

Eileen F. Kopp
H. JoAnn Timmer
IBM Corporation

This paper presents the methodology used at the software development laboratory at IBM for determining the usability of competitive software products. Included is a description of the testing environment and several scenarios and exit questions which are part of the evaluation process.

INTRODUCTION

An IBM goal states that new IBM software be superior to that currently available in the industry, from both IBM and its competitors. IBM has done usability studies of its own products for a number of years. The usability criteria and the technique that IBM uses to evaluate its software products is also used for the evaluation of comparable competitive products. IBM has certain restrictions in regard to the evaluation of competitive software:

1. Competitive software must be acquired and used according to the vendor's terms and conditions. No trade secrets, confidential information or other restrictive contractual obligations can be compromised.

2. 'Evaluation' is limited to the externals of the software panels, messages, reports, dialogs, commands, user documentation, performance, operational characteristics, and so forth. 'Analysis' involves internals (code and logic documentation) and cannot be done by anyone engaged in the development of IBM software. External evaluation is all that is needed to understand usability and functional characteristics.

3. No copies can be made of non-IBM software materials, and evaluation reports have very limited distribution (only within IBM).

This paper presents the generic test plan for evaluating competitive software products.

EVALUATION PURPOSE

The purpose of competitive evaluation is to determine a "best of breed" by evaluating each product and then comparing the results in the usability areas of ease of use, ease of learning, ease of installation, and in usefulness.

Shackel (1984) defines usability as:

> the capability in human functional terms to be used easily (to a specified level of subjective assessment) and effectively (to a specified level of performance) by the specified range of users, given specified training and user support, to fulfill the specified range of tasks, within the specified range of environmental scenarios. (pp. 53–54)

Shackel's definition of usability is one commonly found in the literature (Mills, 1986; Bennett, 1984; Neal & Simons, 1984; Gould & Lewis, 1985). Bennett (1984) further describes usability:

> We can think of usability as relating to mental support for a user. We seek to identify those patterns of system features which will, in actual practice, promote effective user thinking and learning during work in the customer environment. (p. 167)

A product or machine is useful if it does what the users need it to do. Shackel (1984) writes that the usefulness of a product depends:

> upon how well it fulfills its purposes and functions within the specified range of environments for which it was designed, and in relation to an assembly of cost factors. (p. 52)

The results of the evaluations pinpoint difficulties users have with all of the products evaluated and provide usability information which can be applied to the design of new products.

OVERVIEW OF THE EVALUATION

Controlled experimentation is an effective way to derive usability information. Bennett (1984) writes that "usability can only be meaningfully measured during task performance" (p. 167). In a usability evaluation, subjects are asked to complete tasks contained in scenarios. Their performance on the tasks is measured. These measurements are the dependent variables—time and errors. Other dependent data include attitudinal data collected from the subjects through the use of questionnaires. In competitive evaluation, there are two independent variables, task and product. The results of the data analysis give valuable usability information about the product. Bennett (1984) writes:

> Overall usability is often affected by a series of small points or "nits" in the way that the system is used. No one nit is itself enough to cause failure and system rejection, but a whole series of nits can have a devastating effect on user acceptance of the system. (p. 169)

LOCATION AND PHYSICAL FACILITIES

The product evaluations are conducted in the Dallas Usability Labs. Each lab is divided into two rooms: the control room and the studio. The control room is separated from the studio by a one-way mirror. It contains audio and visual equipment that provide observers with a close-up view of the user/software interaction as well as the documentation that accompanies the product. The subject, a representative of the user group, is in a comfortable, attractive studio that resembles the environment where the product would be most likely used.

SOFTWARE AND HARDWARE CONFIGURATIONS

Each product is run on the hardware for which it was designed. The whole system (manuals, reference cards, software, etc.) is evaluated.

MEMBERS OF THE EVALUATION TEAM

Members of the team consist of an administrator, a data logger, and a technical advisor. The administrator is responsible for everything that happens during the test. This person has knowledge of the product being tested and the evaluation procedures. The responsibilities include making sure all hardware/software is available and operational as well as meeting/briefing/ debriefing the test subjects. The administrator also ensures that data are being properly collected.

The data logger uses the PC data logging program to record detailed observations about the subject's actions while the evaluation is going on. The data logger records information needed to gather the following data:

- time spent reading manuals;
- error recovery time;
- number and types of errors made: keystroke, syntax;
- time taken to complete task;
- number of times help screens used; and
- number and type of evaluation team interventions.

The technical advisor is responsible for determining when a subject's request for help should be answered and for answering the help request. The advisor keeps a tally of the help requests made and the comparison of the subject's actions with the command sequence outlined in the script.

SCENARIOS

By definition, comparable products allow users to do similar tasks. A user perceives a "task" as a piece of work or a specific job that can be done with the product, but each "piece of work" must be analyzed before products can be formally evaluated and compared.

The completion of a detailed task analysis of each of the products ensures that only common tasks are included in the scenarios developed for the test sessions. The scenarios, containing related tasks, simulate the way the user will most likely use the product in his or her own environment. Because each of the subjects must learn how to do a task as the first step, the scenarios are structured so that each of the tasks is repeated several times in the attempt to separate learning from doing. Great care is taken to ensure that the scenarios are representative of the real world and that the vocabulary does not include nomenclature of any one of the products. (See Appendix A for sample scenarios.)

For the evaluation team, additional scenario information must be provided:

- probable actions that the subject will take;
- description of the task(s) to be completed;
- the data to be collected throughout the scenario;
- definition of what constitutes the end of the scenario; and

- approximate time required to complete the scenario(s).

SUBJECTS

A minimum of 5 subjects, each representative of the defined user group, are chosen to test each product. The subjects, who have the characteristics of the user group, are obtained from appropriate sources. (See Appendix B for sample user description.)

SUBJECT TRAINING PROCEDURES

No formal training on the product is given to the subjects. After the administrator explains the evaluation procedure, the subjects use the product's training manuals and the on-line help facility to learn how to use the product to complete the scenarios.

DATA COLLECTION

In order to evaluate a product's usability as measured by the criteria contained in the objectives, the type of data to be collected is identified and the method of data collection is established prior to the evaluation itself.

The following data are collected:

- time taken to learn product,
- time spent reading manuals,
- time taken to complete task,
- error recovery time,
- number of times helps screens used,
- number of assistance requests made,
- number and types of errors encountered: keystroke, syntax, and
- number of users who complete task successfully.

The time intervals are measured in minutes and seconds. Cameras, located in the studio, are used so that the test team in the control room can see the subject's use of the keyboard and the manuals. Through the use of the slave monitors in the control room, the test team can also see what happens on the subject's terminal.

Data are collected through the use of the PC data logging program. Using this program, the data logger types in codes for the types of errors made by the subject, help requests, and so forth. These coded observations are automatically correlated with the actual clock time. The analysis of the logs is done by the test team at the end of each evaluation. In addition, the technical advisor and test administrator compare the subject's actions to a script that has been written outlining the optimum command sequence and note any deviations. Subjective attitudinal data are gathered through the questionnaires that each subject completes at the end of each scenario and at the end of the session. The subjects use a Likert scale to respond to such statements as: "Product X is easy to use." (See Appendix C for sample questionnaires.)

DATA ANALYSIS

The data are analyzed in two different ways. First, inferential statistics are used. Multivariate statistics are used to analyze the following variables:

- independent variables;
    task
    products
- dependent variables
    time taken to learn product
    time spent reading manuals
    time taken to complete task
    error recovery time
    number of times helps screens used
    number of assistance requests made
    number and types of errors encountered: keystroke, syntax
    number of users who complete task successfully
    results of attitudinal questionnaire

The mean scores on the attitudinal questionnaire are compared using the appropriate nonparametric test for the number and types of variables.

Second, using a method developed by Lewis (1984), an overall usability rank for each product is calculated in relation to the other products. In Lewis's method, the products are ranked for each measurement according to their scores for the measurement. These ranks are then averaged for each product by totaling the ranks and dividing by the number of ranks. This results in the total overall usability rank for the product. The ranks can be weighted to reflect the importance of the task or the importance of the measurement. These weighted ranks are then totaled and divided by the number of ranks to arrive at the product's total overall usability ranking.

Weighted ranks are used for these evaluations. The variables listed below that are marked by an asterisk are considered twice as important as the other variables. The time variables are not considered as important as the other variables because they can be influenced by outside factors such as typing skill, reading speed, how quickly the technical advisor answers a help request, and so forth.

- time taken to learn the product;
- time spend reading manuals;
- time taken to complete task;
- error recovery time;
- number of times help screens used*;
- number of assistance requests made*;
- number and types of errors encountered: keystroke, syntax*;
- number of users who complete task successfully*; and
- results of attitudinal questionnaires*.

SUMMARY

Certainly, no designer starts out to design a product that is hard to use, but many products end up that way in the eyes of the user. In 1981, Professor A. Chapanis of Johns Hopkins University advanced a simple premise in an IBM symposium. "Ease of use is inversely proportional to the number and severity of difficulties people have in using software."

Product evaluations consistently confirm that "best of breed" can be identified by classifying, counting, and measuring the performance of users and by listening to what they say.

REFERENCES

Bennett, J.L. (1984). Managing to meet usability requirements: Establishing and meeting software development goals, in J.L. Bennett (Ed.), *Visual Display Terminals*, (pp. 161–183), Engelwood Cliffs, N.J.: Prentice-Hall.

Gould, J.D., & Clayton L. (1985). Designing for usability: Key principles and what designers think, *Communications of the ACM, 28*, 300–11.

Lewis, J.R. (1984). Usability comparison of competitive products with ranks, IBM Corporation (Tech. Rep. No. 54 306), Boca Raton, FL: IBM Corporation.

Mills, C.B. (1986). Usability testing in the real world, *Proceedings CHI '86 Conference on Human Factors in Computing Systems*, (pp. 212–15).

Neal, A.S., & Simons, R.M. (1984). Playback: A method for evaluating the usability of software and its documentation, *IBM Systems Journal, 23,* 82–96.

Shackel,B. (1984). The concept of usability, in J.L. Bennett (Ed.), *Visual Display Terminals,* (pp. 45–87), Engelwood Cliffs, N.J.: Prentice-Hall.

APPENDIX A: SCENARIOS

INTRODUCTION

Welcome to IBM

Thank you for your willingness to help us with our evaluation. Remember that we are evaluating the usability of the product you will be using; we are not evaluating you. In fact, you are the most important contributor to our evaluation.

Please proceed through the evaluation package on your own. Some sections may be more difficult for you than others. Please use the manuals and the on-line help to learn how to use the product. Feel free to think aloud while you go through the procedures, as your comments will help us evaluate the product, but ask for help only as a last resort.

At the end of each scenario we would like you to answer a questionnaire. There are no right or wrong answers to these questions. We are interested in your opinions about this product.

We hope you will feel comfortable while you participate in this evaluation. Take a break when you need one.

YOUR SITUATION

You have just been hired as a sales representative at Southwest Enterprises, Inc. The office product, _____ , is an important tool in your work because of its electronic mail and time management functions. Through electronic mail you can communicate with other people in your company. The time management function allows you to schedule meetings and to keep track of your schedule. In the following scenarios, you will be asked to do exercises using _____ .

(Each of the following scenarios would be on a separate sheet of paper followed by the task questionnaire.)

Scenario 1: The first thing you need to do is to check your schedule to see if any meetings have already been scheduled for you for this week. Next, in order to have some idea about the future, look at the whole current month's schedule.

Scenario 2: Your manager told you to attend two meetings. Reserve time on your schedule for the following meetings: − an orientation meeting for new employees on Tuesday, from 3:30 5:00 p.m. −a meeting on Friday from 9:00 9:30 a.m. with R. Smith to discuss the progress being made on a new sales strategy.

Scenario 3: You need to discuss the new product line with J. Roper. Schedule a meeting with her for a time she has available during the next week.

Your manager will be interested in the results of your meeting with Roper. Schedule a meeting with your manager for a time she has available.

Scenario 4: You will need to meet with R. Smith regularly about the development of the new sales strategy. Schedule a reoccurring meeting with Smith for every Wednesday from 10:00 11:00 a.m. Now schedule a reoccurring meeting about the new product line with J. Roper every Thursday from 3:00 3:30 p.m.

Scenario 5: The orientation meeting has been changed from Tuesday from 3:30 5:00 p.m. to the same time on Friday. Delete the meeting from your Tuesday schedule and add it to your Friday schedule.

Something unexpected came up and J. Roper has had to cancel your meeting. Delete that meeting from your schedule.

Scenario 6: You have a dentist appointment next Wednesday at 4 p.m. Put the appointment on your schedule.

You are giving a talk to the P.T.A next Monday. Add that to your schedule.

Scenario 7: Your volleyball team practices Tuesdays and Thursdays from 6:00 7:00 p.m. Add this reoccurring event to your schedule.

You are working on a project with R. Jones. Schedule a reoccurring meeting on Tuesdays at 9:00 a.m.

Scenario 8: You would like to discuss with your manager the project you are working on with R. Jones. Schedule a meeting with your manager for a time she has free.

You need K. Wilson's advice about the above project.

Schedule a meeting with Wilson for a time he has free.

Scenario 9: You have to go out of town on the day you are to meet with K. Wilson. Change the meeting to another day. Delete the canceled meeting from your schedule.

R. Jones cannot meet with you this Tuesday. Cancel that meeting.

Scenario 10: Your schedule has changed several times. Take a look at your schedule for the week.

Next, look at the whole current month's schedule.

Scenario 11: Send a mail message to F. Davis asking for a copy of the procedures for completing a monthly sales report.

Send a mail message to B. Banks asking for expense account forms.

Scenario 12: Read your first mail message. It should be from T. Feldon telling you about a class in nonverbal communication next week and asking you if you would like to attend. Reply to the message saying that you plan to attend.

Read your mail message from S. Wilkins announcing meetings to explain the company's insurance plan. You can go to the 10:00 a.m. meeting or the 1:00 p.m. meeting on Friday. Reply to the message saying you will attend the 10:00 a.m. meeting.

Scenario 13: You realize that P. Burtin in your department might also be interested in the class on nonverbal communication that T. Feldon told you about in the mail message in the last scenario. Forward that mail message to P. Burton. Since you no longer need to see Feldon's note again, delete it. Read the mail message from A. Brown containing last month's sales figures. File the message in the file for monthly sales figures.

Scenario 14: Send the following mail message to M. Small: —Please send me a copy of the new emergency procedures. Thank you.

—Send the following mail message to O. Foley: Would you please send me a copy of your sales projections for this year? Thank you.

Scenario 15: Read the mail message from M. Murray telling about a class in time management. You have already attended such a class. Forward the message to S. Weston and then delete it.

Read the mail message from E. Simon which contains a list of classes. File the message in the classes file and delete it.

Scenario 16: Read and mail message from T. Watson asking you if you are going to attend the time management seminar. Reply that you are not going to attend.

Read the mail message from C. Metcalf asking if you have the manual or the new printer. Reply in the affirmative.

APPENDIX B: SUBJECT CHARACTERISTICS

This product is used by professionals, managers, secretarial and clerical staff. Since the scenarios have been written to reflect the tasks a professional would do, the subject characteristics describe a professional user who would use the product to schedule meetings and appointments, and read, file, delete, and forward electronic mail.

All evaluation subjects must have the following characteristics:

1. be at least 21 years old;
2. have eyesight correctable to 20/40;
3. able to read/understand (American) English written at 8th grade level;
4. have 14 years of formal education;
5. have minimal typewriter keyboard skills;
6. have no specific data processing knowledge or skills;
7. have at least 1 year of business experience;
8. be knowledgeable of general office procedures;
9. be not currently employed by IBM; and be either male or female.

APPENDIX C: ATTITUDINAL QUESTIONNAIRES

The questionnaire administered after each scenario appears in the following format:

Circle the response that most closely matches your opinion.

1. In general, the tasks were easy to do.
   a. Strongly agree
   b. Agree
   c. Neither agree nor disagree
   d. Disagree
   e. Strongly disagree

   Comments_____

   _____ .

The following are the other questions presented in the same format.

2. It was easy to get from place to place during this scenario.
3. When I made a mistake during this scenario, I could correct it easily.
4. The error messages I got were easy to understand.
5. I was able to quickly find the information I needed in the manual.
6. The information in the manual was easy to read and understand.
7. The help screens clearly described what was happening or what I had to do.
8. It took me longer to do this task than I thought it would.

The general attitudinal questionnaire, administered at the end of the evaluation, uses the same format, but focuses on more general, overall responses. These questions include the following:

1. I think computers are easy to use.
2. This product was easy to learn.
3. This product is easy to use.
4. It is easy to make errors when using this product.
5. I usually found the information I needed in the online help.
6. It was easy for me to get from place to place in this product.
7. I was satisfied with the response time when using this product.
8. This product is dependable.
9. The information on the screens made sense. I always knew what I was doing.
10. I was able to find quickly the information I needed in the manuals.
11. The manuals are easy to understand.
12. The examples in the manuals are easy to understand and were helpful.
13. This would be a useful product for a business to have.

Finally, written responses to open-ended questions complete the sub-jective data. (Space is given between questions for the responses.)

1. What features of this product did you like the best?
2. What features of this product did you like the least?
3. What was the most difficult thing you had to learn to use this product?

CHAPTER 14

End-user Computing: A Research Framework for Investigating the Training/Learning Process

Robert P. Bostrom
Lorne Olfman
Maung K. Sein
Indiana University

It is generally accepted that a crucial element of end-user computing success is effective training. Yet, very little research has been conducted in this area. In the absence of any theoretical underpinning, researchers have looked at factors and variables based solely on their intuitive appeal. Past studies and, consequently, the results, have been essentially ad hoc in nature; the potential for integrating the findings into a research tradition is very low.

One reason for this failure on the part of the academic community is the lack of an adequate research framework. This paper aims at filling this void. By drawing upon research findings from such relevant disciplines as educational and cognitive psychology, information systems, cognitive science, and organizational behavior, it proposes a research framework to investigate the training/learning process of end-user computing software. The research issues that surface from examining the framework are discussed.

INTRODUCTION

Beard and Peterson, in this volume, outline five major human-factors research themes. This paper will address one of the categories listed by them, the critical area of end-user involvement. The practice of end users developing, maintaining, and using their own information systems is referred to as end-user computing (EUC). One critical factor that can affect the success or failure of EUC within an organization is training (Cheney, Mann, & Amoroso, 1986).

221

Training for EUC involves several dimensions. End users need to be instructed on system development techniques, database modeling, performing back up and recovery of systems, and security, to name a few. Yet, the most crucial dimension, perhaps, is learning to use EUC software tools. Through the development of an integrated research framework, this paper identifies key variables and discusses key research issues involved in the training/learning process of EUC software tools.

The success or failure of EUC within an organization will ultimately depend on whether end users effectively use EUC software. The key question to be answered then, is: What determines how an end user behaves? Consider an example situation.

An investment manager is currently faced with deciding upon an investment decision from a set of variables involved, each varying in their degree of uncertainty. She needs to explore various scenarios to determine the best alternative. This manager has recently been trained in the spreadsheet/ modeling language, Lotus 1-2-3. She thinks that Lotus 1-2-3 would help her make this decision. She defines a spreadsheet model using the Lotus software and proceeds to check out various scenarios by changing appropriate investment values. However, while doing these "what ifs," she became frustrated when trying to examine scenarios that had already been processed. She did not know that she could save and reaccess the "what if" cases. Consequently, she did not fully compare all scenarios. Overall, this investment manager was very satisfied with her decision and felt that Lotus 1-2-3 was very helpful in this situation, although she did not fully understand the capabilities of the software.

This example demonstrates the major determinants of end-user behavior. The user is engaged in goal-oriented tasks such as choosing between alternative investments. The user has a certain motivation to use available EUC software such as Lotus 1-2-3 and attempts to accomplish the goal as effortlessly as possible. There are certain constraints in this process imposed by the user-system interface, by what the user understands about the software, and by other individual characteristics, such as previous experience with computers. These determinants for user behavior/performance include:

User's task (e.g., problem to solve, decision to make)
User's motivation to use system
User's knowledge (understanding of EUC software)
User-system interface
User's other characteristics
User's behavior/performance

If we want to influence user behavior, we must change one of the determinants. The human-factors literature emphasizes altering or improving the user-system (i.e., man-machine) interface. Alternatively, we can increase the user's knowledge through more efficient teaching methods and increase the user's motivation by showing how the system can be used to accomplish various relevant tasks. The ultimate goal of those focusing on the user-system interface is to develop a system that is idiot proof. Although we agree that better interfaces are badly needed, the objective of achieving error-free interfaces is being regarded as impractical by an increasing number of researchers and systems designers. For instance, Brown and Newman (1985) emphasize this view when they called for "error management" rather than "error avoidance."

More importantly, waiting for an idiot-proof system side steps the difficult issue of the user's understanding of the system and the motivation to use it. We believe these issues cannot be avoided. They are central to developing a user's sense of control over the technology, which is, in turn, essential for effectively using it. Without understanding and motivation, users will not be able to apply EUC software to new situations or to deal with errors and systems malfunctions. We believe understanding and motivation can be achieved through good training.

BACKGROUND

Like each of the previous trends in computing, EUC has grown quickly after entering the scene, seemingly without warning. Now, interest in this phenomenon is booming. It is viewed as a panacea for the huge backlog of requests to information systems (IS) departments for systems development (Alloway & Quillard, 1983). The growth of EUC has been on such a grand scale that some companies have already allocated up to 50% of their computing resource to end users (Rockart & Flannery, 1983). This figure is predicted to rise to 75% for most companies by 1990 (Benjamin, 1982).

The growing number of managers and professionals who are directly using computers, more specifically end-user tools, for the first time (Rockart & Flannery, 1983) is creating a demand for effective educational programs. Although IS departments are providing opportunities for end-user training, it appears that this training is not always successful. Stories of personal computers sitting on employees' desks, not even plugged in, are commonplace in the trade press. Moreover, there are a number of documented cases and, probably numerous undocumented ones, where EUC developed systems have generated erroneous results, causing significant negative impacts on organizations (Davis, 1984).

It is indeed evident that more effective EUC training is needed. In fact, IS managers have identified EUC training as an important area for management and for research (Hartog & Herbert, 1986; Dickson, Leitheiser, Wetherbe, & Nechis, 1984). As noted above, learning difficulties can have serious practical impacts on organizations. These difficulties can be very costly if users can use the computer only when given individual tutorial help. Neither the practitioner nor the research literature has provided much guidance to trainers. This can be attributed to at least three factors.

Firstly, the rapid growth phenomenon itself has made it difficult for researchers to keep up. Previous research on learning to use computers and software focused on procedural oriented languages such as BASIC, FORTRAN, and COBOL, but the software used in EUC is typically nonprocedural, like the fourth-generation languages (4GLs) such as IFPS, FOCUS, and LOTUS 1-2-3.

Secondly, the vendors of 4GLs claim that their products are easy to learn and use. Exploratory research and our experience indicates otherwise. Mack, Lewis, and Carroll (1983) found that learning to use a text processing system can be difficult, time consuming and frustrating for novice users.

Other end-user software such as database and modeling languages, which can be used to model business problems, may be more difficult to learn because of their problem-solving component. During numerous semesters of teaching modeling languages to MBA students, it has become evident to us that students cannot readily grasp the 4GL concepts (Olfman, Sein, & Bostrom, 1986). Although some research has been directed toward how to make EUC tools easier to learn, the issue of motivating students to continue to learn and use these tools has been virtually ignored. In EUC training, especially for novices, initially focusing on the development of appropriate motivational levels may be more important than knowledge acquisition. Research on learning to use computers seems to have lost sight of the research findings that indicate that learning is a function of ability and motivation (see Wlodkowski, 1982 for a review).

The point we want to stress is that no one has stopped to map out a framework of the process involved in learning EUC tools. Our primary goal in this paper is to accomplish this mapping. By doing so, the key variables and interrelationships between these variables can be defined. This will provide a basis for specifying key research areas that need to be addressed in order to develop guidelines for effective EUC training.

The next section of this paper describes an integrated frame of reference for predicting learning outcomes are identified and discussed.

In the last section of this paper, we utilize the proposed framework to discuss important research issues. These issues are directly related to two key questions regarding the design of instruction: How can we make the learning of EUC tools easy? and, How can we motivate end users to use these tools?

A FRAMEWORK OF THE TRAINING/LEARNING PROCESS

Overview

Generally speaking, the end user is one who does not rely directly on the IS department in order to use the computer on the job. In the broadest terms, the end user will utilize computer tools for decision support. This use can range from queries of corporate databases to development and maintenance of systems. The framework presented in this section is specifically geared to discuss the inputs, processes, and outcomes associated with training end users to utilize computer systems and software on the job.

Figure 1 presents a systems view of learning to use a computer software package. The first step is the training process. The inputs to this process are the cognitive characteristics of the trainee, the system/ software to be learned, and the training environment. The outputs of the process are changes in the characteristics of the trainee. The training process includes exposure to the material to be learned and the training environment. The outputs of the process are changes in the character- istics of the trainee. The training process includes exposure to the material to be learned, and exercises to supplement this exposure.

Second and subsequent steps are termed problem-solving processes. They occur if the trainee chooses to apply the new skills on the job. The inputs are the trained user and a specific task that can be supported using the system/software. This set of factors will produce new levels of skill for the user and will also create task-related results. The problem- solving process is repeated as relevant tasks are introduced into the user's world. The focus of this paper is on the first step of the framework, that is, the training process. The following sections describe each of the inputs to the training process and expected outputs from it. Table 1 lists the variables that are described in each of the input and output categories.

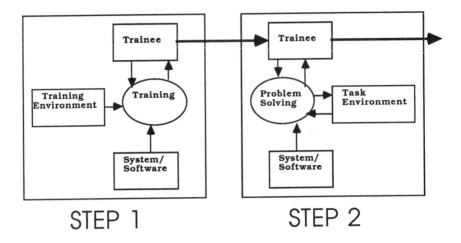

Figure 1. Learning/Using software

INDIVIDUAL/TRAINEE CHARACTERISTICS

What the Trainee Gains From Training

The framework proposed here defines the output of a training process in terms of two outcomes: (a) the trainee acquires a basic understanding of the system defined as an initial accurate mental model of the system, and (b) the trainee leaves with a high motivation to use the system.

It is essential that the trainee has an understanding of the system to be able to use it. However, he or she will use it only if highly motivated to do so. In using the system on the job, the trainee (now a novice user) will learn more about the system. The more the user learns about the system, the more motivated he or she will be to continue to use it. This continuous cycle of learning through using, attributable to high motivation, will result in an end user who can employ the system efficiently and accurately. Thus, the two outcomes of the training process identified by our framework are interrelated. To learn through using the system on the job, the novice user will require support and assistance from other users of his or her organization, as well as the organization itself. The social environment of system use can have a strong influence on the success of the training/learning process (Sein, Olfman, & Bostrom, 1987).

Understanding/Mental Model

A key objective of any training process is to ensure that at the end of the training session, the trainee understands the system well enough to be

Table 1. Trainee Characteristics

◊ MENTAL MODEL OF SYSTEM: M(t)
- Declarative
- Procedural

◊ MOTIVATION TO LEARN/USE SYSTEM
- Enjoyment of using
- Task involvement
- Ease of use
- Usefulness
- Overall attitude

◊ COGNITIVE TRAITS
- Learning style
- Spatial vs. verbal
- Procedurality

◊ MOTIVATIONAL TRAITS
- Self-concept
- Need for knowledge

◊ TASK DOMAIN KNOWLEDGE

◊ OTHER FACTORS

TRAINING ENVIRONMENT

◊ PHYSICAL FACTORS

◊ METHODS
- Conceptual Models: C(t)
- Motivational Planning

SYSTEM/SOFTWARE (t)

◊ EASE OF USE

◊ TYPE OF INTERFACE (e.g., mouse)

◊ TYPE OF LANGUAGE (e.g., 4GL, direct manipulation)

Table 1. Trainee Characteristics

able to use it. But what do we mean by "understanding" the system? Researchers in the area of human-computer interaction have used the concept of mental models to answer this question. Also termed as users' conceptual models (UCM) (Young, 1983; Moran, 1981; Foley, 1980) these are mental or conceptual representations of the system with which the use is interacting. Mental models have been variously defined as a cognitive mechanism (Borgman, 1984), a set of basic concepts (Foley, 1980), the user's knowledge and/or beliefs (Bennett, 1984), and an essential core of knowledge (Owen, 1986).

"Understanding" of the system implies a complete and accurate mental model of the system to be learned. The role of mental models is to facilitate an understanding of how the system works. They aid the user in making inferences about the system (Borgman, 1984), reasoning about it (Foley, 1980; Bennett, 1984; Owen, 1986) and guiding his/her actions (Young, 1983). Although there is general agreement in the literature on the importance of mental models in human-computer interaction, opinion is divided on whether or not users build mental models spontaneously. Moran (1981) feels that, unless explicitly trained, users will not do so. Norman (1981) and Rumelhart and Norman (1981) argue that they will, although the models are apt to be wrong. Nickerson (1981) and Bayman and Mayer (1984) maintain that hands-on experience alone may not produce "useful" mental models.

If anything, the latter views are more alarming. Incorrect models contribute negatively to the interaction process which in turn leads to errors and frustrations (Bayman & Mayer, 1983). Owen (1986) argues that due to the complex nature of the computing domain, acquiring mental models is very difficult for new users. They face a "bootstrapping problem," which means that they must first be taught the primitives of the system. In other words, to help novice users induce mental models, they must be provided with an aid which will convey the basic concepts of the system. Conceptual models of the system to be learned act as such aids and therefore form an important ingredient of training method. They are discussed in detail later in this paper.

Motivation to Learn/Use

An end user typically does not hold a job where the primary function involves continuous use of the computer. A study of EUC usage at IBM's Harrison, NY site found that end users accessed available software for about 90 min per work day (Kublanow, Durand, & Floyd, 1985). One of the questions addressed by this study was: "What motivates managers and business professionals to use office systems [OS]?" (p. 2). It was recognized by the researchers that end users often have a choice of whether or not to use the computer and its associated software. The study concluded that "... use of OS is driven by recognition of applications directly related to the user's work habits." (p. 12).

The relationships uncovered by Kublanow and his colleagues indicate that system/software use is a function of an individual's attitude toward using the software. Davis (1985) used Fishbein and Ajzen's (1975) theory of reasoned action to formulate a conceptual framework for this relationship which he called the technology acceptance model (TAM). In the model (see Figure 2a), he proposes that design features of a software package are reflected in an individual's motivation to use the software, which is subsequently reflected in actual system use. Figure 2b places motivation to use in the context of the training/learning framework. In this view, the system/software and the training environment are inputs to a training process that can produce a motivated user.

To measure the motivation to use construct, Davis (1985) developed a set of scales designed to capture a user's perceived usefulness, perceived ease of use, enjoyment of using, and task importance. An overall scale, termed the attitude toward using, is also included in the measurement model. Davis's model can serve as a valuable tool for assessing the outcome of end-user training. As will be discussed in following sections, the motivational traits of the trainee and the design of the training environment are posited to contribute to the trainee's motivation to learn and use a software package.

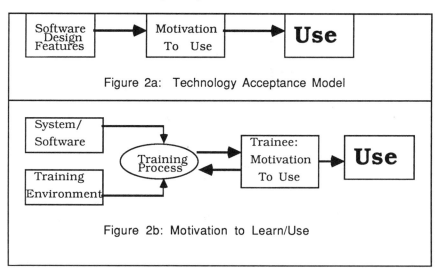

Figure 2a: Technology Acceptance Model

Figure 2b: Motivation to Learn/Use

Figure 2.

What the Trainee Brings to Training

A rich body of literature exists in educational psychology regarding the need to tailor instructional methods to individual aptitudes. Termed Aptitude-Treatment Interaction (ATI), this tradition aims at identifying the relevant aptitudes based on which the instructional materials and methods should be designed. The rationale behind this tradition is articulated succinctly by Pintrich, Cross, Kozma, and McKeachie (1986): "... what the learner brings to the instruction situation in prior knowledge and cognitive skills is of crucial importance" (p. 613). Relevant factors that can be considered as inputs to the training process are cognitive in nature. However, as motivation to use the system is considered a key outcome of training, it is important to know the trainee's sources of motivation, that is, how an individual is motivated. Motivational traits are therefore treated separately from cognitive traits and preferences.

Trainees bring their task-domain knowledge to the training process. They also bring in their referent experiences. These may include any prior interaction with a software package that may be perceived by the trainee to be very similar to the one he or she is being trained on. In terms of the framework, the trainee with prior experience will have an initial mental model of the system prior to entering the training process. This is unlikely to be true for novice users.

Cognitive Traits

Learner cognitive traits can be classified into two types: (a) cognitive style which refers to individual preferences and (b) abilities which refer to basic mental aptitudes. Over the years, researchers in IS have studied a number of cognitive style variables such as dogmatism, risk-taking propensity, field dependency and Myers-Briggs type. Yet, although individual difference variables have consistently accounted for much more of the variance in data than any experimental manipulation (Pennington, 1982; Shiel, 1981), hardly anyone of the cognitive style factors has by itself emerged as a consistent predictor of effective decision-making performance.

A possible explanation for the lack of success of this approach is that none of the studies sought to explain why those factors should be important (Huber, 1983; Taylor & Benbasat, 1980). This can be attributed to the fact that cognitive psychologists have treated these individual differences as "random variance" or noise (Borgman, 1984). Consequently, no theoretical basis exists for examining these variables beyond that they are intuitively appealing.

A cognitive style variable that could influence learning of software is learning style (Kolb, 1971; 1976; 1983). The instrument that measures this construct Kolb's Learning Style Inventory (KLSI) is based on Kolb's experiential theory of learning (Kolb, 1971; Kolb & Fry, 1975). This theory proposes that learning can be modeled as recycling through four modes from concrete experience (CE) to reflective observation (RO) to abstract conceptualization (AC) to active experimentation (AE). Learning takes place as individuals pass through each stage of these cycles, although learners also have preference for a particular stage. By combining the preferences of abstract versus concrete and active versus reflective, the following four learning styles are formed:

1. Converger   AE and AC
2. Accommodator   AE and CE
3. Diverger   RO and CE
4. Assimilator   RO and AC

KLSI has been applied to analyze and describe the learning process in research and development teams (Carlsson, Keane & Martin, 1976), managerial problem solving (Grochow, 1973) and to assess person-job interaction (Sims, 1983). Sein (1987), in his studies of novice learning of modeling language and electronic mail, found that subjects who are convergers performed better in learning tasks than subjects with other learning styles. He also found that those with an active mode of learning performed better than reflective mode learners and that abstract mode learners performed better than concrete learners.

An attempt to define basic ability or aptitude is fraught with philosophical issues. Recent researchers have adopted the information-processing approach which considers aptitude to be a dynamic construct defined in terms of an individual's ability to solve problems (Pintrich et al., 1986). A vast amount of research aimed at identifying dimensions of ability has been generated. Perhaps the grandest scheme is Guilford's 'structure of intellect' concept which proposes that ability or intelligence is composed of 150 factors (Guilford, 1967; 1972; 1982; Guilford & Hoepner, 1971). A host of mental-aptitude constructs have been examined in a learning environment by numerous researchers. Only a handful have been shown to be consistent predictors of learning or problem solving proficiency.

Yet, if learning is viewed as creative problem solving (Polya, 1957; Wertheimer, 1959/1964), those abilities that have been shown to influence problem-solving proficiency could also predict achievement of learning outcomes. An aptitude variable that has been widely examined in different learning and problem solving contexts is visual or spatial ability. Based on Paivio's dual-mode model of memory (Paivio, 1969, 1971, 1974), this stream of research proposes that individuals have varying degrees of visual ability and preference for a visual over verbal mode of processing information. High visual ability has been related with successful solving of physics problems (Larkin, 1980), knowledge acquisition from maps (Thorndyke & Stasz, 1980), efficient decision making (Weissinger-Baylon, R., Hughes, Adams, & Weissinger-Baylon, A., 1980) and analogical problem solving (Pellegrino, 1984). In the area of human-computer interaction, Sein (1987) found that subjects of high visual ability performed better in learning and using a modeling language (IFPS). However, Egan, Bowers, & Gomez (1982) found that visual ability had no bearing on successful use of text editors. One possible reason for these mixed findings could be the use of different instruments to measure visual ability.

We conclude that cognitive factors may not prove to be predictors of learning by themselves. However, in conjunction with such factors as training methods used and the mode of conceptual model provided, they are likely to influence learning. Important variables identified in this section were visual or spatial ability and learning style. Other variables that can be linked to learning software, such as procedurality (Shiel, 1981) and field dependency (Witkin, 1964), also need to be investigated.

Motivation Traits

Educational researchers utilize a number of motivational theories to explain and understand the role of motivation in learning (Keller, 1983; Wlodkowski, 1982; 1985). The theoretical perspective is that each student has a potential for being motivated to learn. This potential, which can be defined across two broad dimensions called self-concept and need for achievement, is an individual trait that can influence success in learning (Wlodkowski, 1982; Pintrich et al., 1986). Researchers have shown that motivating potentials can be installed, or that existing potentials can be tapped to increase learning (Wlodkowski, 1982).

Self-concept implies that "people strive to behave in a manner consistent with a view of themselves" (Wlodkowski, 1982, p. 15). The self-concept characteristic is derived from attributional models of motivation. Some of the more popular models have proposed the concepts of learned helplessness, self-efficacy, and self-worth (Pintrich et al., 1986). In general, each model proposes that students can learn if they have the requisite ability and if they recognize that failure is not contingent on their ability and effort.

Need for achievement "is the functional display of a concern for excellence in work that the individual values" (Wlodkowski, 1982, p. 18). Derived from expectancy-value models of motivation, it implies that learning can be enhanced by relating the material to be learned to relevant criteria important to the trainee. The expectancy-value model is compatible with the concepts provided by attributional models, but "stresses the relationship between goals, expectancies, values, and performance" (Pintrich et al., 1986, p. 616).

Although it is evident that motivational traits influence learning, they have not been examined by researchers in software training. There is a research history in the attitudes literature that focuses on the moderation of attitude changes depending on individual differences (Eagly, 1981). Although this research has been inconclusive in its specific findings, it appears that motivational traits do play a role in predicting learning outcomes.

Other Traits

In addition to cognitive and motivational traits, an individual's previous experiences and knowledge play a role in learning. Empirical studies have found that mathematical background and grade point average (GPA) are significant predictors of success in computer science course work (Butcher & Muth, 1985). The level of understanding gained by trainees learning modeling languages has been shown to be directly related to previous computer experience (Olfman, 1987; Sears, 1986). An explanation may lie in Rosson's (1984) finding that, in a learning situation, subjects with considerable prior experience with software displayed a different pattern of computer use compared to those with little or no experience. This variance in experience could explain varying achievement of learning outcome.

In summary, we reiterate that different trainees bring different cognitive and motivational traits as well as varying degrees of referent experiences. These are of crucial importance in EUC training.

THE TRAINING ENVIRONMENT

The training environment can be viewed from two perspectives. Physical aspects refer to such structural factors as the setting of the training, physical entities involved, and the ambience. Methods refer to strategies that are employed in instructing the learners.

Physical environment design is important, but it will depend on how instructional methods are embedded in the design. The chances of success for a trainee will be greatly reduced if the design does not pay attention to outcomes of the training process other than those of providing a stimulating physical environment. It is for this reason that our subsequent discussion on key research issues focuses on the design of training methods.

Methods of Training

The strategies that need to be adopted in training session can be tied to the two outcomes of training. Conceptual models provide the learner with a basis for forming accurate, initial mental models. Motivational planning and management aims at motivating the learner to use the system and to interact in a meaningful context to further learn about the system.

Conceptual Models

Conceptual models are depictions of the system, developed by an instructor, to convey basic concepts of the system to novice users. They serve users as 'advance organizers' and provide 'ideational scaffolding' (Ausubel, 1968) or anchoring structures and, thus, a basis for forming mental models. Mayer and Bromage (1979) demonstrated that different models produce qualitatively different learning outcomes. Their research draws upon the advance organizer tradition (Ausubel, 1968) which has shown that, for technically complex learning material and for subjects of lower ability as well as less experienced subjects, advance organizers facilitated learning of meaningful concepts about the material to be learned. In the Mayer and Bromage study, the outcomes were reflected in a better performance in creative problem-solving tasks about the to-be-learned system.

Conceptual models can be classified as analogical and abstract. Analogical models represent the target system in terms of another system with which the trainee is familiar. For example, a computer filing system is often described as analogous to an office filing cabinet. Abstract models are synthetic or graphical depictions of the system. Mathematical relations or schematic diagrams are good examples of abstract models.

Conceptual models can also be viewed from a different perspective. di Sessa (1986) identifies three distinct types of models that people use in understanding a computational system in general and a programming language in particular. Structural models refer to the structure of the system and are universal in nature. Functional models are context specific and provide an understanding of the language on the basis of how a command works. Distributed models are confederations of models, that is, an understanding of the language is achieved through multiple partial explanations. DiSessa proposes that each type should be simultaneously cultivated in a learner. The two taxonomies are complementary. Abstract models are basically structural models while analogical models can be both structural and functional.

Motivation Planning/Management

We agree with researchers in the field of instructional design who propose that motivation should be a planned component of the learning environment (Wlodkowski, 1985; Keller, 1983). They propose that tapping into an integrating the findings from motivational research is a necessary part of the training design process. Wlodkowski proposed a time continuum model (TCM) of motivation that shows how motivation can be addressed during various phases of the adult learning process. Keller proposed a motivational approach to instructional design that addresses factors related to the motivation potential of the trainee. The Keller factors that tap into the self-concept dimension of motivation are related to developing confidence in success (expectancy) and managing intrinsic and extrinsic reinforcement (satisfaction). Those factors that tap into the need for achievement dimension are related to connecting instruction to important needs and motive (relevance) and arousing and sustaining curiosity and attention (interest). Figure 3 provides an example of how a high level of motivation can be instilled in a trainee. Prior to, and at the outset of, training, the trainee's negative feelings about using computers (expectancy) are balanced by the need to retain a job (relevance). During training, interest and relevance can be addressed by having the trainee bring his or her own problems to work with; and expectancy can be enhanced through building confidence. After training, satisfaction with the software is important in developing a competent user.

Wlodkowski (1985) and Keller (1983) both provide a number of prescriptive rules for managing motivation during instruction. Similar rules have been applied by Massachusetts Training Associates to produce effective end-user training at Honeywell (Sharrow, Weaver, & Kilduff, 1985). These prescriptions for motivation management need to be tested in a research context. Our thesis is that motivation management can lead to highly motivated trainees: those who will use the target software.

Physical Aspects

Bikson and Gutek (1983) identified three types of instructional settings for end-user software training: group class, one-on-one, and self-

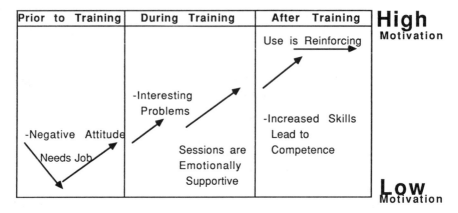

Figure 3. Positive motivation dynamic

instruction. In their survey, they found that over 90% of the trainees surveyed believed that they needed to be trained by instructors and would prefer this over self-instruction. The cost of providing this service is high. Consequently, a large amount of research has been devoted to developing structured, self-instruction materials in the hope that these will be equal to or better than training provided by instructors (e.g., Carroll, 1984 [training manuals]; Anderson, Boyle, & Reiser, 1985 [intelligent computer aided instruction ICAI]).

The design of the physical environment, taken from a technological standpoint, does contribute to the motivation to learn (Wlodkowski, 1982). Technologies such as educational games, audio/video cassettes, programmed instruction, and computer aided instruction (CAI) are possible design alternatives aimed at enhancing a trainee's self-concept. Additional supporting features in software training include training manuals, postclassroom support, and opportunities for advanced learning (Bikson & Gutek, 1983). Another important variable is the time frame devoted to training. In the Bikson and Gutek survey, most respondents believed that more training time was necessary.

THE SYSTEM TO BE LEARNED

A key characteristic of the system that can impact the training outcomes of knowledge and motivation is ease of use (Reisner, 1981). The contention is that a system that is easy to use will also be easy to learn and consequently the likelihood will be greater that the learner's initial mental model will be accurate (Jagodzinski, 1983). At the same time, novice learners will be able to use the system to solve meaningful problems with a minimum amount of training. This will keep them motivated to learn more about the system.

A second issue regarding the system is its applicability in the learner's task domain. For instance, languages of different generations may have different applicability. Modeling languages like Interactive Financial Planning System (IFPS), which is a fourth generation language (4GL), are appropriate for decision support systems (DSS) applications and are more likely to be relevant to an end-user training environment. Conceptual models that stress functionality should be developed for such languages (Riley, 1986).

Training end users in a software language implies more than merely conveying the semantics and the syntax of the language. A language is embedded in a hierarchy of other systems. It works under a particular operating system (OS), which is installed on a particular computer, which may in turn be a part of a large network of machines. Even after weaving through the intricacies of these layers, the learner still has to contend with the architecture or structure of the language before he or she can begin to learn the commands of the language. This is particularly true about 4GLs.

It is essential that the learner get an adequate mental model of the hardware environment and the language architecture in addition to a mental model of the language he or she is learning. Conceptual models must be provided for all the different layers of the system. Icon-based systems and those that are generally classified as direct manipulation languages (DML) (Shneiderman, 1983) shield much of the complexities of the command syntax from the user. They present the user with a visual depiction of the conceptual model of the system. By constantly reenforcing the conceptual model, these systems facilitate the constant enrichment of the user's mental model.

SUMMARY

In this section, we proposed a framework for the training/learning process of an EUC tool. The outcomes of the training were defined as (a) an accurate initial mental model of the software and (b) motivation to use the software.

Training-method variables necessary to achieve these objectives were identified and discussed. Specifically, conceptual models of the software/system to be learned were described as aids in helping trainees form mental models. Motivational planning and management were discussed with the aim of achieving the second objective, that is, motivation to use the system. Trainee characteristics, such as cognitive and motivational traits, ability, and experience were described as influencing factors in attaining the training outcomes both by themselves but, more importantly, through interaction with the training methods.

RESEARCH ISSUES IN END-USER SOFTWARE TRAINING

In developing the training framework described in previous sections, we have identified four key research areas: (a) conceptual models and mental models, (b) training design and motivation to learn/use, (c) system interface, and (d) process of learning.

This section discusses relevant issues in each of these areas. Though cognitive and motivational traits are an integral part of the framework, we believe that studying their impact on the learning outcomes in isolation adds little to our understanding of effective training processes. Drawing upon the attitude/trait interaction (ATI) paradigm from educational psychology, we propose that individual traits can be meaningfully studied only in the context of their interaction with the training environment factors. Accordingly, these variables are discussed within the four areas identified above.

We would, however, like to reemphasize the importance of individual differences in the learning process. This is an area that is "... ripe for empirical investigation" (Carroll & McKendree, 1987, p. 21), and there is a pressing need for research.

CONCEPTUAL MODELS AND MENTAL MODELS

In providing a conceptual framework for the study of mental models, Norman (1983) observes that four entities need to be considered: target system t, conceptual model C(t), mental model M(t) and scientists' conceptualization of mental models C(M(t)). The first three concepts have been described elsewhere in the paper. The fourth, C(M(t)), is the model of the mental models constructed by researchers. The most prominent example of C(M(t)) is the keystroke model for text editors proposed by Card, Moran, & Newell (1982).

Norman's (1983) framework does not provide any role for individual difference variables in the interaction process, nor does it consider the user's prior referent experiences. Jagodzinski (1983) proposes a model of the relationships between the "real world," the computer system, and the user. Though the focus of his model is the design process, it does take into account the user's prior computer experiences and his or her internal representation of the "real world." He reasons that the user will attempt to form an initial mental model of the system by analogically mapping it to his or her pasteferent experiences. For instance, Douglas and Moran (1982) observed that in learning to use a text editor, novices often draw analogies from typewriters.

We have synthesized a cognitive view of the mental model formation process by combining elements of the two frameworks described above and incorporating individual difference factors. This model (Figure 4), firmly embedded in the training framework, identifies a key research issue: How can users be aided in forming mental models? Or, to quote Owen (1986), we need to ".. [understand] more about conditions which foster the development of robust naive theories." (p. 192). The consensus among researchers of the mental model area is that users should be provided with a conceptual model that will help them build mental models (Moran, 1981; Norman, 1981; Young, 1981; Jagodzinski, 1983). What is yet to be resolved is which type of conceptual model should be provided to new users.

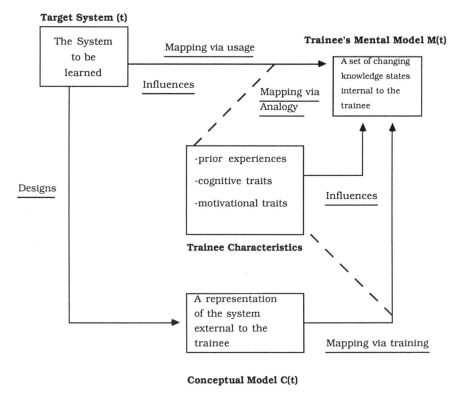

Figure 4. Mental model formulation process

The form of conceptual model used in past research has been almost exclusively analogical. For example, Borgman (1984) trained novice users of an information-retrieval system by representing the computerized system in terms of a card catalogue. She found that their performance (speed and accuracy of retrieval) was slightly better than that of a control group not trained with a model. In training novice users of an electronic mail system, Galletta (1984) also used an analogical model (the system is like a hotel telephone system). He found that the experimental group performed marginally better than the control group that was not trained with a model. A similar pattern of results was obtained by Mayer (1979) in several studies.

It is evident that, although there are theoretical grounds for the efficacy of conceptual models in aiding novice users form mental models, the empirical support has been weak. One reason for this could be the influence of individual difference variables, such as visual ability. A more crucial explanation for the weak findings lies in the shortcomings of analogical models. As Halasz and Moran (1982) pointed out, no ready analogy exists for computing systems. Any analogy used will be inadequate to describe the target system. At some point the analogical mapping breaks down. Yet, users continue to force the mapping from the analogy to the target system leading to erroneous conclusions and consequently, to errors. Halasz and Moran (1982) have recommended using abstract conceptual models instead. Halasz (1975) trained novice users of calculators with an abstract model in the form of a schematic diagram. He found that they performed better than control-group subjects who were not trained with a conceptual model.

The debate between proponents of analogical and abstract models gives rise to the following questions: (a) Are abstract models superior to analogical ones in helping users build mental models? (b) If they are indeed superior, does this advantage exist for different types of systems, tasks, and problems? (c) What roles do individual differences play in the mental model formulation process? These issues were investigated by Sein (1987). In two studies (one using a modeling language IFPS and the other using electronic mail), he trained subjects with abstract and analogical models. Subjects were then measured on comprehension and performance on simple and complex tasks. His findings indicate that abstract models resulted in more flexible and accurate mental models. This was reflected through better performance in complex tasks by subjects trained with the abstract model. He also found that, although high visual subjects performed better than low visual subjects, low visuals were particularly hampered by the abstract model. In contrast, low visuals performed as well as high visuals when provided with the analogical model.

These results are encouraging. But more research is needed before a theory of conceptual models can be formulated or even more general guidelines for training can be developed. The studies need to be extended to other systems, and other individual difference variables need to be examined.

None of the definitions of mental models cited elsewhere in this paper provides an explicit description of a mental model. Bennett (1984) discussed the concept of mental models under five perspectives formal grammar, mental imagery, analogical reasoning, problem space, and schemata. He concluded that it is very difficult to formulate a detailed depiction of mental models. Consequently, good examples of C(M(t)) have been rare.

A fruitful research area is exploring ways to construct C(M(t))s. A possible approach is to synthesize a preliminary C(M(t)) of the system from verbal protocols of expert users of the system. These models can then be validated through verbal protocols gathered from both expert and novice users. Vessey (1985) successfully adopted this approach to build a model of expert debugging of computer programs. Modeling systems such as EMPRINT (Cameron-Bandler, Gordon, & Lebeau, 1985) and ACT* (Anderson, 1983) can provide generalized C(M(t))s that can be used to extract knowledge from users to build specific C(M(t))s for a software environment. Anderson et al. (1985) used ACT* to develop a C(M(t)) of novice LISP users. The applicability of these tools for modeling 4GLs needs to be evaluated.

TRAINING DESIGN AND MOTIVATION TO LEARN/USE

Neither the role of motivation planning nor the measurement of motivation to learn and use software has been directly addressed in the end-user training research literature. The success story reported by Sharrow et al. (1985) about building positive motivation in learners provides support for this approach. A number of research efforts at IBM implicitly address the motivational perspective in training (Carroll, 1984). In designing training materials for word-processing packages, the IBM researchers found that learning can be enhanced by minimizing problems that trainees encounter with the software. Having trainees work with meaningful problems during training was found to be one way of alleviating these problems.

Traditionally, the majority of software training has been aimed at "product features and mechanics" (Karten, 1986, p. 10). The goal of this type of training is to send the trainee away with a knowledge of what the software does. Karten calls this the "I know how it works, but I don't know how to use it syndrome" (p. 10). In terms of the outcomes of training postulated in the research framework, conventional training can be thought of as focusing on the development of software understanding. Training that avoids the issue of demonstrating how to use software on the job is essentially ignoring the fact that enhancing the motivational outcome is also important. The general question that arises is: Can software training be designed to enhance the motivation-to-use outcome as well as the understanding outcome? An answer to this question may be found through the utilization of a concept called personal relevance in software training design. This concept is especially important in the learning process and in the formation and change of attitudes (Ross, McCormick, & Krisak, 1986; Petty & Cacioppo, 1981). The underlying premise is that individuals build their knowledge structures and attitudes on existing scaffolding. Because this scaffolding is highly individualistic, it is developed through experience. A learning environment that is personally relevant can be expected to enhance both training outcomes. Specifically, it can be expected that a personally relevant training session will make it easier to integrate new knowledge and to develop a link between the usefulness of the software and its application to the job.

Olfman (1987) compared a conventional training design (referred to as construct-based training) with a personally relevant training design (referred to as applications-based training) by training groups of users and then measuring their understanding and motivation to use the software. Initial findings indicate that the applications-based training provides a higher level of motivation for novice users.

One training design may not consistently outperform another, due to the role of individual differences and aptitude-training interaction. Therefore a second general question that needs to be examined is What role do individual differences play in affecting the motivation to use outcome of software training? Specific individual difference variables that may impact this outcome are learning style and attitude toward computers.

Hybrids of construct-based and applications-based training are also possible. For example, one method uses construct-based training to teach basic capabilities and syntax, then switches to applications-based training to demonstrate advanced capabilities. The applications-based session(s) often occur at a later date from the initial construct-based training. An alternative hybrid method is that of introducing the software through applications-based training and then switching to a construct-based mode to reinforce the breadth of the language. Olfman

(1987) has taken a first step in the study of the construct-based and applications-based methods in their pure forms.

A third question in the area of motivation management and planning that should be addressed is What roles do components of the training (i.e., overview, presentation materials, exercises, and documentation) play in an individual's subsequent use of the software? Research should be directed toward finding out if one or more of the components is critical to successful training. It may be that software training design can also be focused on enhancing specific aspects. Research reported by Carroll (1984) has been directed toward learning about the role of documentation in training, whereas Davis (1985) has done some preliminary work on assessing the role of videotaped demonstrations. This type of research is most appropriate in a classroom or laboratory setting, where trainees can be easily observed and interviewed. These findings will also contribute to our understanding of the components that can be utilized in creating more effective self-instructional training materials.

THE SYSTEM AND LEARNING

Jagodzinski (1983) argues that the design of a system interface can influence the mental model of a user. The terminal displays and the dialogue should incorporate the conceptual model of the system. Bennett (1984) trained users with different mental models.

Two research areas can be identified. The first, suggested by Jagodzinski (1983), is developing a theoretical basis for the system interface design to convey successfully the conceptual model to the user. The principal of direct manipulation (Shneiderman, 1983) is based on this transparency concept. In this environment, users can acquire a useful mental model of the system that is based primarily on system functions. The ability of a learner to use the system effectively, with a minimum of training, may lead to continuous high motivation. The popularity of icon-based systems can be attributed to this feature. The motivational aspect of direct-manipulation systems is an interesting research question. A more basic issue that needs to be examined is the comparison of direct versus indirect manipulation interfaces. Hutchins, Hollan, and Norman (1985) discuss the relative merits of both types and provide a useful framework for investigation. Research linking system interface with training methods (e.g., conceptual models) is also needed.

A closely related area is the design of programming languages that make their 'flow of control' transparent to the user. Examples of such languages are SOLO (Eisenstadt, 1983) and Graphical database Query Language (GQL) which allows users to specify boolean relations by simply pointing on Venn diagrams (Michard, 1982). As is the case with icon-based systems, these languages make the inherent conceptual model of the system explicit to the user and thus reinforce his or her mental model.

The second research area is concerned with tailoring the system to train novices effectively. The minimalist training concept proposes that learners should be provided with just enough training materials to get them started (Carroll, 1984). In the context of the training framework, this implies that they initially need a minimal mental model. Once they are comfortable with the system, continuous interaction attributable to high motivation will lead to a richer mental model. Carroll and Carrithers (1984) tailored a system so that novice users initially interacted with only a very fundamental subset of the system. Termed 'training wheel', this approach resulted in less frustration and consequently provided a more efficacious training strategy.

THE PROCESS OF LEARNING

The research areas identified in earlier sections address the issue of achieving the desired training outcomes of equipping learners with meaningful mental models and providing them with motivation to use the system. A crucial related issue is how these training inputs are assimilated by the learners. The manner in which the initial mental model of a learner matures into a more cogent, meaningful, and richer form and concurrently how this evolutionary process drives the motivation level of the learner will prove to be a very fruitful area of research.

Perhaps the best way to investigate the learning and use behavior of a system, especially from a cognitive perspective, is a longitudinal study that would track users' behavior over a period of time. Employing this approach, Gilfoil (1982) found that, as novice users of a text editor gain experience, they tend to make fewer and fewer semantic errors, while syntactic error rate remains almost constant. This indicates that the more experienced user's mental model contains higher level constructs of the system. Gilfoil's finding is in accord with those of several research studies about experts' knowledge (Adelson, 1981; Reitman & Reuter, 1980) which have consistently shown that experts organize their knowledge around higher level functional grouping of commands. Several other studies have looked at the typical errors made by novice learners of text editors (Mack et al., 1983; Douglas & Moran, 1982; Carroll, Mack, Lewis, Grischkowsky, & Robertson, 1985). Insights gained in the learning process can prove invaluable in designing training materials. This approach was adopted by Thorndyke and Stasz (1980) in their study of how people acquire map reading knowledge.

OTHER RESEARCH ISSUES

Earlier in the paper, we described the importance of the physical aspects of training. Although we suggested that these aspects are subordinate to the methods of training (conceptual models and motivational planning), research needs to be carried out on how they affect training outcomes.

Of more importance is the social environment of system use. In the context of our framework, factors relating to this issue are more relevant to the second and subsequent steps, that is, problem-solving stage. However, because we emphasize the role of "discovery" mode of learning (i.e., learning through use) in cultivating the link between motivation and knowledge, we would like to mention briefly some of the more crucial elements of the social environment of system use. They are discussed in more detail in Sein et al. (1987).

Brown and Newman (1985) advocated the use of the "larger social environment" to aid understanding of the system. The IS department in the organization can foster interuser communication networks of both a social and a technical nature. Our experience shows that important sources of support for novice users are other colleagues who are more experienced in that particular software. However, in the absence of proper training, novices may become overdependent on these "buddies". Perhaps a greater role can be played by the IS department by providing opportunities and facilities to end users to experiment with the software. They should be able to do so without fear of "crashing" the system on which the software is installed.

Although these notions are intuitively appealing, we have only anecdotal evidence of their effectiveness. More research aimed at providing empirical support for these contentions needs to be conducted.

SUMMARY AND CONCLUSION

In this paper, we have discussed the shortcomings of traditional views of the training process that fail to address adequately its cognitive aspects and almost totally ignore its motivational outcomes. We propose an end-user training framework which identifies two outcomes of training acquiring a mental model of the system and the motivation to use the system. Our framework is based firmly on theories of learner motivation and the current information-processing paradigm in cognitive and educational psychology. The primary thesis of our framework is the belief that learners must be quickly given an adequate base or structure (e.g., conceptual models) to integrate the incoming knowledge, and that their motivation level must be continually managed to achieve the two training outcomes.

We have described the different components of the framework and suggested how they affect other components. Based on these links, we have identified key research areas and reviewed research in the fields of IS cognitive and educational psychology, instructional design, and cognitive science. We have discussed briefly some of the research studies already initiated to investigate the relationships posed in our framework. Conclusions drawn from preliminary analyses of data from these studies argue favorably for utilizing the framework. We recognize that several more studies must be conducted before complete answers to the two major research questions are found: (a) How can we make the learning of EUC tools easy? and (b) How can we motivate end users to learn and use EUC tools? By pointing out several important and interesting research issues in the crucial and neglected area of EUC training, we hope this paper will motivate other researchers.

This Project was supported in part by a grant from the Institute for Research on the Management of Information Systems (IRMIS), School of Business, Indiana University, Bloomington, IN 47405.

REFERENCES

Adelson, B. (1981). Problem solving and the development of abstract categories in programming languages. *Memory and Cognition, 9*, 422–433.

Alloway, R.M., & Quillard, J.A. (1983). User managers' systems needs. *MIS Quarterly, 7*, 27–41.

Anderson, J.R. (1983). *The architecture of cognition*, Cambridge, MA: Harvard University Press.

Anderson, J.R., Farrel, R., & Sauers, R. (1983). Learning to program in LISP. *Cognitive Science, 8*, 87–129.

Anderson, J.R., Boyle, C.F., & Reiser, B.J. (1985). Intelligent tutoring systems. *Science, 228*, 456–462.

Ausubel, D.P. (1968). *Educational psychology: A cognitive view*. New York: Holt, Rinehart & Winston.

Bayman, P., & Mayer, R.E. (1983). Instructional manipulation of user's mental models of electronic calculators. *International Journal of Man-Machine Studies, 20*, 189–199.

Bayman, P., & Mayer, R.E. (1983). A diagnosis of beginning programmers' misconceptions of BASIC programming statements. *Communications of the ACM, 26*, 677–679.

Benjamin, R.I. (1982). Information technology in the 1990's: Long range planning scenario". *MIS Quarterly, 6,* 11–32.

Bennett, K.B. (1984). *The effect of display design on the user's mental model of a perceptual database system.* Unpublished doctoral dissertation, The Catholic University of America, Washington, DC.

Bikson, T.K. & Gutek, B.A. (1983). Training in automated offices: An empirical study of design and methods. In J.I. Rijnsdorp & T.J. Plomp (Eds.), *Training for Tomorrow, Proceedings of IFAC/IFIP 1983 Symposium, XX,* 129–143.

Borgman, C.L. (1984). *The user's mental model of an information retrieval system: Effect on performance.* Unpublished doctoral dissertation, Stanford University, Palo Alto, CA.

Brown, J.S., & Newman, S.E. (1985). Issues in cognitive and social ergonomics: From our house to Bauhaus". *Human-Computer Interaction, 1,* 359–391.

Butcher, D.F., & Muth, W.A. (1985) Predicting performance in an introductory computer science course. *Communications of the ACM, 28,* 263–268.

Cameron-Bandler, L., Gordon, D., & Lebeau, M. (1985). *Know How.* San Rafael, CA: FuturePace, Inc.

Card, S.K., Moran, T.P., & Newell, A. (1982). *The psychology of human-computer interaction,* Hillsdale, NJ: Erlbaum.

Carlsson, B., Keane, P., & Martin, J.B. (1982). R & D organizations as learning systems. , 1 *Sloan Management Review, 17*

Carroll, J.M. (1984). Minimalist training. *Datamation, 30,* 125–136.

Carroll, J.M., & McKendree, J. (1987). Interface design issues for advice-giving expert systems. *Communications of the ACM, 30,* 14–31.

Carroll, J.M., & Carrithers, C. (1984). Training wheels in a user interface. *Communications of the ACM, 27,* 800–806.

Carroll, J.M., Mack, R.L., Lewis, C.H., Grischkowsky, N.L., & Robertson, S.R. (1984). Exploring a word processor. *Human-Computer Interaction, 1,* 283–307.

Cheney, P.H., Mann, R.I. & Amoroso, D.L. (1986). Organizational factors affecting the success of end-user computing. *Journal of MIS, 3,* 65–80.

Davis, G.B. (1984). *Caution: User developed systems can be dangerous to your organization. (MISRC-WP-84–04),* Duluth, MN: University of Minnesota, MIS Research Center.

Davis, F.D., Jr. (1985). *A technology acceptance model for empirically testing new end-user information systems: Theory and results.* Unpublished doctoral dissertation, Massachusetts Institute of Technology, Cambridge.

Dickson, G., Leitheiser, R.L., Wetherbe, J.C., & Nechis, M. (1984). Key Information systems issues for the 1980s. *MIS Quarterly, 8,* 135–159.

diSessa, A.A. (1986). Models of computation. In D.A. Norman & S.W. Draper (Eds.), *User Centered Systems Design,* Hillsdale, NJ: Erlbaum.

Douglas, S.A., & Moran, T.P. (1982). Learning text editor semantics by analogy. *Proceedings of the Conference on Human Factors in Computer Systems,* Gaithersburg, MA, 207–211.

Eagly, A.H. (1981). Recipient characteristics as determinants of responses to persuasion. In R.E. Petty, T.M. Ostrom, & T.C. Brock (Eds.), *Cognitive responses in persuasion,* Hillsdale, NJ: Erlbaum.

Egan, D.E., Bowers, C., & Gomez, L.M. (1982). Learner characteristics that predict success in using a text editor tutorial. *Proceedings of the Conference on Human Factors in Computer Systems,* Gaithersburg, MA, 337–340.

Eisenstadt, M. (1983). A user-friendly software environment for the novice programmer, *Communications of the ACM, 26,* 1058–1064.

Foley, J.D. (1980). Methodology of interaction. In R.A. Guedj (Ed.), *Methodology of Interaction,* Amsterdam: North Holland.

Galletta, D. (1984). *A learner model of information systems: The effects of orientating materials, ability, expectations and experience on performance, usage and attitude.* Unpublished doctoral dissertation, University of Minnesota, Duluth.

Gilfoil, D. (1982). Warming up to computers: A study of cognitive and affective interaction over time. *Proceedings of the Conference on Human Factors in Computer Systems*, Gaithersburg, MA, 245–250.

Grochow, J. (1973). *Cognitive style as a factor in the design of interactive decision-support systems.* Unpublished doctoral dissertation, Massachusetts Institute of Technology, Cambridge.

Guilford, J.P. (1982). Cognitive psychology's ambiguities: Some suggested remedies, *Psychological Review, 89,* 48–59.

Guilford, J.P., & Hoepner, R. (1971). *The analysis of intelligence.* New York: McGraw-Hill.

Guilford, J.P. (1967). *The nature of human intelligence,* New York: McGraw-Hill.

Guilford, J.P. (1972). Thurstone's primary mental abilities and structure-of-intellect abilities, *Psychological Bulletin, 77,* 129–143.

Halasz, F. (1975). *Mental models and problem solving in using calculators.* Unpublished doctoral dissertation, Stanford University, Palo Alto.

Halasz, F., & Moran, T.P. (1982). Analogy considered harmful. *Proceedings of the Conference on Human Factors in Computer Systems,* Gaithersburg, MA, 383–386.

Hartog, C., & Herbert, M. (1986). Opinion survey of MIS managers: Key issues. *MIS Quarterly, 10,* 351–361.

Huber, G. (1983). Cognitive style as a basis for MIS and DSS designs: Much ado about nothing. *Management Science, 29,* 567–579.

Hutchins, E.L., Hollan, J.D., & Norman, D.A. (1985). Direct manipulation interfaces. *Human-Computer Interaction, 1,* 311–338.

Jagodzinski, A.P. (1983). A theoretical basis for the representation of on-line computer systems to naive users. *International Journal of Man-Machine Studies. 18,* 215–252.

Karten, N. (1986). End user demand requires new approach to training. *Data Management,* 11–19.

Keller, J.M. (1983). Motivational Design of Instruction. In C.M. Reigeluth (Ed), *Instructional design theories and models: An overview of their current status,* (pp. 386–434), Hillsdale, NJ: Erlbaum.

Kolb, D.A. (1976). *The learning style inventory: Technical manual.* Boston, MA: McBer and Co.

Kolb, D.A. (1983). *Experiential learning: Experience as the source of learning and development,* Englewood Cliffs, NJ: Prentice-Hall.

Kolb, D.A., & Fry, R. (1975). Toward an applied theory of experiential learning. In G.L. Cooper (Ed.), *Theories of group processes,* New York: John Wiley.

Kublanow, S.M., Durand, D.E., & Floyd, S.W. (1985). *Measurement of office system use.* Boulder, CO: IBM-University of Colorado Joint Study.

Larkin, J.H. (1980). Studying how people think: An application in the science classroom. In R.O. Yager (Ed.), *What research says to the science teacher.* National Science Teachers Association, Washington, DC.

Mack, R.L., Lewis, C.L., & Carroll, J.M. (1983). Learning to use word processors: Problems and prospect. *ACM Transactions on Office Information Systems, 1,* 254–271.

Mayer, R.E. (1979). Can advance organizers influence meaningful learning? *Review of Educational Research, 49,* 371–383.

Mayer, R.E., & Bromage, B.K. (1979). Different recall protocols for technical experts due to advance organizer. *Journal of Educational Psychology, 72,* 209–225.

Michard, A. (1982). Graphical presentation of boolean expression in a database query language: Design notes and an ergonomic evaluation. *Behavior and Information Technology, 1,* 279–288.

Moran, T.P. (1981). An applied psychology of the user. *Computing Surveys, 13,* 1–11.

Nickerson, R.S. (1981). Why interactive computer systems are sometimes not used by those who might benefit from them. *International Journal of Man-Machine Studies, 15,* 469–483.

Norman, D.A. (1981). Problem with unix. *Datamation, 27,* 139–150.

Norman, D.A. (1983). Some observations on mental models. In A.L. Stevens & D. Gentner (Eds.), *Mental models,* Hillsdale, NJ: Erlbaum.

Olfman, L. (1987). *A comparison of construct-based and applications-based training methods for DSS generator software.* Unpublished doctoral dissertation, Indiana University, Bloomington.

Olfman, L., Sein, M., & Bostrom, R.P. (1986). Training for end-user computing: Are basic abilities enough for learning? *Proceedings of the 22nd Annual Computer Personnel Research Conference,* Calgary, AB.

Owen, D. (1986). Naive theories of computation. In D.A. Norman & S.W. Draper (Eds.), *User centered system design,* Hillsdale, NJ: Erlbaum.

Paivio, A. (1969). Mental imagery in associative learning and memory. *Psychological Review, 76,* 241–263.

Paivio, A. (1971). *Imagery and verbal processes,* New York: Holt.

Paivio, A. (1974). Language and knowledge of the world. *Educational Researcher, 3,* 5–12.

Pellegrino, J.W. (1985). Anatomy of analogy, *Psychology Today, 19,* 49–54.

Pennington, N.P. (1982). Cognitive components of expertise in computer programming: A review of literature. (Tech. Rep. 46), Ann Arbor: University of Michigan, *Cognitive Science Technical Report Series.*

Petty, R.E., & Cacioppa, J.T. (1981). Effects of Rhetorical Questions on Persausion A Cognitive Response Analysis, *Journal of Personality and Sociology, 40,* 432–440.

Pintrich, P.R., Cross, D.R., Kozma, R.B., & McKeachie, W.J. (1986). Instructional psychology, *Annual Review of Psychology, 32,* 611–651.

Polya, G. (1957). *How to solve it.* New York: Doubleday.

Reisner, P.E. (1981). Human factors studies of database query languages: A survey and assessment. *Computing Surveys, 13,* 13–31.

Reitman, J.S., & Reuter, H. (1980). Organization revealed by recall order and confirmed by pauses. *Cognitive Psychology, 12,* 559–581.

Riley, M.S. (1986). User understanding. In D.A. Norman & S.W. Draper (Eds.), *User centered system design,* Hillsdale, NJ: Erlbaum.

Rockart, J.F., & Flannery, L.S. (1983). The management of end user computing, *Communications of the ACM, 26,* 776–784.

Ross, S.M., McCormick, D., & Krisak, N. (1986). Adapting the thematic context of mathematical problems to student interests: Individualized versus roup-based strategies, *Journal of Educational Research, 79,* 245–252.

Rosson, M.B. (1984). The role of experience in editing. In B. Shackel (Ed.), *Human-Computer Interaction Interact '84,* (pp. 45–50), Amsterdam: North-Holland.

Rumelhart, D.E., & Norman, D.A. (1981). Analogical processes in learning. In J.R. Anderson (Ed.), *Cognitive skills and their acquisition,* Hillsdale, NJ: Erlbaum.

Sears, J.A. (1986). *Business modeling systems: Comparing learning performance and identifying learning complexity.* Unpublished doctoral dissertation, University of Arizona, Tucson.

Sein, M.K. (1987). *Conceptual models in training novice users of computer systems: Effectiveness of abstract vs. analogical models and influence of Individual Differences.* Unpublished doctoral dissertation, Indiana University, Bloomington.

Sein, M.K., Olfman, L., & Bostrom, R.P. (1987). Training methods for end-user computing: Cognitive, motivational and social issues. *INFOR Special Issue on End-User Computing.*

Sharrow, J., Weaver, V., & Kilduff, K. (1985). Appreciation and confidence: A study in micro training. *Information Center,* 44–47.

Shiel, B.A. (1981). Psychological study of programming. *Computing Surveys, 1,* 02–119.

Shneiderman, B. (1983). Direct manipulation: A step beyond programming languages. *IEEE Computer, 16,* 57–69.

Sims, R.A. (1983). Kolb's experiential theory: A framework for assessing person-job interaction. *Academy of Management Review, 8,* 501–508.

Taylor, R.N., & Benbasat, I. (1980). A critique of cognitive styles and results. *Proceedings of the 1st International Conference on Information Systems,* Philadelphia, PA.

Thorndyke, P.W., & Stasz, C. (1980). Individual differences in knowledge acquired from maps. *Cognitive Psychology, 12,* 137–175.

Vessey, I. (1985). Expertise in debugging computer programs: Situation-based versus model-based problem solving. *International Journal of Man-Machine Studies, 23,* 459–494.

Weissinger-Baylon, R., Hughes, W., Adams, S., & Weissinger-Baylon, A. (1980). Analyzing execution decision making processes: The methodological contribution of visual mental imagery protocols. *Proceedings of the 1st International Conference on Information Systems,* Philadelphia, PA.

Wertheimer, M. (1959). *Productive Thinking.* New York: Harper and Row.

Witkin, H.A. (1964). Origins of cognitive style. In Scheere,E. (Ed.), *Cognition: theory, research, promise,* (pp. 172–205), New York: Harper and Row.

Wlodkowski, R.J. (1985). *Enhancing adult motivation to learn,* San Francisco: Jossey-Bass.

Wlodkowski, R.J. (1982). *Motivation: What research says to the teacher.* 2nd Ed. National Education Association of the United States, Washington, DC.

Young, R.M. (1983). Surrogates and mappings: Two kinds of conceptual models for interactive devices. In D. Gentner & A.L. Stevens (Eds.), *Mental models,* Hillsdale, NJ: Erlbaum.

SECTION VIII

The End User

The end user has certain characteristics and attributes which impact the development, design, and implementation of a management information system (MIS). These attributes include cognitive information-processing style, locus of control, level of management, level of expertise, power base, attitude toward the MIS and attitude toward the analyst/designer.

Human information processing capabilities and preferences interact with information presentation modes. There are several typologies of cognitive information processing which have been utilized in MIS research including Jungian, cognitive complexity theory, field dependency, hemispheral lateralization, and whole brain theory. The key thrust of all of them is to identify a consistent style of information processing and performance. There is empirical evidence that there exists an interaction effect between cognitive type and information presentation and other system attributes. For example, certain types seem to prefer and understand graphic presentations of information better than tabular and vice versa.

The paper included in this section is "A Human Information-Processing Model of the Managerial Mind: Some MIS Implications" by William M. Taggart of Florida International University, Department of Management. This paper presents a whole-brain model of the mind, measurement issues, and the impact of this model upon such issues as information processing, management styles, and information presentation preferences.

CHAPTER 15

A Human Information Processing Model of the Managerial Mind: Some MIS Implications

William M. Taggart
Florida International University

Today, much of the interest in human information processing (HIP) assumes the dual-mode, rational/intuitive view of style. The dual-mode model follows from the work of Joseph Bogen and Roger Sperry. By incorporating the research of Paul MacLean and Ward Halstead and Aleksandr Luria, the dual model can be expanded to a whole-brain metaphor for understanding the managerial mind in management information systems.

The Bogen/Sperry, MacLean, and Halstead/Luria views can be integrated as a whole-brain HIP model:

Frontal left (planning)   Frontal right (vision)

Left neocortex (logic)   Right neocortex (insight)

Reptilian (ritual)   Limbic (feeling)

This view of human information processing accounts for a broader range of manager behavior in the computer context. In addition to logic and insight; ritual and planning and feeling and vision play important roles in the everyday affairs of management. This whole-brain metaphor enhances the dual-mode, rational/intuitive view of processing style in organizations.

The measurement of HIP style and the application of the results are the practical consequences of the extended model. Tools for measurement are summarized and applications are discussed in the areas of

analyst development, analyst education, and management development. Progress in the first two and the last one are tied closely together.

INTRODUCTION

I have found it convenient and significant for practical purposes to
consider that these mental processes consist of two groups which I shall
call *non-logical* and *logical* (emphasis added). (Chester Barnard, 1966, p.
302)

Nearly 50 years ago, Chester Barnard, a management practitioner and
theoretician, described what he considered to be two ways of thinking
necessary in the "everyday affairs" of a manager. In the 1970s, research
results became widely known that provided scientific support for what
had been personal observation and speculation. This has come to be
understood as the left/right hemisphere model of human information
processing (HIP).

The importance of balance and flexibility is the most significant aspect
of the scientific support for ideas that have long been understood by the
perceptive manager. The HIP model highlights the imbalance in our
education for managers and analysts and the inflexibility that both
display in their everyday activities. This has been clearly stated for
managers by Peters and Waterman (1982) in *Search of Excellence* where
they observe "The numerative, rationalist approach to management
dominates business schools . . . . It is right enough to be dangerously
wrong, and it has arguably led us seriously astray" (p. 29). If the West
lags behind its Japanese competitors, the root cause may lie in an
imbalanced, inflexible emphasis on the logical processes of management
and systems to the relative exclusion of the non-logical.

That both ways of thinking are important was well put in a
Handlesman (1983) cartoon of two business men, perhaps computer
professionals, chatting in their favorite cocktail lounge. One says to the
other "My left hemisphere couldn't agree more with what you're saying,
but my right hemisphere intuits it's all a load of rubbish" (p. 160). Even
though our rational side praises the quantitative approach, our intuitive
side suspects that it is "rubbish" when used in isolation. To extend the
practical application of the human information processing model, we
should seriously rethink our implicit, dual-mode view of management
style. With an enhanced metaphor, we can be specific about ways to
restore balance and flexibility to the managerial mind and our approach
to it as we develop more sophisticated management information and
decision support systems.

LEVELS OF ANALYSIS

The human information processing (HIP) approach can be applied at several levels of understanding. Four levels are summarized in Figure 1: body, brain, mind, and consciousness. A brief discussion of these four illustrates the scope of the levels and focuses on the level of this paper. Beginning at the bottom, bodily processes involve magnificent examples of information processing. The unravelling of the genetic code in the structure of DNA represents one of the exciting adventures of 20th century science. For some years endocrinology has understood the role of the pituitary gland's secretions and their control over the hormones of the other glands that continuously regulate vital bodily functions.

The body can be viewed as support for the human nervous system of which the brain (biocomputer) at the second level of analysis is the crowning glory. New findings about the nature and role of the neurotransmitter in the nervous system are flooding from the laboratory. In addition, the work of the neurophysiologist that suggests major psychological functions of the human brain merits attention. The work of MacLean, Sperry, and Luria is of special interest. We will return to this level in the next section.

At the third level, mind exists distinct from the human brain. This view accepts Wilder Penfield's (1975) argument for the existence of mind. Penfield touched and experimented with more living human brains than any other scientist. He concluded, from a lifetime of observation, that brain mechanisms alone cannot account for human behavior. When Barnard spoke of logical and nonlogical thinking, he was referring to mental activities, not biochemical processes in the brain. Historically, the mind of man is at the center of philosophical inquiry. Most philosophies imply some model of the mind. Of particular interest to the author is Lao Tsu (1972) as expressed in the Chinese classic *Tao Te Ching* translated by Gia-Fu Feng and Jane English. The options are numerous, however. Charles Hampden-Turner's (1981) *Maps of the Mind* surveys the variety of philosophical statements on the nature of the human mind.

Finally, at the consciousness level, man recognizes his distinctive ability to do and know that he is doing at one and the same time. Julian Jaynes (1976) explained *The Origin of Consciousness in the Breakdown of the Bicamerel Mind*. His hypothesis assumes a special association between the speech area in the left hemisphere and the corresponding area in the right. Once consciousness awakens within the human mind, how does it evolve for the species? Rupert Sheldrake (1981) has proposed a bold hypothesis in *A New Science of Life* that suggest "morphonogentic fields" for each species with which individual consciousness communicates.

LEVELS OF ANALYSIS IN
HUMAN INFORMATION PROCESSING

CONSCIOUSNESS (SPIRIT)	Evolution of human consciousness (Sheldrake-A New Science of Life)
	Origin of consciousness (Jaynes-The Bicameral Mind)
MIND	Nature of man (Lao Tsu-Tao Te Ching)
	Functions of the human mind (Barnard - Mind in Everyday Affairs)
BRAIN (Biocomputer)	Functions of the human mind (MacLean, Sperry, and Luria- Neuropsychology)
	Effects of neurotransmitters on Excitation and inhibition in the nervous system (Neurophysiology)
BODY	Effects of hormones on body function (Endrocrinology)
	Genetic code in the DNA structure (Genetics)

Figure 1.

This hypothesis offers an explanation for the mental evolution of the human species.

THE HUMAN BIOCOMPUTER

A "whole-brain" basis for human information processing in management begins at the level of brain functions. To illustrate the brain basis for a HIP model, Figure 2 describes the functional components of the human biocomputer in levels beginning with the lower (older) brain functions at the top and the higher (newer) at the bottom of the figure. The brain has evolved by adding more sophisticated behavior patterns on earlier, more primitive levels.

We share our oldest brain with the reptiles. Its territorial drive focuses on survival. The lizard moves into the sunlight to warm its cold-blooded circulation. The neomammalian brain evolved as the limbic system extended beyond the reptilian, adding a sense of nurturing for the offspring of the species. The mother cat's "licking" attention to her kittens brings limbic functioning into "soft" relief.

The emergence of neocortex in man is associated with the idea of human "intelligence." Transcending instinct, intelligence emerges in its lowest forms when neocortex develops. In all animals except primates, this intelligence is considered primitive. In the successively higher forms of primates, the increasing size of the neocortex correlates with an increased intellect. More distinctly than for the lower brain structures, the neocortex divides into left and right hemispheres connected by a complex bundle of nerve fibers. The most recent outcroppings of the neocortex are the frontal lobes. The relative size of the frontal lobes compared to the rest of the neocortex provides a rough measure of intelligence. Because they are part of the hemispheres, the frontal lobes have the distinctive division into right and left halves. Three major lines of neuropsychological research can be aligned with the biocomputer diagram in Figure 2:

The Triune Brain (MacLean, 1978)
    Neocortex, Limbic, and Reptilian
The Bilateral Brain (Bogen, 1969; Sperry, 1975)
    Left Hemisphere and Right Hemisphere
The Frontal Brain (Halstead, 1947; Luria, 1973)
    Frontal Lobes and Posterior Lobes

Each line of research emphasizes a different orientation of biocomputer function without excluding the findings of the others. These are not

FUNCTIONAL COMPONENTS OF THE HUMAN BIOCOMPUTER

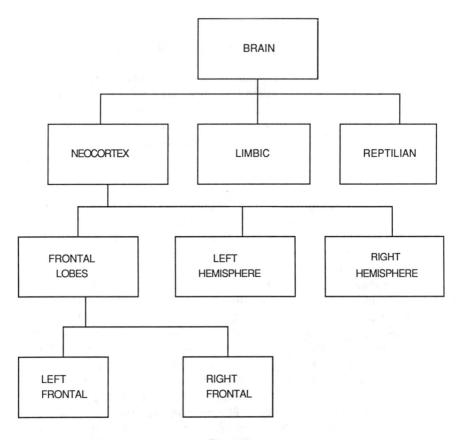

Figure 2.

competitive models. But, due to the limited focus of each, no one has pulled the themes together into a whole-brain model of the human biocomputer. These researchers can be studied from their original writings, but in each case popularizations offer more direct access to the ideas. Carl Sagan (1977) discusses the triune brain in the *Dragons of Eden* as does Robin Beebe (1980) in *The Evolving Angel*. Thomas Blakeslee (1980) clarifies the left/ right distinctions in *The Right Brain*, and Sally Springer and George Deutsch (1981) summarize the research in *Left Brain, Right Brain*. David Goodman (1978) explains the frontal brain model in *Learning from Lobotomy* as does Maya Pines (1983) in *The Human Difference* and David Loye (1983) in *The Sphinx and the Rainbow*.

These three lines of research can be linked together as a whole-brain model by grouping the biocomputer diagram components from Figure 2 in the "physiological" arrangement shown in Figure 3. From bottom to top, the three levels of MacLean's triune brain are reptilian, limbic, and neocortex. For the left/right hemispheres of Bogen and Sperry, note the division down the middle of the neocortex. Finally, the Halstead/Luria emphasis divides the neocortex horizontally into frontal and posterior parts. This whole-brain model of the biocomputer blends the findings of all three research efforts for a comprehensive understanding of human information processing.

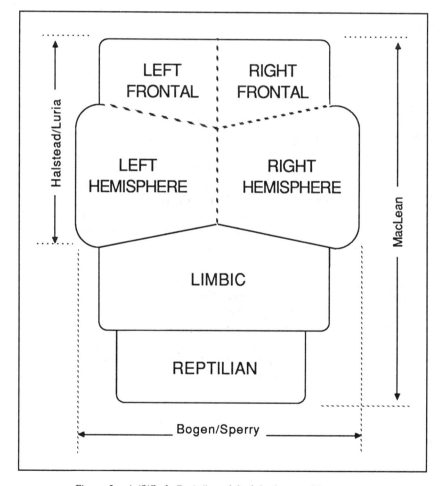

Figure 3.   A "Whole-Brain" model of the human biocomputer

WHOLE-BRAIN HUMAN INFORMATION
PROCESSING

Using the biocomputer diagram of Figure 3, the whole-brain model of human information processing in Figure 4 highlights the rational and intuitive styles. These correspond respectively to Barnard's logical and nonlogical thinking. The rational style is left mode thinking whereas the intuitive is right mode. The term *mode* is used, rather than *hemisphere*, to avoid implying that rational thinking is exclusively or even primarily a left-brain activity. Similarly for the right mode, the intuitive style is not exclusively or perhaps even primarily right-brain processing. For most, if not all, sophisticated human behavior, many parts of the nervous system become involved to some degree.

The researchers from whom the whole-brain model is drawn have written about the broader implications of their scientific findings. Bogen (1977) and MacLean (1978) have eloquently discussed the educational implications of their research. Borrowing from their carefully reasoned implications, Figure 4 associates a primary mode of the rational style with three parts of the left brain and a primary mode of the intuitive style with the three parts of the right brain. The rational arc swings through the left frontal, left hemisphere, and the reptilian parts of the biocomputer; the intuitive arc swings through the right frontal, right hemisphere, and limbic parts. This association emphasizes that the older reptilian brain falls more in line with the rational style, whereas the newer limbic brain aligns more closely with the intuitive style.

Semantic analysis and synthesis were used to name the three modes of the two styles as well as to select elements of the whole-brain metaphor. The words (elements) were derived from a study of 100 pairs of terms suggested by writers and thinkers (e.g., Bogen, 1977, p. 135; Hampden-Turner, 1981, p. 89) that correlate with the rational/intuitive differences. A sharp contrast in term pairs focused on the basic left/right distinction. Distinguishing the left frontal from the right frontal was based on a weak contrast compared to the left/right differences. The selection of words to clarify the reptilian and limbic modes recognized that the limbic builds upon the more primitive reptilian.

The elements of the rational and intuitive styles listed in Figure 5 provide specific descriptors of the information-processing emphasis of each mode. Notice the relatively sharp contrast in terms for the logic and insight modes:

Analyze   Synthesize
Sequence   Pattern
Control   Release

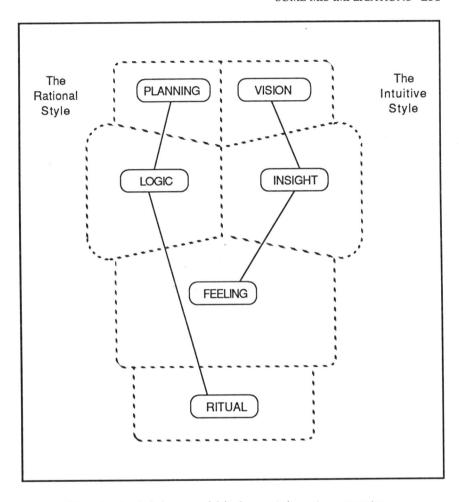

Figure 4.   A whole-brain model for human information processing

The planning and vision descriptors are weakly contrasted:

Propose	Imagine
Predict	Foresee
Design	Invent

Finally the terms for feeling build upon those for ritual:

Possess	Express
Conform	Share
Prohibit	Associate

Taken together, the descriptors for the six modes in Figure 5 provide a whole-brain psychological metaphor for the managerial mind.

MEASUREMENT OF HIP STYLES

Individual styles can be measured in terms of the whole-brain metaphor. The first question in undertaking this measurement is determining the approach to use. One study (Robey & Taggart, 1981) identifies three approaches: (a) physiological monitoring of brain wave patterns, (b) inference of style from observed behavior, and (c) self-description inventories. This section high- lights a self-description inventory called

The Rational Style   **The Intuitive Style**

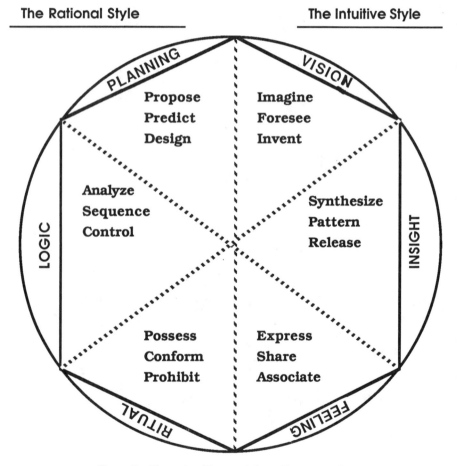

Figure 5. Elements of human information processing

the HIP Survey. The validity of self-description inventories to assess individual differences can be checked by monitoring brain-wave patterns. Some initial comparisons of style assessment and brain wave patterns are reported in a study of managerial decision styles and cerebral dominance (Taggart, Robey, & Kroeck, 1985). A discussion of the relative merits of the three approaches and the link between the first and third are beyond the scope of this paper.

Among others, one self-description inventory is tentatively supported by monitoring brain-wave patterns. The *Human Information Processing Survey* and companion *Strategy and Tactics Profiles* (Torrance, Taggart, & Taggart, 1984) describe an individual's style. The strategy profile represents HIP style in one of four categories and the tactics profile provides a process view of problem-solving style. (The latter is not discussed here.) Figure 6 represents a strategy profile based on the results of the 40 item HIP survey. Using the standard scores as the basis for classification, this profile represents the integrated category. The determination of the four strategies is explained in the administrator's manual (Taggart & Torrance, 1984):

1. Rational: Uses logic for most situations
2. Intuitive: Uses insight for most situations

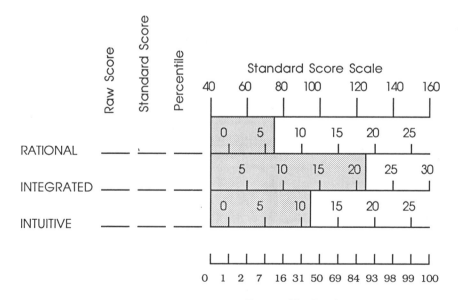

Figure 6. Human information processing strategy profile

3. Integrated: Uses logic and insight
4. Mixed: Uses logic or insight

Care must be exercised in interpreting the differences among the strategies and their implications, especially the distinction between integrated and mixed. The manual provides background for this purpose.

The present HIP survey assesses only rational, integrated, and intuitive styles. To move beyond this dual-mode interpretation to the whole-brain model, the survey is being extended to distinguish the three rational and the three intuitive modes. The present survey is used to approximate a six-mode profile. An example of a whole-brain HIP strategy appears in Figure 7. Using percentile scores from the HIP survey, three axes are defined on the Figure 5 diagram of the elements of HIP. This revision of the strategy profile describes processing style in terms of ritual and logic, planning and vision, and insight and feeling, using, respectively, the results of the rational, integrated, and intuitive HIP survey measures. The profile in Figure 7 illustrates a heavy reliance on the vision and insight modes to the relative exclusion of planning, logic, ritual, and feeling.

APPLICATION OF HIP STYLE MEASUREMENT

Among others, the HIP strategy and tactics profile information can be used in three areas: (a) analyst development, (b) analyst education, and (c) management development. In analyst development, the feedback provides a personally revealing means for understanding one's approach to problem solving. This can be extended to gain an appreciation of how others differ slightly or significantly from one's own approach to day-to-day situations. A clear example of the development value can be seen in the personal growth process.

In Carl Jung's (1971) *Psychological Types*, sensing and intuitive ways of perception are described, along with thinking and feeling means for making judgments. One of these four psychological functions typically dominates. The personal growth process, referred to as individuation, involves bringing all four aspects into conscious and unconscious balance. There is an association of sensing and thinking with the rational style and intuition and feeling with the intuitive. Applying the Jungian idea of growth, analyst development implies bringing all modes of the whole-brain metaphor into flexible balance in their behavior. The significance of this perspective for the systems development process has been presented in detail (Kerola & Taggart, 1983).

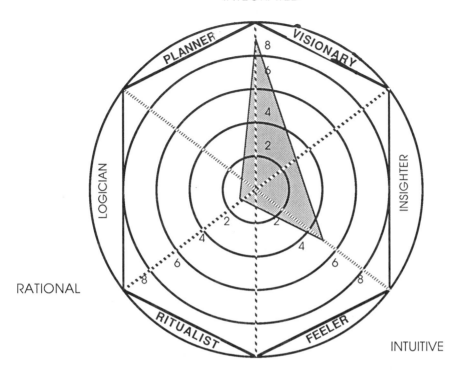

INTEGRATED

Figure 7. HIPS personal strategy profile

Western education is based primarily on the rational style. Ritual, logic, and planning are emphasized. Much less attention is given to the intuitive modes of feeling, insight, and vision. The arts-related courses in which these modes are emphasized are the first to be cut when the budget ax falls. In a similar manner, when parents note a decline in their children's basic test scores, compared to those of children in other schools, the cry goes out for "back to basics" reading, writing, and arithmetic.

There is no quarrel with the need for sound, rational-style education. But the whole-systems analyst requires balanced attention to the rational and intuitive sides of education. A glance at either the Association for Computing Machinery (ACM) or Data Processing Management Association (DPMA) curriculum guidelines for information-systems education quickly indicates the absence of this balance. The case for moving away from the "half-brained" approach to educate the whole analyst was presented earlier (Taggart, 1982).

In addition to educating the whole analyst, HIP profiles suggest that analysts and managers have unique strategies. Analysts should develop skills in the whole-brain development and presentation of their projects so that the material will be available to managers with different styles. Whole-brained instructors encourage students to become whole-brained. In analyst education, we should have people nurturing whole people rather than rationalists begetting rationalists ad infinitum.

For management development, the consequences of the dual-mode model are presented in *Minds and Managers: On the Dual Nature of Human Information Processing and Management* (Taggart & Robey, 1981). The HIP strategy and tactics profiles are especially useful in training and development in the areas of decision making, leadership style, team building, and communication skills. A new business curriculum has been developed to enhance these personal needs from the whole-brain point of view. This work is reported in *Decision Styles Education: An Innovative Approach* (Taggart, Robey, & Taggart, 1982) which describes a course that restores balance and flexibility to management education. This course demonstrates the application of the whole-brain metaphor to the managerial mind. A similar offering should become a required part of the MIS curriculum.

CONCLUSION

The whole-brain model outlined here establishes a human informationrocessing basis for understanding the managerial mind and a systems outlook for approaching it. This exploratory metaphor draws from the triune, bilateral, and frontal brain lines of neuropsychological research. This paper highlights the major features of the HIP model in terms of levels of analysis and the biocomputer as well as the styles, modes, and elements of whole-brain manager and analyst behavior.

The consequences of not coming to grips with the implications of this model have been clearly stated by Kahlil Gibran (1923):

> Your reason and your passion are the rudder and sails of your seafaring soul. If either your sails or your rudder be broken, you can but toss and drift, or else be held at a standstill in mid-seas (emphasis added). (p. 50)

Reason (rational style) and passion (intuitive style) are the twin companions of successful managers and computer professionals.

Reason is expressed in terms of its planning, logical, and ritual modes, whereas passion has its visionary, insightful, and emotional modes of expression. Managers and systems analysts who neglect planning, logic, and ritual lack direction as they "toss and drift," whereas those who undervalue vision, insight, and feeling lack momentum as they are "held at a standstill." Whole-brain managers and whole-brain systems professionals should blend the six modes of management in proportions appropriate to each situation.

REFERENCES

Barnard, C.I. (1966). *The functions of the executive.* Cambridge, MA: Harvard University Press.

Beebe, R.V. (1980). The evolving angel: Educating the triune brain dromenon. *A Journal of New Ways of Being, 3,* 28–32.

Blakeslee, T.R. (1980). *The right brain: A new understanding of the unconscious mind and its creative powers.* New York: Anchor Press/Doubleday.

Bogen, J.E. (1969). The other side of the brain II: An appositional mind. *Bulletin of the Los Angeles Neurological Societies, 34,* 135–162.

Bogen, J.E. (1977). Some educational implications of hemispheric specialization. In M.C. Wittrock (Ed.), *The human brain.* Englewood Cliffs, NJ: Prentice-Hall.

Gibran, K. (1923). *The prophet.* New York: Alfred A. Knopf.

Goodman, D.S. (1978). Learning from lobotomy. *Human Behavior, 7,* 44–49.

Halstead, W.C. (1947). *Brain and intelligence: A quantitative study of the frontal lobes.* Chicago, IL: The University of Chicago Press.

Hampden-Turner, C. (1981). *Maps of the mind.* New York: Macmillan.

Handlesman, J.B. (1983, March). Cartoon, *Playboy,* 160.

Jaynes, J. (1976). *The origin of consciousness in the breakdown of the bicameral mind.* Boston, MA: Houghton Mifflin.

Jung C.G. (1971). *Psychological types.* Trans. by H.G. Baynes, (revision by R.F.C. Hull of original work published 1923), Princeton, NJ: Princeton University Press.

Kerola, P., & Taggart, W.M. (1983). Human information processing styles in the information systems development process. In J. Hagwood (Ed.), *Evolutionary information systems* (pp. 63–86). Amsterdam: North-Holland.

Lao Tsu. (1972). *Tao Te Ching.* (G. Feng and J. English, Trans.), New York: Vintage Books.

Loye, D. (1983). *The sphinx and the rainbow: Brain, mind and future vision.* Boulder, CO: Shambhala.

Luria, A.R. (1973). The frontal lobes and the regulation of behavior. In K.H. Pribam & A.R. Luria (Eds.), *Psychophysiology of the frontal lobes.* New York: Academic.

MacLean, P.D. (1978). A mind of three minds: Educating the triune brain. In J.S. Chall & A.F. Mirsky (Eds.), *Education and the brain.* Chicago, IL: The National Society for the Study of Education.

Penfield, W. (1975). *The mystery of the mind: A critical study of consciousness and the human brain.* Princeton, NJ: Princeton University Press.

Peters, T.J., & Waterman, Jr., R.H. (1982). *In search of excellence.* New York: Harper and Row.

Pines, M. (1983). The human difference. *Psychology Today, 17,* 62–68.

Robey, D., & Taggart, W.M. (1981). Measuring manager's minds: The assessment of style in human information processing. *Academy of Management Review, 6,* 375–383.

Sagan, C. (1977). *The dragons of eden: Speculations on the evolution of human intelligence.* New York: Random House.

Sheldrake, R. (1981). *A new science of life: The hypothesis of formative causation.* Los Angeles,

CA: J.P. Tarcher.

Sperry, R.W. (1975). Lateral specialization in the surgically separated hemispheres. In B. Milner (Ed.), *Hemispheric specialization and interaction*. Cambridge, MA: The MIT Press.

Springer, S.P., & Deutsch, G. (1981). *Left brain, right brain*. San Francisco, CA: W.H. Freeman.

Taggart, W.M. (1982). The other half of the systems development process: Are we half-brained systems professionals? *Computer Personnel, 9*, 17–22.

Taggart, W.M., & Robey, D. (1981). Minds and managers: On the dual nature of human information processing and management. *Academy of Management Review, 6*, 187–195.

Taggart, W., Robey, D., & Taggart, B. (1982). Decision styles education: An innovative approach. *Exchange: The Organizational Behavior Teaching Journal, 1*, 17–24.

Taggart, W., & Torrance, E.P. (1984). *Administrator's manual for the human information processing survey*. Bensenville, IL: Scholastic Testing Service.

Torrance, E.P., Taggart, B., & Taggart, W.M. (1984a). *Human information processing survey*. Bensenville, IL: Scholastic Testing Service.

Torrance, E.P., Taggart, B., & Taggart, W.M. (1984b). *Strategy and tactics profiles*. Bensenville, IL: Scholastic Testing Service.

APPENDIX

Using Integrated Software on Microcomputers to Foster User Acceptance and Understanding of Management Science Tools in Decision Support Systems

Edward J. Szewczak
Southern Illinois University

Using integrated software to illustrate management science tools in decision support systems can be an effective way of imparting an understanding of how management science tools work dynamically. The approach advanced here can be utilized to complement traditional textbook-based instruction as well as basic input/output software designs by opening up the usual "black box" of contemporary computer-assisted instruction. It reveals the process of management science model solution, thereby fostering both an understanding, as well as an acceptance, of management science tools. A linear programming example is used to demonstrate the approach.

Deintinger (1983) presented a microcomputer-based approach to teaching linear programming (LP) which addressed the issues of learning as well as acceptance of management science (MS) tools. His concern was with overcoming the obstacles to the effective presentation of LP material manually using the traditional method of blackboard instruction. His approach was contemporary in three important respects:

1. The use of an Apple II microcomputer.
2. The use of classroom monitors to display the microcomputer monitor screen.
3. Interactive capability which allowed the user to experiment with the instructional program by choosing the locus of the pivot operation.

Deintinger's (1983) approach was important because it demonstrated that contemporary microcomputer technology could be used to improve on traditional teaching techniques. And, although he addressed LP specifically, it is clear that the approach can be used to teach any MS tool. It assumed a basic input/output design. Basic input/output design is premised on the belief that, if the primary objective of a user is to solve problems, then an input/output design which effectively shelters the user from the details of a software program's manipulation of input data to produce output information should be evaluated as "easy to use" and hence as desirable (Turban & Erickson, 1985). Virtually all of the MS software produced for use with microcomputers today employs a basic input/output design and may be acquired along with an accompanying textbook,(e.g., Burns & Austin, 1985; Dennis & Dennis, 1986; Erickson & Hall, 1986; Lee & Shim, 1986; Render & Stair, 1986).

Integrated software developments suggest that Deintinger's (1983) approach has room for significant improvements. One particular short-coming of his approach is the display of the output of only a particular MS tool. The microcomputer's program's workings remain opaque to the user. That is, the user sees the results of his or her decision but not the process leading to the results. A full understanding of a MS tool requires not only an appreciation of output but also a good grasp (a) of the details and assumptions of a model and (b) of the details of model solution.

If a user is a newcomer to MS analyses and/or mistrustful of the outputs of MS analyses because he or she is not familiar with the details of MS model solution processes, then a different form of software design is needed to help such a user accept MS for use in problem solving. In short, basic input/output software designs assume user acceptance of MS when, in fact, in the case of newcomers to MS, the key to learning with a view toward subsequent use is acceptance through understanding.

The mere use of MS software to solve problems by users does not indicate user acceptance of MS. A user may not understand the details of a particular MS tool, yet still accept the results of a MS analysis because of an implicit faith in computer output. This phenomenon is present in industry and represents a potential pitfall for practicing executives (Turban & Erickson, 1985).

Users need to be educated so as to avoid this pitfall. But, our responsibility extends even beyond users to systems designers. Users improperly educated in MS become managers who intentionally or unintentionally thwart the efforts of systems designers who attempt to incorporate MS tools in computer-based management information systems (MIS). The result is what has been called the "Type IV" implementation error, that is, the error of developing a MIS which is technically correct but which is not used by the managers it was developed for (Schultz & Slevin, 1985). This issue is an integral issue in the implementation of MIS (Lucas, 1981). The key to solving this aspect of the Type IV error problem is acceptance, that is, a willingness to embrace MS tools and their applicability to solving problems.

A DYNAMIC APPROACH

Integrated software (such as Lotus 1-2-3) can be used on microcomputers to demonstrate dynamically how a MS tool works at the level of detail of model solution. Emphasis can be placed on understanding the process of MS, not merely on identifying relevant inputs and interpreting outputs (important as these may be), as in the case of basic input/output software designs.

Because digital computers are responsible for the growth and proliferation of MS tools, we want end users to use computers when learning about MS. Yet, the temptation on the user's part to "let the computer do it" is great, especially when the problem at hand is to get the novice user over the initial hurdle of understanding how these tools work. If we can demonstrate "how the computer does it" using computers, then the temptation to be static can be overcome and users can be helped along toward understanding.

Integrated software offers a way to view MS dynamically using "macros". Macros are programs which execute operations automatically by reading a "record" of the keystrokes one would use to perform the operations manually (Ridington & Williams, 1985). Although the basic idea behind macros is to save the user the trouble of performing numerous (and at times, repetitive) keystrokes, they can be used for more advanced purposes. By using macros, we can make integrated software perform in ways which demonstrate how a given MS tool (say, LP) works. And we can write the macro program in such a way that the user controls the pace of the program as it executes. The real value of using macros is that macros transform abstract concepts into concrete events on the terminal screen right before the user's eyes.

The emphasis in this approach is on instruction. We are not concerned with developing, say, a general purpose program to do linear programming with n decision variables and m constraints. Instead, we take an example and make it "come alive" through the use of macros. Typically, the example will be small. But, this is so much the better, because ideally we want the example and demonstration of a MS tool to fit on the microcomputer display screen.

AN LP EXAMPLE

The following LP example uses a model from a popular textbook (Cook & Russell, 1981) and is implemented using Lotus 1-2-3 (Version 2). The initial tableau (which is also the initial microcomputer screen display) is presented as Figure 1 in the context of Lotus 1-2-3's spreadsheet option. Each element of the initial tableau can be referred to in terms of columns and rows which define cell locations. For example, the character string "solution" occupies cell I5, and the c1-z1 value can be referred to as cell D17. Macros can be used to create and store cell contents (numbers, characters, and formulas), to light up and dim cells, to erase cell contents, and to move the cursor.

All that is needed to begin the dynamic demonstration of the simplex method is to type Alt-Z (i.e., hitting the Alt key and the Z key together on the microcomputer keyboard). This fact is indicated by cell A20, which is "lit up" to attract the student user's attention. Typing Alt-Z will invoke the LP macro program which will begin to execute. There are three iterations needed to solve the model. In the interest of brevity, only the relevant details of the first iteration are discussed below. The details of the other two iterations are similar and can easily be inferred

A1:   READY:

A	B	C	D	E	F	G	H	I	J	K
		c_j	200	500	0	0	0			
	c_B	Basis	x_1	x_2	s_1	s_2	s_3	Solution	Ratio Test	
	0	s_1	0	1	1	0	0	40		
	0	s_2	1.2	4	0	1	0	240		
	0	s_3	0.5	1	0	0	1	81		
		z_j	0	0	0	0	0	0		
	c_j	$-z_j$	200	500	0	0	0			

To begin simplex method, type Alt-z.

Figure 1. Initial display in Lp example

by the reader. (The text of the LP macro covering the demonstration of just the first iteration is given in the Appendix. Interested readers can acquire the full text by writing the author.)

As the LP macro executes, it demonstrates the steps of the simplex method by directing the student's attention to relevant items in the tableau. First it announces its intention to accomplish a task, then follows by using color to emphasize a given item. It does this by exploiting the Lotus 1-2-3 feature of "lighting up" a cell's contents when the cell's protection is disabled. On my terminal screen, the cell's contents turn from white to green.

What the user experiences as the LP macro executes is detailed in the following steps. The author apologizes to the reader for requiring him or her to exercise more than the usual amount of imagination required to follow the steps. Ideally, the steps themselves would progress dynamically on the visual medium of the microcomputer display screen. The reader is urged to bear with the restrictions imposed by the medium of print.

1. After the user invokes the macro with Alt-Z, the macro replaces the contents of cell A20 with "Find pivot column:" After a 5 second pause, the macro lights up cell E17 (i.e., the c2-z2 value 500), designating the pivot column. The macro then replaces the contents of cell A20 with "To continue do a carriage return."

2. After the user presses the return key, the macro replaces the contents of cell A20 with "Find pivot rows:" After a 5 second pause, the macro begins to perform the ratio test by displaying the relevant ratios in cells J8 (i.e., 40/1), J10 (i.e., 240/4), and J12 (i.e., 81/1). It then lights up cell J8 to designate the least ratio, hence the pivot row. The macro then replaces the contents of cell A20 with "To continue do a carriage return.".

3. After the user presses the return key, the macro replaces the contents of cell A20 with "Enter new variable into basis:" After a 5 second pause, the macro replaces the s in cell C8 with an x, the 1 in cell C9 with a 2, and the 0 in cell B8 with 500. The macro also lights up each of these three cells. The macro then replaces the contents of cell A20 with "To continue do a carriage return." At this point, the microcomputer display screen appears as in Figure 2. The shaded cells are the ones lit up during macro execution.

4. After the user presses the return key, the macro replaces the contents of cell A20 with "Revise pivot row using pivot element:" It then returns the lit up cells (E17, J8, C8, C9, B8) to their original color. Next, it replaces the contents of cell A20 with "Pivot element:" After a 5 second

A1:   READY:

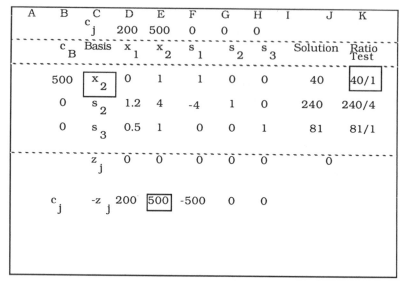

To continue do a carriage return.

Figure 2. Display after new variable enters basis

pause, the macro lights up cell E8, designating the pivot element (i.e., 1). Then the macro replaces the contents of cell A20 with "To continue do a carriage return.".

5. After the user presses the return key, the macro proceeds to revise the pivot row. The user watches as the cursor moves from cell D8 to cell I8, one cell at a time, and performs the needed revision. When finished revising the pivot row elements, the macro replaces the contents of cell A20 with "To continue do a carriage return."

6. After the user presses the return key, the macro replaces the contents of cell A20 with "Revise remaining rows:" After a 5 second pause, the remaining rows in the tableau are revised. After each row's revision is completed, the macro prompts the user to do a carriage return before proceeding to the next row's revision.

7. When all row revisions are completed, the macro replaces the contents of cell A20 with "End of 1st iteration." At this point, the microcomputer display screen appears as shown in Figure 3.

8. After a 10 second pause, the macro prompts the student to do a carriage return. The macro then proceeds with the demonstration of the second iteration. After announcing the completion of the second iteration, it prompts the user to do a carriage return. It then proceeds with

A1:

A	B	C	D	E	F	G	H	I	J	K
		c_j	200	500	0	0	0			
	c_B	Basis	x_1	x_2	s_1	s_2	s_3		Solution	Ratio Test
	500	x_2	0	1	1	0	0		40	40/1
	0	s_2	1.2	4	-4	1	0		240	240/4
	0	s_3	0.5	1	0	0	1		81	81/1
		z_j	0	0	0	0	0		0	
	c_j	$-z_j$	200	0	-500	0	0			

End of 1st Iteration.

Figure 3. Display at end of 1st iteration

the demonstration of the third iteration. (For brevity's sake, the details of these two iterations are omitted.)

9. After announcing the completion of the third iteration, the macro prompts the user to do a carriage return. It then replaces the contents of cell A20 with "The solution is optimal," thereby announcing the end of the analysis.

BENEFITS AND OPTIONS OF THE APPROACH

The dynamic, macro-based approach enables the user to see how MS tools work dynamically. It has the added benefit of involving users in the dynamic demonstration.

After the demonstration is completed, the user can explore the results of the macro execution. The user merely has to cursor to any cell to examine the formula stored there, which is displayed in the first line of the Lotus 1-2-3 control panel. The stored formulas (which can be created and stored during macro execution) contain the information needed to solve the problem. Thus the relation between the macro demonstration and textbook exposition can be noted and learning effected through a comparison of static and dynamic material. Any MS tool that can be exemplified using the basic spreadsheet format provided by Lotus 1–2–3 can be addressed. Linear regression can be exemplified using a table of X, Y data. Linear programming can be exemplified using tableaus. Other MS tools such as moving averages, exponential smoothing, expected value, transportation models, sensitivity analysis, critical path method (CPM), and simulation are fair game for this approach.

The LP macro is actually of the "no-frills" variety. Its features can easily be altered and other features can be added, according to taste. Among the more interesting features which can be incorporated in MS macros for educational purposes are:

1. The addition of [Wait] statements at select points of a macro program to slow the execution down. Lotus 1–2–3 executes very quickly, and instructors may choose to add slack to make their macros proceed at a slower pace. Instructors may also choose to allow some periods of slack pace. Instructors may also choose to allow some periods of slack to be longer than others for emphasis. The LP macro uses [Wait] statements after the display of its intention to begin a new major step in its execution (e.g., after "Find pivot column:").

2. The stoppage of the macro execution at critical points of the demonstration. Use of [?] in the macro allows students to enter a(ny) keystroke to get things moving again. Instructors may wish to have comments appear to the student at these breakpoints to elucidate the material or simply to provide directives. The LP macro uses the directive "To continue do a carriage return."

3. The addition of key breaks in the macro execution to allow students to offer input to the program. This allows for an interactive session where student responses to programmed prompting can be checked for desired accuracy. This option makes the macro writing more complex. But the instructor may feel that the additional programming effort is worth it in terms of learning effectiveness. A good discussion of programming interactive macros appears in Ridington and Williams (1985).

4. The use of more than one macro to allow the user more options. In the LP macro, one obvious candidate is another macro to provide the option to return to the initial tableau. Once invoked, the user could elect to run through the entire analysis again.

CONCLUSION

By dynamically demonstrating the process of MS model solution, programs written using integrated software can be used to complement basic input/output software designs. These programs can help users by increasing their understanding of the details of model solution. The approach enjoys certain benefits from the perspective of transferability. Any organization with integrated software and microcomputers can implement the approach. Programs can be adopted in toto from other organizations. Or they can be adopted and adapted to fit the needs of the adopting organization. Finally, programs can be developed in-house from scratch, to suit the teaching objectives and styles of training centers.

The dynamic demonstration of MS in the context of computer-assisted instruction offers many avenues for approaching the issue of fostering user acceptance of MS which are not available with basic input/output design software. The macro-based approach offers educators a free hand in developing unique and creative ways to help users gain an understanding and acceptance of MS which will help them in the management of organizations.

REFERENCES

Burns, J.R., & Austin, L.M. (1985). *Management science models and the microcomputer*, New York: MacMillan.

Business Week. (1984, September). How personal computers can trip up executives.

Cook, T.M., & Russell, R.A. (1981). *Introduction to management science*, Englewood Cliffs, NJ: Prentice-Hall.

Deintinger, R.A. (1983). Teaching linear programming on a microcomputer, *Interfaces, 13*, 30–33.

Dennis, L.B., & Dennis, T.L. (1986). *Microcomputer models for management decision-making*, St. Paul, MN: West Publishing.

Erickson, W.J., & Hall, O.P. (1986). *Computer models for management science*, Reading, MA: Addison-Wesley.

Lee, S., & Shim, J. (1986). *Micro management science*, Dubuque, IA: William C. Brown.

Lucas, H.C. (1981). *Implementation*, New York: Columbia University Press.

Ploch, M. (1984). Micros flood campuses, *High Technology, 4*, 47–49.

Render, B., & Stair, R.M. (1986). *Microcomputer software for management science and operations management*, Boston, MA: Allyn & Bacon.

Ridington, R.W., & Williams, M.M. (1985). *Using macros*, Bowie, TX: Brady Communications.

Schultz, R.L., & Slevin, D.P. (1985). A program of research on implementation. in R.L. Schultz & D.P. Slevin (Eds.), *Implementing Operations Research/Management Science*, New York: American Elsevier.

Turban, E., & Erickson, W. (1985). Selecting operations research software for classroom microcomputers, *Computers & Operations Research, 12*, 383–390.

Author Index

A

Aamodt, M.G., 138, 140, *145*
Abelson, R., 171, *180*
Ackoff, R.L., 85, *99*
Adams, S., 232, *250*
Adelson, B., 244, *246*
Ahituv, N., 84, *99*
Ajzen, 229
Alloway, R.M., 1, *5*, 223, *246*
Alty, J.L., 15, *21*
Amoroso, D.L., 221, *247*
Anderson, J.R., 236, 241, *246*
Andriole, S.J., 15, *21*
Argyris, C., 190, 191, 193, *194*
Asher, H.B., 88, *99*
Atwood, M., *81*, 104, *115*
Austin, C.M., 270, *277*
Ausubel, D.P., 234, *246*

B

Bailey, E.K., 17, *24*
Bailey, J.W., 17, *24*
Bair, J.H., 192, *194*
Barber, G.R., 15, *21*
Barnard, C.I., 254, 256, *267*
Barnard, P., 16, *23*, 25
Barton, B., 33, *40*
Barton, M., 33, *40*

Bass, B.M., *204*
Bass, L.J., 15, *21*
Bateman, R.F., 15, *21*
Bayman, P., 228, *246*
Bazerman, M., 190, *194*
Beard, J.W., *163*
Beebe, R.V., 258, *267*
Benbasat, I., *21*, 230, *250*
Benjamin, R., 137, *146*, 223, *246*
Bennett, J., *180*, 208, 209, *213*
Bennett, K.B., 228, 241, 243, *247*
Berrisford, T., *146*
Beynon, M., *21*
Biermann, A.W., 14, 15, *21*
Bikson, T.K., 235, 236, *247*
Bin Yao, S., *133*
Bjorner, D., 121, *133*
Black, J.B., 14, 15, *22*
Blakeslee, T.R., 258, *267*
Blanchard, K., 196, 197, *205*
Blanning, R.W., 88, *99*
Blaser, A., 15, *22*
Bogen, J.E., 253, 257, 259, 260, *267*
Bolt, R.A., 14, 15, *22*
Bologna, J., 191, *194*
Bonczek, R.H., 84, *99*
Borgman, C.L., 228, 230, 240, *247*
Bostrom, R.P., 137, 138, 141, 142, 143, *145*,
    146, 224, 226, 245, *249*
Bowers, C., 232, *247*

Boyle, C.F., 236, 241, *246*
Brand, S.D., 30, *40*
Branscomb, L., 69, 71, *80*
Brockman, 18
Brod, C., 15, *22*
Bromage, B.K., 234, *248*
Brown, J.S., 172, *180*, 223, 245, *247*
Brown, P.J., 15, 18, *22*, 150, *163*
Bruenenfelder, T.M., 17, *24*
Bryan, W.L., 32, *40*
Burns, J.R., 270, *277*
Burns, T., 195, *204*
Butcher, D.F., 233, *247*

C

Cacioppa, J., 242, *249*
Cameron-Bandler, L., 241, *247*
Campbell, D., 75, 78, *80*
Card, S.K., 15, 18, *22*, 34, *40*, 238, *247*
Carey, T., 66, 71, 72, *80*
Carlson, E.D., 84, *100*
Carlsson, B., 231, *247*
Carrithers, C., 15, *22*, 244, *247*
Carroll, J.M., 15, *22*, 224, 236, 238, 241, 243, 244, *247*, *248*
Carter, E., 195, *204*
Cerullo, M.J., 1, *5*
Cerveny, R., *99*
Chandrasekaran, 169, 170, *179*, *180*
Chang, C.L., *133*
Chapanis, A., 8, 9, 12, *22*
Chapin, R., 71, *80*
Chaw, P., *80*
Cheney, P.H., 221, *247*
Cherrington, M., 86, *99*
Chervany, N.L., 140, *146*
Choobeineh, J., 125, *133*
Cirillo, D.J., 192, *194*
Clancey, W.J., 170, *180*
Clowes, I., 15, *22*
Cockton, G., 15, *22*
Cofer, C.N., 85, *99*
Cole, D., 30, 31, *40*
Conlon, E., 190, *194*
Cook, S., 16, *23*
Cook, T.M., 272, *277*
Cooke, T., 75, 78, *80*
Coombs, M.J., 17, *24*
Cooper, E., 32, 34, *40*
Cotton, I.W., 31, *40*

Courtney, J., 68, *80*, 84, 88, *99*, *100*
Cross, D.R., 230, 231, 232, 233, *249*
Cuff, R., 66, 72, *80*
Culnan, M.J., 5, 8, *22*
Curtis, B., 15, *22*
Cushman, W.H., 150, *163*

D

Danzin, A., *194*
Davis, F.D., Jr., 229, *247*
Davis, G.B., 223, 243, *247*
Dehning, W., 15, *22*
Deintinger, R.A., 267, 268, *275*
De Jong, P., 120, *133*
deKleer, J., 172, *180*
Dennis, L.B., 270, *277*
Dennis, T.L., 270, *277*
De Sanctis, G., 68, *80*
Deutsch, G., 258, *269*
Dexter, A.S., *21*
Dickson, G.H., 140, *146*, 224, *247*
Dickson, G.W., 185, 186, 187, 188, 190, 192, 193, *194*
diSessa, A.A., 234, *247*
Dix, A.J., 15, *22*
Doddington, G.R., 31, *40*
Douglas, S.A., 239, 244, *247*
Dray, W., 175, 177, *180*
Dreyfus, H., 21, *22*
Driscoll, J.W., 184, *194*
Dunker, K., 85, *99*
Durand, D.E., 228, *248*

E

Eagly, A.H., 233, *247*
Edmondson, W.H., 16, *23*
Egan, D.E., 232, *247*
Ehrlich, K., 15, 18, *22*
Eisenstadt, M., 244, *247*
Embley, D.W., 121, *133*
Emshoff, J.R., 85, *99*
Erdman, H., 151, *163*
Erickson, W.J., 270, *277*
Essig, H., 15, *22*

F

Faerstein, P.H., 192, *194*
Farrel, R., 241, *246*

Fishbein, 229
Flannery, L.S., 223, *249*
Floyd, S.W., 228, *248*
Foley, J.D., *80*, 228, *247*
Forsen, G., 33, *40*
Foster, A., *180*
Fountain, A.J., 15, 18, *22*
Fowler, J.F., 15, *22*
Fowler, J.H., 15, *22*
Friesen, P.H., 196, *205*
Fry, R., 231, *248*
Fuerst, W., 69, 72, 73, 78, *81*

G

Gaines, B.R., 10, *22*
Gaines, R.S., 33, 37, *40*
Gaither, N., 168, 173, *180*
Galbraith, J., 183, *194*
Galitz, W.O., *22*, 185
Galletta, D., 240, *247*
Genter, D.R., 32, 34, *40*
Gibran, K., 266, *267*
Gilfoil, D., 244, *248*
Gilford, D., 71, *80*
Glen, J.A., 15, *22*
Gomez, L.M., 232, *247*
Good, M.D., 15, 18, *22*
Goodman, D.S., 258, *267*
Goodman, P.S., 190, *194*
Goos, G., 15, *23*
Gordon, D., 241, *247*
Gould, J.L., 208, *213*
Green, T., 16, *23*
Greenberger, M., *194*
Greenwood, F., 183, *194*
Greenwood, M., 183, *194*
Griest, J.H., 151, 160, *163*
Grischkowsky, N.L., 244, *247*
Grochow, J., 231, *248*
Grued, R.A., 16, *23*
Gruenberg, 12
Guilford, J.P., 231, *248*
Gutek, B.A., 235, 236, *247*

H

Habinek, J.K., 17, *24*
Hahn, W.V., 14, 16, *23*
Halasz, F., 240, *248*
Halstead, W.C., 253, 257, 258, *267*

Hall, O.P., 268, *275*
Hammer, J.N., 184, 185, *194*
Hammer, M., 120, *133*
Hammond, N., 16, *23*
Hampden-Turner, C., 260, *267*
Handelsman, J.B., 254, *267*
Hansen, W., 104, *115*
Harrison, M., 16, *23*
Harter, N., 32, *40*
Hartmanis, J., 15, *23*
Hartog, C., 224, *248*
Hasling, D.W., 170, *180*
Hedberg, B., 195, *205*
Heidlage, J.F., 15, *21*
Helman, D., 168, *180*
Hempel, C.G., 175, 177, *180*
Heppe, D.L., 16, *23*
Herbert, M., 224, *248*
Herot, C.F., 16, *23*
Hershey, D., 196, 197, *205*
Hevner, A.R., *133*
Hewitt, C., 15, *21*
Hicks, G.P., *163*
Hill, I.D., 16, *23*
Hiltz, S.R., 16, *23*, 150, *163*
Hoepner, R., 231, *248*
Holland, J.D., 243, *248*
Holsapple, C.W., 84, *99*
Hopkins, C., *22*
Hora, S.C., 84, *99*
Houghton, R.C., Jr., 16, 18, *23*
Huber, G., 230, *248*
Huchingson, R.D., 9, 12, *23*, *62*
Hughes, W., 232, *250*
Hulme, C., 16, *23*
Hultman, K.E., *205*
Humpress, 33
Hussain, D., 11, 12, *23*
Hussain, K.M., 11, 12, *23*
Hutchins, E.L., 243, *248*

J

Jacob, R.J., 16, 18, *23*
Jagodzinski, A., 236, 238, 239, 243, *248*
James, P.N., 191, *194*
Jarke, M., 17, *25*
Jaynes, J., 255, 256, *267*
Jensen, R.L., 86, 88 *99*
Johnson, P., 16, *23*
Johnson, W., 85, *99*

Jones, C.B., *133*
Jones, R., 32, *41*
Jones, S.J., 15, 18, *22*
Judson, A.J., 85, *99*
Jung, C.D., 141, *146*
Jung, C.G., 264, *267*

K

Kahneman, D., 85, 86, 96, *100*
Kaiser, K.M., 138, 141, 142, 143, 145, *146*
Karten, N., 241, 242, *248*
Kasper, G.M., 86, *99*
Kasschau, R.A., 16, *23*
Keane, P., 231, *247*
Keller, J.M., 232, 235, *248*
Kennedy, T., 71, *81*
Kerola, P., 264, *267*
Kidd, A., 16, *23*
Kilduff, K., 235, 241, *249*
Kilmann, R.H., 85, *99*, 140, 141, 142, 143, *146*
Kimbrough, W.W., 138, 140, *145*
Klein, M.H., 151, *163*
Klensin, J., 71, *81*
Kneppreth, N., 160, *163*
Kofer, G.R., 183, *194*
Kolb, D.A., 231, *248*
Koppa, R.J., *62*
Kosy, D.W., 178, *180*
Kozma, R.B., 230, 231, 232, 233, *249*
Krisak, N., 242, *249*
Kroeck, 263
Kublanow, S.M., 228, *248*

L

Lachman, R., 16, *23*
Ladd, I., 121, *133*
Lampen, L.J., *62*
Langer, P., *205*
Lao Tsu, 255, 256, *267*
Larkin, J.H., 232, *248*
Larson, J., 120, *133*
Latremoville, S.A., 150, *163*
Laughery, K.R., 16, *23*
Lawler, E.E., 199, *205*
Lawrence, P., 195, *205*
Laxas, K., 71, *81*
Lebeau, M., 241, *247*
Lee, S., 270, *277*

Lefkovitz, H.C., 120, *133*
Leifler, R., 137, 139, 140, 142, *146*
Leitheiser, R.L., 224, *247*
Lewis, C.H., 244, *247*
Lewis, C.L., 224, 244, *248*
Lewis, J.R., 212, *213*
Libby, R., 86, *99*
Lickorish, A., 150, *164*
Lisowski, W., 33, 37, *40*
Lorsch, J., 195, *205*
Loy, S.L., 86, *99*
Loye, D., 258, *267*
Lucas, H.C., 271, *277*
Lum, V.Y., *133*
Luo, D., 120, *133*
Luria, A.R., 253, 256, 257, 259, *267*

M

Maass, S., 15, *22*
Macaulay, L.A., 15, *22*
Mack, R.L., 224, 244, *247, 248*
MacLean, A., *25*
MacLean, P.D., 253, 256, 257, 259, *267*
Maguire, M., 66, 71, *81*
Maier, J.J., *41*
Makey, J.D., 30, *40*
Malone, T.W., 16, *23*
Maniha, J., 195, *205*
Mann, R.I., 221, *247*
Mannino, M.V., 125, *133*
Mansour, 196
March, J., 195, *205*
Martin, J., 10, 14, 16, 18, *23*, 231, *247*
Martin, M., 69, 70, 72, 73, 74, 78, *81*
Mason, R., 137, *146*
Mayer, R.E., 228, 234, 240, 246, *248*
McCain, C., *205*
McCormick, D., 242, *249*
McFarlan, F.W., 137, 138, 139, 140, 142, 143, *146*
McKeachie, W.J., 230, 231, 232, 233, *249*
McKendree, 238, *247*
McKenney, J., 137, 138, 139, 140, 142, 143, *146*
McLean, 86, *99*
McGrath, J., 68, 74, 75, 77, *81*
Meissner, P., 31, *40, 41*
Michard, A., 244, *248*
Miller, D., 196, *205*
Mills, C.B., 16, 208, *213*

Mintzberg, H., 85, *99, 205*
Mitroff, I.I., 85, *99*, 137, 141, *146*
Mittal, S., 169, *180*
Monk, A., 16, *23*
Monzeico, H., 62, *81*
Mook, D., 75, *81*
Moran, T.P., 15, 18, 22, 34, 40, 228, 238, 239, 240, 244, *247 248*
Morland, D.V., 16, *23*
Mumford, E., 17, *23*
Murrell, 12
Muter, P., 150, *163*
Muth, W.A., 233, *247*
Myers, 141

N

Naffah, N., 16, *24*
Neal, A.S., 208, *213*
Nechis, M., 224, *247*
Nelson, M., 31, 33, *40*
Nesdore, P., 66, *81*
Neumann, S., 84, *99*
Newcomb, T.M., 20, *24*
Newell, A., 15, 18, 22, 34, 40, 85, *99*, 238, *247*
Newman, S.E., 223, 245, *247*
Newsted, P.R., *163*
Nickerson, R.S., 228, *248*
Norman, D.A., 16, 18, *24*, 32, *41*, 228, 238, 239, 243, *248, 249*
Norman, M.A., 18, 22
Nystrom, P., 196, *205*

O

Odiorne, G.S., 191, *194*
Olfman, L., 224, 226, 233, 242, 245, *249*
Olson, G., 71, *81*
Olte, F.H., *24*
O'Neill, H., 104, *115*
O'Reilly, C.A., 183, *194*
Osborne, D.J., 12, 16, *24*
Otte, F.H., 16, *24*
Otway, H.J., 185, *194*
Owen, D., 228, 239, *249*

P

Paivo, A., 232, *249*
Palko, K.D., *62*

Paradice, 88
Parkingson, 72, *81*
Payne, J.J., 16, *23*
Pellegrino, J.W., 232, *249*
Peltu, M., 185, *194*
Penedo, M.H., *133*
Penfield, W., 255, *267*
Pennington, N.P., 230, *249*
Perrow, C., 195, *205*
Peters, T.J., 254, *267*
Peterson, T.O., *163*
Petty, R.E., 242, *249*
Pines, M., 258, *267*
Pintrich, P.R., 230, 231, 232, 233, *249*
Ploch, M., *277*
Polya, G., 231, *249*
Pondy, L., 183, *194*
Pounds, W.F., 84, 85, *100*
Power, B.L., 190, *205*
Pracht, W.E., 86, *100*
Press, S.J., 37, *40*
Pruitt, 85

Q

Quible, Z., 184, 185, *194*
Quillard, J.A., 1, *5*, 223, *246*

R

Raiffa, H., 84, *100*
Raisinghani, D., 85, *99*
Ramsey, H., *81*
Ramsey, R., 104, *115*
Reed, C.E., *163*
Reid, P., 16, *24*
Reiser, B.J., 236, 241, *246*
Reisner, P., 16, 17, 18, *24*, 236, *248*
Reitman, J.S., 244, *249*
Reitman, W.R., 85, *100*
Reitman-Olson, W., II, 17, *24*
Render, B., 270, *277*
Rennels, G., *180*
Rennick, R.J., 31, *41*
Reuter, H., 244, *249*
Ridington, R.W., 271, 276, *277*
Riley, M.S., 237, *249*
Ritchie, R.A., 15, *21*
Roberts, P.S., 17, *24*
Robertson, S.R., 244, *247*
Robey, D., 196, *205*, 262, 263, 266, *267, 268*
Rockart, J., 137, *146*, 223, *249*

Rodman, R.D., 15, *21*
Ross, S.M., 242, *249*
Rosson, M.B., 233, *249*
Rowe, A.J., 85, *100*
Rubin, D.C., 15, *21*
Rumelhart, D., 32, *41*, 228, *249*
Runciman, C., 15, *22*
Rushinek, A., 151, *163*
Rushinek, S., *163*
Russell, R.A., 272, *277*

S

Sachman, H., 10, *24*
Sagan, C., 258, *267*
Sage, A.P., 84, 86, 87, 88, 93, 97, *100*
Sales, G., 150, *164*
Saloway, E., 15, 18, *22*
Salvendy, G., 17, *24*
Sauers, R., 241, *246*
Savage, R.E., 17, *24*
Schaie, W.R., *205*
Schank, R., 171, *180*
Schneider, M.L., 17, *24*, *25*
Schultz, R., 271, *277*
Scott Morton, M.S., 137, *146*
Sears, J.A., 233, *249*
Sein, M., 224, 226, 231, 240, 245, *249*
Selander, S., 66, 72, *81*
Shackel, B., 8, 18, *24*, 208, *214*
Shaffer, L.H., 32, *41*
Shaffer, L.J., 34, *41*
Shapiro, N., 33, 37, *40*
Sharrow, J., 235, 241, *249*
Sheldon, A., 196, *205*
Sheldrake, R., 255, *267*
Shepherd, P., 86, *99*
Sheppard, S.B., 17, *24*
Shiel, B.A., 230, 232, *249*
Shim, J., 270, *277*
Shneiderman, B., 1, 3, *6*, 8, 11, 14, 17, 18, 24, 237, 243, *250*
Shortliffe, E., 168, *180*
Shu, N.C., 121, *133*
Sime, M.E., 17, *24*
Simmon, J.K., 185, 186, 187, 188, 190, 192, 193, *194*
Simon, H.A., 84, 85, *99*, *100*, 183, *194*, 195, *205*
Simons, R.M., 208, *213*
Simpson, H., *81*

Sims, R.A., 231, *250*
Sisson, N., 71, *81*
Slack, W., *163*
Slevin, D.P., 271, *277*
Smith, J.J., 17, *25*
Snowberry, K., 72, *81*
Spence, R., 16, *23*
Sperry, R.W., 253, 256, 257, 259, *267*
Spillane, R.J., 32, 33, *41*
Sprague, R.H., 84, *100*
Springer, S.P., *268*
Stair, R.M., 270, *277*
Stalker, G., 195, *204*
Starbuck, W., 196, *205*
Staron, R., 31, 33, *40*
Stasz, C., 232, 245, *250*
Stealey, S.L., *62*
Sterling, L., 179, *180*
Stewart, T., 71, *81*
Stohr, E.A., 17, *25*
Student, K.R., *205*
Studer, R., 121, *133*
Stutz, J., 151, *163*
Sutcliffe, A.G., 17, *25*
Swartout, W.R., 170, *180*
Switchenko, D.M., 150, *163*

T

Taggart, B., 263, 266, *268*
Taggart, W.M., 262, 263, 264, 265, 266, *267*, *268*
Taylor, I.A., 85, *100*
Taylor, R.N., 230, *250*
Theoret, A., 85, *99*
Thimbleby, H.W., 16, 17, *23*, *25*, *81*
Thomas, E.A., *41*
Thomas, J.C., 12, 17, 20, *25*, 69, 71, *80*
Thompson, J., *205*
Thorndyke, P.W., 232, 245, *250*
Torrance, E.P., 263, *268*
Treurniet, W.C., 150, *163*
Trollip, S.R., 150, *164*
Tsichritzis, D., 121, *133*
Tullis, T., 72, *81*
Tung, F.C., *133*
Turban, E., 270, *277*
Turner, J.A., 17, *25*
Turoff, M., 16, *23*
Tushman, M., 183, *194*
Tversky, A., 85, 96, *100*

U

Umphress, D., 33, 36, *41*

V

Van Cura, L.J., 160, *163*
van der Veer, G.C., 16, *23*
Vassiliou, Y., 17, *25*
Vessey, I., 241, *250*
Vitols, V.A., 31, *41*
Volkema, R.J., 86, *100*

W

Wallace, V., *80*
Walther, G., 104, *115*
Wang, M.S., 84, *100*
Warfel, J., 30, *41*
Wartik, S.P., *133*
Wasserman, D., 71, *81*
Waterman, R.H., Jr., 254, *267*
Watson, H., 196, *205*
Weaver, V., 235, 241, *249*
Wegstein, J., 31, *41*
Weinberg, G.M., 14, 17, *25*
Weiner, J.L., 170, *180*
Weissinger-Baylon, A., 232, *249*
Weissinger-Baylon, R., 232, *250*
Wertheimer, M., 231, *250*
Wetherbe, J., *146*, 224, 247
Whieldon, D., 103, *115*
Whinston, A.B., 84, *99*
White, K.B., 137, 138, 139, 140, 141, 142, 143, *146*

White, N., 17, *25*
Whiteside, J.A., 15, 18, *22*
Wickens, C.D., *25*
Widman, L., *180*
Willeges, B., *81*
Willeges, R., *81*
Williams, G., 33, 36, *41*
Williams, M.M., 271, 276, *277*
Wilson, M., 17, *25*
Winograd, T., 168, *180*
Wismer, J.N., *205*
Wise, B.D., 178, *180*
Witkin, H.A., 232, *250*
Wixon, J.R., 15, 18, *22*
Wlodowski, R.J., 224, 232, 233, 235, 236, *250*
Wolstein, A.S., *62*
Wood, H., 30, *41*
Wood, M., 196, *205*
Woodard, J.P., 31, *41*
Woodman, 12
Woodson, W.E., 11, *25*
Wright, P., 150, *164*
Wyman, J., 137, *146*

Y

Yao, 121, *133*
Young, R.M., 228, 239, *250*

Z

Zloof, M.M., 120, *133*
Zmud, R.W., 4, 6, 137, *146*
Zoeppritz, M., 15, *22*

Subject Index

A

Abstract models, 240
Acceptance of change models, 199–200, 204
Access control, 29
Adaptive audience models, 65
Alternate user processing paths, 68
Analogical models, 240
AND/OR graphs, 167
Artificial intelligence, 168
Attitude toward change, 197
Audience directed model, 65

B

Biases in problem formulation, 82, 87, 95–98
Browsing, 106

C

Casual users, 72
Causal modeling, 88
Cognitive partitioning, 32
Cognitive traits, 230–232
Cognitive styles, 141–143
Computer use, 160
Computer simulations in human factors, 75
Conceptual models, 234–235, 238
Criteria for determining MIS success, 1, 2

D

Data flow diagram, 3
Data redundancy, 97
Determinants of user behavior/performance
    task, 222
    motivation, 222
    knowledge, 222
    interface, 222
    user characteristics, 222
Digraph, 34
Direct manipulation techniques, 63
Display enertia, 105, 111
DSS, 82, 269

E

Ease of recall, 96
Encoding strategies, 48
End user facility committee (EUFC), 120
End user, 251
End-user computing (EUC), 221–223
End-user involvement, 18, 181–182
Engineering psychology, 9
Ergonomics, 12, 27
Escape mechanisms, 68, 74
Executive pacer, 32
Experimental simulations in human factors, 75

F

FAR (False Alarm Rate), 35
Feasibility study, 2
Federal Bureau of Investigation, 31
Field studies in human factors, 74
Form model, 122
Form Definition Interface (FDI), 125
Form templates, 122
Form Manipulation Interface (FMI), 131
Form types, 122
FORMFLEX, 124–132
Function keys, 44, 61

G

Gambler's fallacy, 96

H

Help function, 73
HIP styles
  rational, 263
  intuitive, 263
  integrated, 264
  mixed, 264
History of human factors
  preinformation systems, 9
  postinformation systems, 10–11
Human factors taxonomy, 4–5, 7, 13–18
Human factors definition, 11–13, 28
Human factors coaching, 78
Human factors in MIS, 80
Human Engineering Laboratory, 43
Human factors engineers, 27
Human information processing, 253
  levels of analysis in, 256
  limbic processing, 257
  reptilian processing, 257
Human-computer interface, 10
Human-machine interaction, 14
Human-machine interface designs
  form-filling, 117–120
  menu-selection, 117
  command languages, 117
  question/answer, 117

I

Inference modeling, 169
Information, attributes, 1

Information presentation, 18, 147–148, 149, 163
Interface specification tools, 14, 101–102
IPR (Imposter Pass Rate), 35

J

Jungian cognitive types, 141–143

K

Key displacement, 51
Keyboards, 44–56
Keypad, 44
Keystrokes, 32
Knowledge acquisition, 88

L

Laboratory experiments in human factors, 75
Left brain/right brain theory, 254
Locus of control, 147

M

Man-machine systems, 10
Mental anchoring, 95
Menu-driven systems, 106
Microwriter, 55–61
MIS, 1, 4, 7, 11, 28, 137, 251, 253
Motivation to learn/use system/software, 228–229, 232

N

Natural languages, 63
Naturalist, 167
Novice users, 3, 8, 73

O

Office automation, 3, 190
Office personnel functions
  information capture, 183
  information processing, 184
  information storage, 184
  information retrieval, 184
  information dissemination, 184

P

Paper and pencil questionnaires, 149
Participative change cycle, 197
Passphrases, 30
Passwords, 30
Path analysis, 91
Presentation format, 150
Problem space, 85
Project structure, 143
Project teams, 138
Prototyping tools, 101
Psychological model, 34
Psychology of keystroking, 32

Q

Quick reference guides, 61

R

Resistance to system change, 183, 185–187, 195
  dysfunctional behaviors
    aggression, 188, 190
    projection, 188, 192
    avoidance, 188, 193
Response time, 73
Reversible actions, 105
Rule Definition Interface (RDI), 127
Rule-based expert systems, 167

S

Scenarios in software usability evaluation, 210, 214–217
Screen entry format, 107
Scripts, 171
SDLC (System Development Life Cycle), 2
Self-fulfilling prophecies, 96
SmartSLIM, 83, 89
Software engineering, 103, 104–105
Static Identity Verifier (SIV), 30

Statistical inference, 88
Symbolic trace facility, 168
System analyst, 19, 135–136
System-user documentation, 18, 165–166

T

Task completion, 165
Task/team considerations, 140
Templates, 46
Test of Behavioral Rigidity (TBR), 197–199
Texas Transportation Institute, 43
Theories of explanation
  by trace, 168–169
  by inference modeling, 169–170
  causal, 178–179
  envisioning, 171–173
  functional, 177–178
  genetic, 177
  script-based, 171
  what-if, 175–177
Time stamp, 38
Time-and-motion studies, 9
Training environment, 233–234
Training design, 241
Training/learning process framework, 225–228
Triggering mechanisms, 66

U

Usability of software, 207–208
User acceptance, 31, 269
User Computer Interface (UCI), 43
User "friendly," 10, 103
User identification, 31–33

V

Voluntary system usage, 3

W

Walkthroughs, 135
Whole-brain model, 259–262